As Far as Yesterday: Memories and Reflections

EDWARD
WAGENKNECHT

As Far As
Yesterday

MEMORIES
AND
REFLECTIONS

UNIVERSITY OF OKLAHOMA PRESS
NORMAN

A complete list of the publications of Edward Wagen-knecht will be found in the Appendix.

The paper on which this book is printed bears the watermark of the University of Oklahoma Press and has an effective life of at least three hundred years.

Library of Congress Catalog Card Number: 68–15690

Copyright 1968 by the University of Oklahoma Press, Publishing Division of the University. Composed and printed at Norman, Oklahoma, U.S.A., by the University of Oklahoma Press. First edition.

PREFACE

IN THE FIRST VOLUME of his autobiography, *Left Hand, Right Hand!* (Atlantic–Little, Brown, 1944), Sir Osbert Sitwell wrote wisely:

> I do not pretend to tell the reader everything, only to paint for him in a setting a portrait, of which, as in a surrealist picture, many diverse incidents compose the features. I leave the skeletons in their cupboards, and the flesh in its clothing, and walk where I will. I claim the right, moreover, to jump forwards and look backwards as I choose.

I have stolen my title from a phrase thrown off in passing by one of my favorite writers, Robert Nathan, this time in his charming play, *Juliet in Mantua* (Alfred A. Knopf, 1966). But though *As Far as Yesterday* is much the most personal book I have ever written or shall ever write, it is not an autobiography. Many periods and aspects of my life are completely untouched, and a glance at the table of contents will show that the focus is often upon others. Nearly all the more personal chapters deal with my childhood and youth, and even here I am more concerned with what I remember than with myself remembering.

As Far As Yesterday

I realize that I might have written much more fully about the personalities of my parents and relatives (not brothers and sisters, for I was an only child), but it has never been my way to share intimacies, particularly intimacies involving other persons, with the world. And as to the family I established, this, happily, belongs not to yesterday but to today. Some readers may feel that in that case I should have done better to let this kind of writing alone. As to that, I cannot pretend to be an unprejudiced judge. In any case, I prefer to content myself with dedicating these pages to all those persons, living and dead, in the family and out of it, who have loved me and whom I have loved.

EDWARD WAGENKNETCHT

West Newton, Massachusetts
April 10, 1968

CONTENTS

vii

As Far as Yesterday: Memories and Reflections

Wie aus der Ferne längst vergang'ner Zeiten.
The Flying Dutchman

. . . Memory can lead
The harassed mind back to the scenes it lov'd
In years departed . . .
JOHN GREENLEAF WHITTIER

Long ago, sweetheart mine,
Roses bloomed as ne'er before.
EDWARD MACDOWELL

Unto thee
Let thine own times as an old story be.
JOHN DONNE

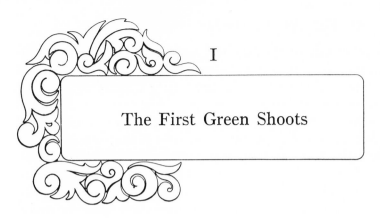

I

The First Green Shoots

THE BEST PLACE to see the park was from the front room windows. They were fascinating in themselves, for they had very wide sills on which a small boy could play quite comfortably, and very substantial indoor shutters, the like of which existed nowhere else in the house, and which it was great fun to unfold out of their side-frames and fasten together, making the room as dark as could be. But your mother would not let you do this very often, for fear you might tear the lace curtains, and anyway when you closed the shutters you could not see the park.

Directly across the street there was, in the very early days, a greenhouse, and beyond that on the other side of the road that ran through the park, there was an artificial lake. Off to the south, on Nineteenth Street, where the park ended, St. Anthony's Hospital loomed up, an overwhelming building indeed, partly because it suggested sickness and suffering, which were things you did not like to think about, and partly because its affairs were administered by nuns, who, in those days, were awesome beings to you, not, I think, because of any religious prejudice, but because you did not understand them, and because you hated, and were always to hate, the color black.

As Far As Yesterday

The other side of the lake the park went on, past the natatorium, as far west as Albany Avenue, but northwards it extended for a considerably greater distance. In a manner of speaking there were indeed two Douglas Parks. The "new" park, which was the part that your house on California Avenue faced, ended at Ogden Avenue, but on the other side of that spacious thoroughfare, the "old" park stretched on as far as Twelfth Street.

When I was very small, the superintendent of the greenhouse was a friend of my father's. He was a man with a very keen interest in politics, and when election time drew near, he would come over to ask whether he might put up pictures of his favored candidates in our front windows. My mother was considerably less enthusiastic about this than I was, but she always said yes because she did not wish to be uncivil and also, I think, because she enjoyed the flowers the superintendent gave us from time to time. I cannot believe that those posters in a third-story window really decided any Chicago elections.

Neither the greenhouse nor the lake was with us long. First the one came down; then the other was filled in. Oddly enough, I cannot recall the actual process of change. They were simply there, and then they were gone.

The greenhouse was replaced by an attractive planting of shrubs and lawn, and we did not miss it, but the loss of the lake meant a distinct decline in picturesqueness. I can remember walking home from school in the afternoon, along its eastern shore, with the reddest of red suns sinking over it into the West. When it was filled in, it was replaced by a large treeless meadow which was the widest piece of open country I saw anywhere during my early childhood. Thereafter when I wished to get west of the park to Lawndale, where my aunts lived, I would often take a short cut across the meadow. Up until now we had been obliged to walk north on California Avenue as far as Sixteenth Street, where we would cut into the park along a gravel path which led over a dear little hill with a massive, fascinating willow tree at the top of it, and out upon Ogden Avenue leading west.

4

The First Green Shoots

This area, too, suffered change. Facing Ogden Avenue, but set well back from it into the "new" park, when I first knew the region, was a large conservatory, quite as impressive as those which still survive in Lincoln and Garfield Parks. Since the park itself was comparatively new, it cannot have been there long. It was pulled down nevertheless when I was still very young, and the space it had occupied plus a good deal more, clear from the path over the hill almost west to Albany Avenue, was laid out in a large garden. At the western end a huge peristyle was erected, towering over a pool of water lilies and goldfish (I think this must have been the first construction of poured concrete that I ever witnessed); east of the peristyle it was all garden, flat in the middle but reaching up a sloping embankment on the south side. We may have missed the conservatory but we made good use of the garden, for both my parents and I liked to walk there of an evening, and I can still never see cockscomb nor smell tuberoses without thinking of that place. One fall night there came an early frost and the next evening the flowers were all wilted and black and dead. I think this must have been about my first sharp experience of mutability.

That was about all there was in the "new" park; the old one was both larger and more interesting. The lake here was never filled in, and a large refectory and boathouse were built on its north bank. In front of the boathouse there were more gardens, leading down from a terrace, which I quite arbitrarily associated in my mind with the gardens at Versailles. I am afraid some of my associations were almost as farfetched as those of the girl in Walter de la Mare who always thought of her godmother along with crocodiles!

Farther over, near the western end of the Twelfth Street side of the park, there was a mineral spring, whose water tasted exactly like rotten eggs. I could never believe that anything so nauseating could be so "good for you" as people said it was.

But of course the best things in the park as elsewhere were not the regulation sights but little out-of-the-way places that you

5

had sought out for yourself and never mentioned to anybody. There was a little island in the lake which teased me unmercifully because I had no way of reaching it. I saw it thousands of times, and I have no idea why I remember it one time in particular, when my cousin and I came upon it—shrouded in cold and mist unless my treacherous memory has added these elements—toward the end of a long Sunday afternoon walk. In those days I had never seen Arthur Rackham's pictures for *Peter Pan in Kensington Gardens*, but when I did I immediately recognized my island, and I have never looked at them since without having my island come back to me. There was also a little bridge, spanning a narrow arm of the park lake, which, for no reason that I can pin down, I identified in my mind with one of the sites in *Black Beauty*, thus making it one of the many places where I could enjoy the actual and the imaginary together.

Once, in a manner of speaking, I managed to get myself "lost" in the park. The California Avenue side was rather heavily wooded, and I used to love to run between the bushes, imagining myself off somewhere in the great woods. One evening I traveled thus, while my father and mother walked sedately on the sidewalk, and when I finally emerged at Sixteenth Street, they were nowhere in sight. If I had had the brains I was born with, I should simply have followed them down the gravel path, which was the only direction in which they could possibly have gone. Moreover I knew my way home as well as I knew my own name, and I knew the way to where they were going just as well. Instead, quite illogically, it came over me that I was "lost." I kept repeating the word to myself, "selling" myself the idea of lostness, so that I might savor it to the full, and finally burst into noisy tears. I do not know how long this continued, but shame turned it off, as suddenly as one can flick a switch, when a girl somewhat older than I was suddenly appeared and asked me in astonishment if I did not know the way home. I was too ashamed to answer her questions except in monosyllables, but all at once I was completely self-possessed again, and even a little curt.

6

The First Green Shoots

Like the White Queen, I had had my emotional orgy and felt quite all right again. Very shortly, too, my mother returned, and in the fewest possible words, indicated that she thought it time for me to be moving along, which I did, with a great inward sense of relief supervening, but with a laconicism which not only matched but far and away surpassed hers. I suppose it was all another example of my lifelong tendency to shun physical adventure but to explore to the utmost the adventures that lie in the world of the imagination.

On Sunday afternoons my mother and I generally went to the house of my aunts (until I was nine, my grandmother too was there), and this of course meant the walk through the park of which I have already spoken. In those days gypsies still came through our part of Chicago occasionally, begging and telling fortunes. My mother, who took very little stock in such things, generally locked the door if she saw them coming, and once a gypsy woman who had been thus excluded terrified me by hammering on the door, and cursing, and spitting against it. I do not know how she knew we were within, and I am not quite sure why I was frightened; I *may* have feared that she possessed supernatural powers, but I think the naked malevolence with which I must then have been making one of my first encounters was a more important element. On another occasion, however, my mother did have her fortune told by a gypsy, who informed her that one Sunday afternoon, as she walked through the park, she would find a large sum of money, tied up in a red bandana handkerchief. "Don't try to find the owner," she said; "he would only waste it in gambling," which seems to me a dubious sort of morality. Since we *did* go through the park every Sunday afternoon, and since the gypsy had no means of knowing this, we were much impressed, and we looked for that handkerchief many an afternoon, but alas! it never appeared.

Occasionally, though not often, we would meet a balloon-man, and then the earth turned into fairyland, but you could never seize it for long, for either you would lose your hold on the gas-filled balloon, and it would sail away into the heavens, which was at least romantic to watch while it lasted, or else the gas would gradually seep out of it in the course of a day or two, and it would look like something that had died, which was not romantic at all. One Sunday afternoon we encountered an itinerant photographer who wanted to take a picture of the little boy standing on the grass under the trees. The little boy never said no to an opportunity to be photographed, and I still have the picture, which shows him in white starched "waist," tight dark pants and stockings, and a really enormous white sailor hat. Though he looks melancholy enough to suggest that he had just come home from his father's funeral and was preparing to leave to attend his mother's, I am sure this does not mean a thing; he must have been having the time of his life.

If the photographer brought the charm of novelty, the popcorn man's charm was familiarity. He was inevitably stationed at the Albany Avenue end of the park, and there, every Sunday, I had to buy a box of Cracker Jack to take to my Aunt Frances. I wouldn't have eaten it for love nor money; as a very small child, I refused to touch either candy or ice cream; the ban on candy did not last long, but I was much slower in coming to the ice cream. Nevertheless it was terribly important that I should buy that Cracker Jack, and Sunday would not have been Sunday without it. I really do not think affection for my aunt had anything to do with it. I was attracted to the popcorn man, and for some reason or other I enjoyed making the purchase.

In those days, every day of the week had its own color and atmosphere for me. My favorite days were Sunday, Monday, Thursday, and Saturday. I liked Tuesday, Wednesday, and Friday much less. Why this should have been it is hard to say. I suppose most children like Saturday and Sunday for obvious reasons; you still hear people say that it "feels" or "doesn't feel" like Sunday. But Monday is proverbially "blue"; I have never been able to understand this; for me Monday always has an air

8

of freshness and expectancy. When I saw a particularly clear and fresh-looking picture in one of my childhood fairy books, I said, "That looks like Monday" and I still know what I meant. I may have disliked Tuesday because that was the day the washer-woman came, and this meant a certain amount of confusion, detested by my fastidious soul, but surely my mother's ironing on Wednesday and cleaning on Friday could not have upset things sufficiently to spoil these days.

I find it difficult to tell how far back I can remember. There seem to be great differences between people in connection with this matter; some apparently remember little or nothing before they went to school, while others can go back almost to the dawn of consciousness. Marilyn Monroe used to think she could remember herself in a long baby dress, crawling over the grass at the age of nine months. I do not believe I can go back quite that far. Once, when I was still being carried, my mother took me to visit her family at the old house on Thirteenth Street, before they moved to Sawyer Avenue, west of Douglas Park. When we left the Elevated at the Twelfth Street station, it was beginning to rain. So my mother walked under the structure to Thirteenth Street, and before we left the shelter told me to call my aunt, so that she could come and open the door for us and we should not have to stand in the rain. I shouted at the top of my small lungs, and, strange to relate, my aunt did hear me and came to the door. It seems to me that I can remember all this. It even seems that I was as proud as Chantecleer when he crowed the sun up. But since I heard my mother talk about it later, I cannot be sure. On the other hand, I was told a great deal about how I used to play on the couch with my mother's father who died just before I turned two, and none of this ever caused me to suppose that I had any recollection of him.

There are other things about which I can be sure. I have told elsewhere[1] how I examined the newspaper the night of the

[1] In my *Chicago* (University of Oklahoma Press, 1964), 59–60.

9

As Far As Yesterday

Iroquois Theater fire, when I was still three months short of being four years old. Two other recollections, hitherto unrelated, are possibly of greater interest.

Habitually we did our shopping in our own neighborhood, but one day, while I was still in my buggy, my mother stopped at a food store on Ogden Avenue, west of the park, to make a purchase. I remember that I had my monkey with me in my buggy. Strictly speaking, he was not what is generally called a stuffed animal. He had been printed in colored inks on cloth, cut out, sewed, filled with cotton, and fitted out with a stiff cardboard base on which he could stand. I loved him passionately, played with him until the ink was all worn off and he had become a shapeless lump, and mourned him for years after I had lost him. Why I should connect him with this moment at the grocery store, I do not know, but such is the fact. And this is something that nobody could have told me about, for nobody else knew how I felt about it.

The other experience took place in my own home. One weekday we were visited—my mother and I—by two of her sisters. They had no sooner arrived than I was driven to the kitchen by childhood's perpetual preoccupation—to get a drink of water. I was still in dresses, I remember very clearly, and I was so small that I had to get a kitchen chair and drag it to the sink before I could reach the faucet. While I was thus engaged, somebody called to me from the front room. It made me feel very important to think that I could not even leave the room long enough to get a drink of water without being missed and needed and called back. I answered, "Just a minute," hurried through my drink, and toddled as quickly as I could move through the long hallway which joined the kitchen to the front part of the flat. "What is it?" I asked. "What do you want?" But by this time, my mother and my aunts were busy talking about something else, and they did not even answer me. I was as furious as I have ever been in my life. And this, too, is the kind of thing I could not possibly have been told.

10

The First Green Shoots

My devotion to my monkey must not be taken to indicate that I was the kind of boy who plays with dolls. I hated dolls. I hated them with a fierce and consuming hatred. I suppose this was my way of expressing my manliness—about the only one I can think of as ever having engaged in—and I have no idea why I should have felt as I did, for I cared much more for girls than for boys. But give me a toy in the form of any animal, or even of a human being involving the grotesque or the fantastic, and I was gone. I remember that I cherished Aunt Jemima and her family, who came in the same form as the monkey (of course for the purpose of advertising Aunt Jemima's Pancake Flour), and, even more, Sunny Jim, a Yankee Doodle kind of figure who was the symbol of a then popular breakfast food whose name I cannot recall.

It seems to me that advertising was more imaginative in the days of my youth than it is now, and I am sure nobody ever followed it more devotedly than I did. It was not that I gave a hang for any of the products that were being advertised; my interest was in the advertisements themselves. There were, for example, the "little nigger boys," as I fear I must then have called them, who were known as the Gold Dust Twins, and who belonged to a popular washing powder; there was a charming little boy who represented the merits of a breakfast food called Apeteizo (since I could not say that, I called him "the Dady Boy"), and, best of all, there were the gorgeous colored clowns of the Zu-Zu Ginger Snaps. Here, again, I had no interest in the product (I disliked ginger snaps), but every spring the Elevated platforms blossomed out with gorgeous posters of the little clowns that I would have given my eyeteeth to possess. These were as much a part of the coming of spring for me as the leaves on the trees or the brilliant yellow of the dandelions against the bright green grass in the yard.

The posters were beyond my reach, but newspapers and magazines were not. My aunt, who conducted a dressmaking business, took in all the women's magazines (much more given to patterns in those days than the survivors are now), and whenever I went

11

to her house, I would go through them, shears in hand, with "Can I have this?" and "Can I have that?" Santa Claus and the Corticelli silk thread kitten were the special objects of my devotion (since the kitten was always the same I do not know why it did not occur to me that one example was as good as a thousand), but nobody could ever tell what would strike my fancy. It did not even need to be a picture. I loved the Gothic type in which the Chicago department store called The Fair printed its name in those days, and when it was abandoned for a more modern, more severe design, I felt as though I had been personally assaulted. I may have been extreme in this, but I do not think I was unique, or if I was, advertisers have certainly wasted a great deal of money. How much has the fox terrier listening to "His Master's Voice" coming out of the phonograph contributed to the prosperity of the Victor Company? or the Piper who does not adorn nearly as many title pages as he ought to nowadays to that of Houghton Mifflin Company? I suppose nobody will ever really know.

It will be perceived that atmosphere was often much more important to me than anything concrete, and I am as sure that this is true as I am that I could never completely communicate my feelings on the subject to another person. Why, for example, should one particular stroll through a place that had seemed commonplace enough on a thousand other occasions be touched with wonder? I do not know, but I am sure that this kind of thing has happened to me, and I am sure, too, that, on occasion, some very ordinary thing has suddenly become wonderful enough to justify the whole business of living. Of course, all this applies to other things besides the sense of place. We can analyze the effects achieved by a great writer, for example, and we can pool our impressions of him, but how can I be sure that you "feel" either Dickens' novels or the pictures "Phiz" made for them quite as I do? May we not, in this aspect, be inhabiting quite different worlds which merely lie side by side?

I do not know that I have ever really found adequate recog-

12

nition of this feeling of mine anywhere in literature except in two passages in the stream-of-consciousness writers—one in Virginia Woolf and the other in Dorothy Richardson. "For Heaven knows why," wrote Mrs. Woolf, in *Between the Acts*, "just as we have lost faith in human intercourse some random collocation of barns and trees or a haystack and a waggon presents us with so perfect a symbol of what is unattainable that we begin the search again." Exactly! And Dorothy Richardson cuts even deeper when she makes her heroine, Miriam Henderson, observe that "what is much more astonishing than things behaving after their manner is that there should be anything anywhere to behave. Why *does* this pass unnoticed?" Going up the stairs in *Backwater*, Miriam feels a "curious buoyancy rising within her."

> For a second, life seemed to cease in her and the staircase to be swept from under her feet. . . . "I'm alive." . . . It was as if something had struck her, struck right through her impalpable body, sweeping it away, leaving her there shouting silently without it. I'm alive. . . . I'm alive.

There is a certain poetry about such an experience, and poetry involves both insight and acceptance. The poet as poet does not really wish to change anything; he is too busy accepting it. But the trouble with life at first hand is that it is forever slipping out from under you and never consents to repeat itself exactly. "I wish I could do that again" we are forever saying, but we never can. On the other hand, we *can* read a book or see a film or play a phonograph record over and over again, and thus escape, in a measure, from the tyranny of transience. The twenty-fifth time you read *David Copperfield* or watch *The Birth of a Nation* or hear Caruso sing one of his great arias, you are beyond both critical judgment and surprise. It really does not even make much difference any more whether it is "good" or "bad." It *is*, and, as Shakespeare would put it, you are content to have it ever "do nothing but that."

I am told that when my father's parents came to Chicago from

13

As Far As Yesterday

Germany in 1868, they hesitated between buying a lot on State Street or on West Eighteenth Street! They chose Eighteenth Street, alas, and lived there, in a cottage that has been pointed out to me, until some time in the nineties when they built the house on California Avenue in which I was born. It was a three-story red brick, with a huge attic above, running the whole length of the house, and it was surmounted by a heavy slate roof, with a mansard type of construction coming down over the attic story in the front. My grandparents lived in the middle, and the bottom story was rented out to a variety of people who, during the fifteen years I inhabited the house, ranged all the way from the excellent to the unspeakable. We called the first floor the "basement," but it was not a basement actually; the house had no basement; it merely lay below the level of the street. In many parts of Chicago houses were built before the level of the street had been determined; when the streets were graded, therefore, the lowest story sometimes found itself below street level, and you had to descend a flight of steps from the sidewalk to reach it. This was the case with our house, though here you had to climb another flight to reach the second story, which was the main entrance, and then, of course, still another, indoors, to the third story, where we lived.

Wooden sidewalks were constructed on the street level, and in some places you could look down through the cracks into the prairie below. Though I cannot remember it, this was probably true where we lived, for I can remember when both the cement sidewalk and the asphalt street paving were laid. Contemporary with the wooden sidewalks was a wooden-block type of paving for the streets, the blocks being held together with tar. When a block broke or was injured in some way, a hole would get started, and it was a great temptation to a small boy to kick at it and make it larger, watching the wood shred fascinatingly around it.

The under-the-sidewalk area harbored, I am told, a vigorous rat population in some parts of Chicago, and I am sure human

14

rats must also have employed it for sundry nefarious purposes, but for some strange reason I was never, as a child, in the least afraid of anything I met out of doors. There were still plenty of horses on the streets in those days, and no horse whom I could reach ever escaped being petted and fondled by me. I do not know why I was never kicked or bitten, but it simply did not occur to me that this could happen. You had to bring my imagination into play before you could scare me, and I was desperately afraid of a dark room indoors. Our attic, for example, was a fearsome place, though its dark shadows fascinated me even while they repelled.

I was more original, however, in the population I assigned to the closets in our three bedrooms. The front and the back bedroom closets were both inhabited by witches, each with a clearly defined personality. The witch in the front bedroom was cadaverous and tireless, and there were no limits to her malignity. She had a large family, and she was forever working away at some task, I know not what. But the witch in the back bedroom, who lived alone, was fat and lazy, and had a sallow complexion. She dressed entirely in white, with a curious sort of hood on her head. I know because, one night, I saw her in a dream. My mother was ironing, and I was engaged in some childish deviltry when she suddenly came out of the bedroom and announced that she was going to take me away. Though my mother regretted it, she seemed to feel that I had brought it upon myself, and in any case I gathered that there was nothing she could do about the matter. The witch, as always, was too lazy to be really dangerous, and she finally waddled off lackadaisically, saying, well, maybe she wouldn't do it this time. But the middle bedroom, where I slept, had a closet inhabited by devils of assorted sizes, all quite as lobster-red as Mephistopheles in *Faust*. One was as large as a full-sized adult, and from here they graduated down to the smallest you could conceive. As long as you kept the door of the closet tight shut, you were safe from the larger devils—I some-

15

times got up out of bed in a cold night to check it—but the trouble was some of the little ones could get out through the keyhole, and I did not know how to protect myself against these.

I am not saying, of course, that I actually believed any of this. I never really wiped out the line between fact and imagination. But I am sure there must have been times when I half believed it, and I think it gave me pleasure as well as terror to do so. Where it all came from I have no idea. The witches in the fairy stories I read certainly contributed, but I do not believe that they were altogether responsible. Nobody had ever told me anything of the kind—I am sure of that—nor had I ever been punished by being put in a dark room.

On the whole, however, I do not think the witches and the devils tormented me half so much as my own sins. These characteristically took the form not of overt actions but of "bad thoughts," generally of a most fantastic character, thoughts which I was sure I had no right to think but which would sometimes cross my mind uninvited. I had the idea that I ought to tell my mother about these things and secure her forgiveness, but I knew too that I could not do this because I should be too ashamed. Yet if life was ever to be right again, ultimately I would be obliged to do so, and therefore I must not forget them. For this reason, it was my habit at one time to recall them all to my mind, one by one, before going to sleep at night!

If this gives the impression that my life as a child was grim or that I was, as such things go, an unhappy child, I can only assure the reader that the impression is wholly erroneous. It is true, of course, that we did without a good many things which people today take for granted and regard as indispensable, but since this was the common lot at the time, it never occurred to us to complain about it. And my awareness that I am much better off now than I was in the days of my youth does not prevent me from looking back to the days gone by as if they had been lived in a kind of Arcadia.

For example, our house had been built before gas was laid on

16

The First Green Shoots

California Avenue, and in the beginning lighting had been achieved by the then omnipresent kerosene lamp. When the gas came through, which was before my time, the house was piped, but no gas fixtures were placed in the bedrooms! In a bedroom, one slept, and why did one need light for that? About the only time this caused any serious inconvenience was when you (generally meaning me) were sick and for such emergencies the old kerosene lamp had to be kept ready.

For that matter, our gas illumination was not itself what could be called brilliant. The "mantle" on the gas fixture in the dining room gave a fairly decent light except that it was always burning out, but in the kitchen there was only a small naked flame by which I wonder how anybody ever managed to see anything. I wonder whether the absence of adequate illumination in the house I grew up in had anything to do with establishing my life-long disinclination to work at night. Is it even possible that if the lights had been brighter, I might not have gone to the movies quite so often? Even today, when people ask me, "How do you manage to get so much work done?" (which is about the only question anybody ever does ask me), I always reply that my success, such as it is, has been due to two things: I don't play golf, and I never work after dinner.

For heat we depended upon the cookstove in the kitchen and the "heater" in the dining room, which burned anthracite, and which, come spring, would be taken down and packed away until next winter. This meant that in really cold weather, it was too cold to dress in my bedroom; I would jump out of bed, grab my clothes, and make for the dining room. Many of these old heaters were picturesque affairs. Ours had a kind of Hail Columbia figure on the top, and I loved to watch the red coals shining through the isinglass windows.

Our street lights were of gas, and every night, as dusk fell, we could watch the man come round with a long pole to turn them on. There were electric lights in the park, however, and before the house next door was built, my bedroom window looked out

17

to where a very bright light burned at a junction of two roads in the park. This light was blue, and there was something about it that seemed to belong to fairyland. For many years of my adult life I did not see any street lights of that color; of late years something like them has been reappearing on superhighways.

When you were sick and had to stay in your bedroom all the time, it was less pleasant of course, but there were compensations, for though I had my share of childish ailments, I was not often in great distress; I had excellent care, and I enjoyed being coddled. Then, too, sickness always brought Dr. McKee, and to see him was as great a joy as any child could ask.

I wonder how many families there are today who sustain as intimate a relationship to the family physician as was ours to Dr. C. William McKee. I think he must virtually have adopted the family when he pulled my mother through a dangerous siege of typhoid fever a year or two before I was born. (He charged her twenty-five dollars, and when she paid him, he gave her a dollar back "to buy ice cream.") When I finally arrived on the scene, which I was a pretty long time in doing, he practically moved in with us until it was over. I suppose modern doctors know a good many things which he did not know, though I must say that whenever conflicting diagnoses appeared in our family history, he was always right and the other diagnostician was always wrong. He was a huge man of preternatural gentleness (when the horses that drew his carriage were too old for service, he would put them out to pasture in the country until nature claimed them), gloom vanished before his robust and infectious gaiety, and his kindness was matched only by his withering scorn for meanness and cruelty. I am sure he had never heard of either psychiatry or psychosomatic medicine, but he practiced both with skill and distinguished success, unattended by any of the vagaries which frequently attach to them today, yet his great power was that he knew the secrets which reveal themselves to love alone. He was, I am sure, the first great man I ever encountered, and he remains one of the greatest. Until he retired from

18

practice in Chicago and went to live in California when I was about twenty, no other doctor ever touched me, and I can still remember how desolate both my mother and I were the night we climbed the steps to his office for the last time and he told us the news. I saw him last in 1932, when my bride and I, on our honeymoon, visited him at Long Beach.

Our flat had an important annex in the shape of a large back porch, and the view from here was very different from what we saw out the front windows. The neighborhood was peculiar in that though it overlooked the park, an industrial district had grown up in the back, and at the end of the block, just beyond Nineteenth Street, the elevated tracks of the Burlington Railroad crossed California Avenue running east and west. We were not close enough to the factories to see them, but we could hear their whistles (and those of the trains too, of course), and it still seems to me that a factory whistle is what ought to be on hand to announce the achievement of noon. When the wind was just right —or, rather, wrong—there was also at times an odd and pungent smell, which I was told came from "the vinegar works," but I have no idea where the vinegar works were, and I am not sure I should have found the odor unpleasant if I had not gathered somehow that it was not the kind of thing one was expected to relish.

One day, when I was still so small that I could look over the porch railing only by standing on the first of the steps which led up to the attic, a train going by suddenly emitted a hideous toot, which so startled me that I banged my chin on the railing and bit my tongue; I can still remember the sharp pain. A much happier memory goes back to one afternoon when I woke up from my nap (I must have been very young, for I gave up napping very early) and came out to the porch to find my mother sitting on the steps. As I appeared in the doorway, still half drugged with sleep, she turned her head toward me and said, "Hello," so very kindly and sweetly and with such a beaming smile, that my heart was warmed within me. I had never, God knows, had any reason to doubt that my mother loved me, but I never realized it more gratefully than in that moment.

Summer evenings at home were generally spent on the porch, for summer evenings in Chicago can be very hot, and having the gaslight on can make them even hotter. I have never been fond of night, and since having nothing to do is hell to my temperament, I could become very restless and melancholy under these conditions.

The best of all the planned occasions or festivities in our home came of course at Christmas time. Or, more exactly, on Christmas Eve; for that was when I received my gifts from father and mother; Christmas Day was spent west of the park, where I received more gifts from others. Only, of course, I got them from Santa Claus too—the gifts from my parents at any rate; I am not sure about the rest. I have never credited myself with the possession of a metaphysical mind, but I must have believed in Santa Claus for a longer period than any other child in the recorded history of this planet, and I experienced no difficulty at all in reconciling the apparently contradictory ideas that my parents should be thanked for what Santa Claus brought. It was all a little like what Walter de la Mare says about phenomena in general. They can be frightfully "real," but "it doesn't follow . . . that they didn't mean something else too."

Our front room could be shut off from the dining room by sliding doors which I found as fascinating as the blinds in the front room windows, but they were hardly ever closed except for a day or two before Christmas. Then the tree would be installed (reaching clear to the ten-foot ceiling), and I was told that if I were to "peek" Santa Claus would be very angry. I always respected his feelings, though I recall my mother once voluntarily offered me a brief glimpse through the crack, of which I availed myself with a clear conscience, for I knew that Santa Claus and my mother understood each other perfectly. And so the time dragged on to Christmas Eve (it never went so slowly at any other period), and then, as soon as we had had our dinner, the sliding doors would be opened, my mother would say, always in exactly the same tone, "Oh, Santa Claus has been here already!" and I would go in to wonderland.

I believe that in most homes Santa Claus merely leaves the gifts and takes his departure. I should like to record here that at our house he also trimmed the tree; it is pleasant to remember that one has received such special service. There were no electric lights on our tree, for there was no electric power in the house, but there were any number of beautiful red, blue, green, and yellow candles, and the smell of their wax is forever associated for me with Christmas. Once in a while a burning candle would catch a branch of the fir, and that meant another delightful smell. I never had any doubt that my parents were fully able to deal with the situation thus created, and I do not believe the thought of fire hazard ever occurred to me.

My gifts, arranged about the base of the tree, were toys and books. I never received "useful" things for Christmas, and I still think it a "gyp" to make a pretense of Christmas giving to your children out of something you would have to buy for them just the same even if there were no Christmas at all. I had magic lanterns and steam engines and every kind of building blocks there were, being, as always, completely indifferent to everything that suggested practical utility, like the steam engine, and enthralled by whatever smacked of fantasy. I remember with pleasure some very substantial circus toys, made of wood which had been carefully jointed so that they could be made to assume any desired stance, and gaily attired—the clowns, at least—in real clothes. But there was one thing I had to have every Christmas while I was small, and this was "The Stubborn Donkey." He was made of tin and attached to a cart driven by a clown; when you wound him up, he reared backwards, kicking, and the clown reared back to avoid his hoofs. His only shortcoming was that his spring always wore out much too soon. Does anybody except me remember him?

II

The Color of Spring

I HAVE SO FAR WRITTEN of the immediate world into which I was born—the house in which I lived and the park which served as its front yard—but there were other worlds around this, and it does not seem unnatural to describe them thus, for each had a personality of its own.

Go south on California Avenue and you soon came to Twenty-Second Street, a busy shopping thoroughfare extending as far west as Kedzie Avenue, and predominantly Czech (or, as we called it then, Bohemian) in its culture. We sometimes bought there, but the street was more important to me because it held several motion-picture theaters.

Extending your explorations a few more blocks south, you would come to two institutions which were to play some part in my life. As far back as I could remember, St. Mark Evangelical Lutheran Church, which my grandparents attended, stood on South California Avenue, and every Saturday evening I would hear a lengthy performance of its bells, reminding people that tomorrow it would be time to go to church. Later, near Marshall Boulevard, which swept grandly into Douglas Park at Nineteenth Street, the vast classical building of the Carter H. Harrison High

22

The Color of Spring

School would be erected just in time for me to have part of my intermediate education there. Even before that, Marshall Boulevard was not without its varied interests: it was a parkway; it had a large Elevated station, with the tracks very high indeed to permit them to cross the Burlington embankment, which was itself elevated; and there were a number of institutions, including a home for the blind, who forever made one feel sad and almost frightened when one encountered them poking their way about the streets with their sticks.

Another unit was formed by the area lying just north of us between Eighteenth Street and Ogden Avenue. This was not much more than two blocks wide, running from California Avenue to Fairfield to Washtenaw, for beyond that the area of industrialization soon began. On Eighteenth Street were the food stores where we generally traded, and after 1907, when he married, my mother's younger brother, for whom I was named, lived and raised part of his family there. My father's only brother lived with his family on California Avenue, near Sixteenth Street. On Fifteenth Place, just beyond Washtenaw, was the Ambrose Plamondon School, which I attended for eight years, and on Ogden Avenue itself, just east of California, was my first neighborhood movie theater, about which I have written at some length elsewhere.[1]

This area, too, could be extended, a few blocks farther north, across Ogden Avenue and on towards Twelfth Street, to take in the Douglas Park Methodist Church (now the Arnold Memorial), where I went to Sunday school, and later to church and Epworth League. This was situated, first, on Washtenaw Avenue, then, after this building was sold, temporarily in a store at the corner of West Twelfth Street and Fairfield Avenue, and finally in a new church on Fairfield, not far north of Ogden.

You could, however, travel eastward along Ogden Avenue, and this would bring you shortly, over a vast viaduct crossing

[1] In *The Movies in the Age of Innocence* (University of Oklahoma Press, 1962).

23

railroad tracks and freight yards, to where Ogden Avenue and Twelfth Street crossed. This was another shopping center and a considerably larger and older one than the others with which I was familiar.

The final world which I inhabited was the only one that was actually cut off from the others by any distinct line of demarcation. This, as I have already said, was Lawndale, west of the park.

I shall speak, first, of the area I saw least of—the region around the intersection of Ogden Avenue and Twelfth Street. Perhaps because I knew it less well than the others, it still wears a somewhat richer or more romantic patina for me. It was closer to downtown, and the business conducted there seemed to be upon a somewhat larger scale. Furthermore, it was beginning to run down. I cannot define the quality of the charm which often exists in such a neighborhood (before the decline has gone beyond a certain point), but I am sure everybody knows that it can exist. Perhaps it is merely the enrichment contributed by the sense of past glory (that was rare enough anywhere in Chicago so that you were always inclined to cherish it wherever it appeared); perhaps it was rather the feeling that before decay can set in, there must be something there that *can* decay!

The atmosphere which hovers for me around this neighborhood is a Saturday-night atmosphere. For a long time my shoes were bought there, and, for some reason, this was always on Saturday night. There was also a popular and well-known clothing store known by the undignified appellation of "Little Jake's." The neighborhood boasted three motion-picture theaters, and I could still tell you some of the films I saw here—Edwin August in Edison's newspaper drama, *The Big Scoop*; the great Italian spectacle, *Satan; or, The Drama of Humanity*; and Marguerite Snow in *Carmen*. Not, alas, Thanhouser's *Paul and Virginia* and Kalem's *The Kerry Gow*. I got my only chance to see these in this neighborhood, but I did not get beyond the posters; my own incapacity blocked me on *The Kerry Gow*, and I do not remember what stood in the way of *Paul and Virginia*. Thanhouser's

24

poster for it was a reproduction of Cot's beautiful painting, *The Storm*, one of the most popular canvasses in the Metropolitan Museum; the aesthetic snobs who wish to put "Art Seminars in the Home" have recently reached a new "high" in cultivating hypocrisy among their victims by advertising it as the kind of thing which nowadays one is not "supposed" to admire. I think this was the first time I ever encountered *The Storm*; consequently I always took it for granted that it represented Paul and Virginia; this may be true, but I now realize that I really have nothing beyond the Thanhouser poster to support the identification.

The most distinctive institution in the area under consideration was, however, Merz's Drug Store. It was quite the largest drug store I had ever seen, and my interest in it was not medical but feline, for Merz's housed the largest cat I had ever seen or probably ever was to see. He was a huge Angora who presided over the establishment from his own special throne, where he rested gracefully upon his cushion and condescended to acknowledge the homage of his many adorers. I suppose he was one of the most distinguished citizens of the West Side, and when, in the course of time, he was gathered to his fathers, his throne was undisturbed and his living presence replaced by a life-sized portrait of himself hung reverently above it.

The most exciting night I ever spent in this area, however, was Election night of the year 1908, when William Howard Taft was elected President of the United States. This was not only before the days when radio and later television brought us blow-by-blow election returns in our homes; it was even before they were given, as the 1916 returns were for me, in motion-picture theaters. So my mother and father and I stood with I know not how many others and watched the returns thrown by a large magic lantern upon an immense screen across the square. I enjoyed every minute of it, even the long, cold, damp walk home over the viaduct afterwards, but though I was glad our man had won, I am not sure that I was not even more interested in the pictures of the various celebrities of the day which occupied the screen between the receipt of the various returns.

In the early days, Lawndale, where my aunts lived, was a more elegant neighborhood than the one we inhabited, and it held many attractions for me besides those furnished by the house itself and the various film theaters along Ogden Avenue.[2] Though it has now fallen upon evil days, spacious Ogden Avenue is surely in itself one of the noblest streets in Chicago, and I always found it stimulating to window-shop there, especially on a brisk winter evening.

On Sunday nights we were habitually at the house in Lawndale, as members of a rather large family group, and I can still see the Sunday-night supper, with sausages, cheese, hard-boiled eggs, and hot German potato salad with vinegar and fried bacon. In some respects, my Aunt Frances and her husband inhabited a somewhat wider world than we did; especially were they great opera- and theatergoers, and when the talk turned to this area, I was all ears. Judged by my standards at that time, the conversation was stimulating, and I think I profited by it. There was an agreeable atmosphere of *Gemütlichkeit* and good humor also, and it is still pleasant to me to recall those Sunday evenings of which so few survivors are left now.

My Aunt Augusta had the largest "library" in the family—largely fiction, some of it standard, some selections from the popular novels of the day—and I cannot have gone to her house many times, once I had grown old enough to handle books, without gravitating to the bookcase. Two volumes in particular never failed to draw me. One was Harpers' "Becky Sharp Edition" of Thackeray's *Vanity Fair*, illustrated with photographs of Mrs. Fiske and her supporting cast in character and with scenes from her production of the play. The other was a cheap but pretentious unauthorized edition of Whittier's *Poems*, with a padded, soft, squishy leather cover, which contained a number of pieces which the poet had excluded from the Houghton Mifflin editions.

[2] Some of which I have described in *The Movies in the Age of Innocence*.

26

The Color of Spring

What drew me to *Vanity Fair* was a hideous photograph of Miss Crawley (the very book lies open on the desk before me as I write) facing page 96. And what drew me to the Whittier was a morbid and (so far as the mature Whittier at least is concerned) eminently uncharacteristic poem called "Suicide Pond." For years I hardly ever went to my aunt's bookcase without getting unholy shivers from both the picture and the poem. One verse in the latter I never forgot:

Twined as in mockery round the neck of that suicidal girl.

It was certainly a strange, unhealthy introduction to one of the most wholesome of poets.

This story has a sequel, or, rather, two of them. Growing up, I grew away from these addictions, and for a number of years I must have let them rest. Then, one day, I suppose during my early college years, by which time my aunt and her books and I were all in Oak Park, I opened *Vanity Fair* once again, and this time I also read the cast of Mrs. Fiske's production. And I do not believe that anything in literature could at that moment have given me a greater start than one line I encountered here:

Miss Crawley . . . . IDA WATERMAN

For, many years after she had appeared with Mrs. Fiske in *Vanity Fair*, Ida Waterman had become a character woman in motion pictures, and in this aspect she had played the old ladies in a number of Mary Pickford's early films. There I had encountered her, and by this time I had become very fond of her, for she was a handsome woman whose aspect was both regal and kindly. It was amusing indeed to think that it should have been she who, in "Miss Crawley" make-up, had so terrified my infancy.

I can see even yet that the make-up was stagy and ugly enough to be repulsive to a child, though there would not seem to be anything there to justify my extreme reaction. The point is, however, that one can never tell how a child will be affected by such a thing—or, for that matter, by anything. In her autobiography,[3] Marjorie Bowen tells how she was terrified by Wordsworth's "Lucy Gray." And in this case, the final grueling touch that pushed the impression over the edge of the endurable was the quite innocent detail that she "never looked behind."

The impression that "Suicide Pond" made upon my mind was more reasonable, especially when one remembers that I had cause to entertain a more than normal horror of self-destruction. When I was working on my *John Greenleaf Whittier: A Portrait in Paradox*,[4] I learned the name and the story of the pathetic heroine of this poem. But I did not tell it there, and I shall not tell it here or elsewhere, for it is the kind of story that should never be told except in the guise and under the protection of fiction. Suffice it to say that the poor girl was like Tess of the D'Urbervilles in the sense that a brute and a prig undid her between them.

I wonder how many pictures survive in my memory from these early years, stemming from events in themselves of no moment, which in some cases perhaps registered only in my consciousness, which at least I have never forgotten, though letting go my hold upon a million other much more vital things, and which at any rate now survive in my memory alone. And the same thing must be true, though often, I am sure, not to the same degree of intensity, of virtually everybody else who lives upon this earth.

I can see my grandmother coming out into the hall as far as the head of the stairs with my mother and me, as we prepared to go home, one afternoon in 1909, and standing there smiling at us as we descended. A day or two later I was told that she was very ill, and within a week she was dead. She had passed out of my life with that smile at the head of the stairs. Take another memory centered in the same area but about as different from this as any could well be. One day I paused on the lower level to

---

[3] *The Debate Continues, by Margaret Campbell, Being the Autobiography of Marjorie Bowen* (Heinemann, 1939).

[4] Oxford University Press, 1967.

pick up the evening paper. On the front page was a picture of Harry K. Thaw, photographed in his jail cell while on trial for the murder of the great architect Stanford White.

At that time, as I shall soon make clear, my interest in the newspapers was largely confined to the comic sections; I think the first news event I ever really read up in the papers was the sinking of the *Titanic* in 1912. But though I was too young to read about the Thaw case, I did hear my elders talk about it, and I was well aware both that it was something very scandalous and that it was attracting a great deal of attention.

We have become so inured to violence and scandal now that it must be hard for the present generation to realize what a shock the Thaw-White case created and for how many, many years it was kept fresh in living memory. When Evelyn Nesbit Thaw took the stand in her husband's defense and told, accurately or not, the story of her relations with Stanford White, it is hardly too much to say that she divided America into pro-Evelyn and anti-Evelyn factions. Compared to this, the interest taken in the sordid and senseless crime out of which Truman Capote has recently made so much capital, was largely synthetic.

As such connoisseurs in the field of crime-writing as William Roughead, Edmund Lester Pearson, and Edgar Lustgarten have always realized, murder is not interesting in itself. It interests us when it involves mystery, when it reveals human nature *in extremis*, or when the motives and the personalities of the people concerned challenge our powers of analysis or appeal to our sympathies. In the Thaw-White case, the murderer himself was interesting only to the pathologists—and to the sociologists who saw in him an example of what an influence toward degradation great wealth can be when it is employed without intelligence—but the victim was a man of genius who had created beauty which enriched all our lives and who died in the floodtide of his great creative powers, and the "woman in the case" was one of the most beautiful girls of her time.

Many years later, when she was asked what she thought life

29

had taught her, Evelyn Nesbit replied that she had learned that only two things were fundamentally important—the love of God and boundless pity for everything that lived. Queried further as to her regrets, she replied that, in the sense in which that term is generally employed, she regretted nothing. What happens to a human being in this world, she went on (I am quoting from memory) depends upon whether or not he has the character needed to resist temptation at the time he encounters it. She, who had been brought up without religion, so that she did not even know whether she believed in God or not, did not have it; consequently what happened to her was inevitable. Being what I was then, she concluded in effect, I could have learned what I know only as I learned it. But it had to be learned, and it was worth the price.

For various reasons, I do not believe that Evelyn's spiritual pilgrimage always moved in so single and straightforward a line as this statement would indicate, but there can be no question as to its general direction. There was never anything cruel or mean about her, and whatever wrong choices she may have made, she never said, "Evil, be thou my good." I did not know until after her death, on January 18, 1967, that she had finally become a Catholic. By that time she had outlived most of the persons who had been interested in her, but I for one was glad to know that her stormy life had ended in peace in the bosom of Mother Church.

I have so far said nothing about the great change which came over Lawndale when Chicago's expanding Jewish population began to overflow the ghettoes around Maxwell Street where it had hitherto been centered and gradually took over the community. I remember one evening just before dinner when I was still young enough to be playing with some other children in a sand pile which had been left by a neighboring builder on Sawyer Avenue, and a little girl turned to me and asked, "Are you a Jew or a Christ?" (she pronounced it with a short *i*). It was the first time it had ever occurred to me that such a question could be asked. When I replied that I was a Christian, she pointed out another boy in the group and said kindly, "That's what he is too," as if she wished to assure me that I need not feel inferior for not being a Jew. There were no Jews at all in the grade school I attended until my last years there, when two Jewish families moved into the community, and the boys involved, incidentally, almost at once became the closest companions I had in school.

I am sure that I have been guilty of much wrong and of much more stupidity during the years of my life, but I think I can claim that I have always kept myself reasonably clear of the demons of social, racial, and religious prejudice. When I was in my second summer, I was very sick with what in those days was called "summer complaint," and Dr. McKee prescribed that my mother take me on a lake cruise. She did, and I promptly proceeded to disgrace myself by conducting a shameless love affair in public with the Negro stewardesses, toward whom I would reach out my arms whenever they hove in sight. I don't know whether they were flattered by the "white chile's" obvious infatuation, or whether I really did possess outstanding charms in those days, but they followed my embarrassed mother and me all over the boat. And I know, too, that all through my early childhood I considered Negroes much more interesting and attractive than white people.

At a large university on the Pacific Coast, I once heard G. K. Chesterton lecture on "The Ignorance of the Educated." In the course of the evening he managed to touch upon almost all the types of ignorance represented in the audience, and I amused myself by glancing about the hall at my fellow faculty members seated here and there. At one minute he would be treading on Professor ———'s corns, a few rows ahead of me on the main floor, and a few minutes later he would be up in the first row of the balcony mangling Professor ———'s bunions. I never saw so heavy a man get around so quickly. I will not pretend that my own toes were never stepped on, but I was used to it, and I found all the comfort I needed by observing that the lecturer's own

31

prejudices were not completely invisible at all times. I was, however, not at all surprised to learn next morning that most of my colleagues were under the impression that they had heard a miserable lecture. They had, on the contrary, heard a superb one, of which many of them stood in desperate need, but God had denied them the ears of understanding.

Chesterton told the story about George Stephenson, who invented the locomotive, and the farmer who asked him what would happen if a cow should get on the track. Stephenson replied that that would be too bad for the cow. This is always cited as a very clever answer. It was, on the contrary, an extremely stupid answer. Those who admire it have already brought the world to the brink of destruction and may yet well succeed in destroying it altogether. Stephenson's answer was based on the unspoken assumption that locomotives are more important than cows, and that therefore when the interests of cows come into conflict with those of locomotives, the cows ought to be sacrificed. But this is criminal lunacy, and no man who is unable to see through it ought to be allowed to roam at large.

Not so very many years have passed since Chesterton gave this lecture, and locomotives are already much less important to the world than they were then, but the importance of cows has not declined. In different forms, the Stephenson heresy still prevails, however, and we can now look forward to the supersonic plane, which may well make it impossible for any sensitive person to continue to live on this planet except in soundproof caves underground. Moreover, we are already in secure possession of many other blessings. Cigarette-smoking may cause lung cancer, emphysema, heart disease, and phlebitis, but, after all, since the tobacco industry is so very important in our economy, and since we have far too many people in this country anyway, might it not be better not to say anything about it? Industry is progressively poisoning our air and our water, thus killing off its potential customers, but industry never takes the long view of

32

anything, and it is still tough for any living creature who gets in the way of any machine. It seems a shame, too, that we have to kill every man, woman, and child in Vietnam to save them (whether they wish to be saved or not) from a hypothetical monster called Communism—and certainly this hurts us much more than it does them, for we Americans are a sensitive people, and, like Mrs. Gummidge, we feel things more than other people do—but isn't it better to be dead than red (especially for other people)? and how can anybody doubt that God in His wisdom has authorized us to choose for all mankind?

Chesterton distinguished sharply between two kinds of ignorance. One kind is represented by *The Winter's Tale*, in which Shakespeare erroneously presented Bohemia with a seacoast. This has occasioned a good deal of commentary from people who happen to know that Bohemia has no seacoast, and much of this commentary has been informed with obvious gusto. The commentator can hardly conceal his glee at having found Shakespeare out! He was ignorant of something that we know! What could possibly put us into a better conceit of ourselves?

Yet this kind of ignorance does no harm whatever. Suppose Shakespeare had known that Bohemia had no seacoast. How could this knowledge have advantaged him in any way? What use could he have made of it in his life as an Elizabethan Englishman? *The Winter's Tale* would certainly not have been a better play for his knowing it. On the contrary, he would have been deprived of a particular effect which, as it was, he employed to advantage.

Stop worrying about the seacoast of Bohemia—such was Chesterton's counsel. It does not matter one iota. But there are other kinds of ignorance which matter a great deal. If, for example, your ignorance takes the form of believing that because somebody has a different color skin from your own, or wears a different slant to his eyes, or adheres to a different creed, he must be inferior to you, and that you, therefore, have a divine commission to rule over him—that is the kind of ignorance you had better watch out for, for such ignorance can drench the world in blood and turn this earth itself into a hell.

The Jews in Lawndale cut down the trees for firewood and tramped out the grass in the parking strips. They removed the doorknobs and the light fixtures from the flats they rented and sold them for junk. They allowed the drains in their sinks to become clogged with debris, and when you went into their kitchens, you would see the sink full of water to the brim with fishtails and other remains of food products floating in it. I know because my aunt owned her house in Lawndale for some time after she had moved out of it and gone to Oak Park, and when I was in my teens I used to go in and collect the rent for her.

Obviously this was a situation ideally calculated to inspire racial and religious prejudice. But the dreadful mistake which many persons made was that they supposed that these people were behaving as they did because they were Jews. The truth of the matter is of course that they were behaving thus because they were peasants. They had not yet learned how to live in an American city. They, or their fathers, had come from Polish and Russian villages (most of the older members of the community had not even learned to speak English), and when they first came to America they had been herded into slums where it would have been impossible for anybody to live in any other way than they were living. They were now in the first stage of their escape from the slums, but they did not yet know any better than to take the slums with them. All this was straight sociological conditioning, and it had nothing whatever to do with their being Jews. I am sure that most of us would have been astonished if we had been told that their children and grandchildren would have made their adjustment with complete success and that, long before the date at which I am writing, some of these would have made important contributions to American welfare and become distinguished citizens in music, science, philanthropy, and many other areas of our corporate life.

34

The Color of Spring

I am not saying that I reasoned all this out to myself as a child. I was no sociologist, nor was I ever to become one. I am saying that, at no time in my life, have I ever accepted or rejected human beings on a wholesale basis. I do not judge anybody as a member of a group. To me he is never anything but himself.

Norah Lofts once told me that she herself had an incurable tendency always to turn blue against a red background and red against a blue. I am sure the same thing is true of me, and I am sure too that this has contributed importantly to saving me from being contaminated by the prejudices I encountered. But I must in all fairness add that, generally speaking, I got on well with the Jews with whom I was brought into contact, frequently finding them much more reasonable and agreeable than Christians.

I have come now, finally, to the area just north and east of my house which contained the Plamondon School. Here, too, as I have already said, we generally bought our provisions. Grocery stores and butcher shops had not yet combined in those days; the ones we patronized habitually stood side by side at the corner of Eighteenth Street and Washtenaw Avenue. And only half a block away was the candy-novelty store where I wasted many pennies and where I loved to climb in the old willow before the door.

Again, I display the romanticist. Each year, shortly before Christmas, one of the grocer's sons would take over one of the store windows to create a winter scene. Using sheets of cotton batting for his snow and little cardboard buildings and miniature figures of various kinds, he would create a complex and enchanting scene of winter activities.

Now my indifference to sports and games has always been absolute; not only have I never *played* baseball or football, but I have never even *witnessed* a contest. (I used to wonder whether I was unique in this, but when I read Channing Pollock's autobiography, I learned that there were two of us at least.)

I did not stop to ask myself why I was so enthralled by the aesthetic (if you can call it that) depiction of activities that I would never have thought of looking at in actuality. My sympathies have always been wider in art than they are in life, and I am willing to read about a great many things in which I do not wish to share. Perhaps this may be one reason why I have never "identified" with characters of fiction as some people say they do. I will match my enjoyment of fiction and drama with that of anybody else on earth, but I always keep my distance. I am conscious of myself *and* of the character, and when it comes to the theater, I am also conscious, even in moments of intense emotion, of both the character *and* the actor. There is a three- (or four-) fold relationship here: the playwright and the actor create the character who is brought to me to apprehend. It seems to me that anyone who fails to do these things fails to understand the difference between life and art, and I should think his relish of both would be impaired. I suppose the little scene which so charmed me in the grocer's window was very crudely done compared, say, to the enchanting dioramas of Miss Louise Stimpson in the Boston Public Library, but that is no matter. I wonder how many grocery stores there are in the world now (or "supermarkets," for that matter) in which anybody would take the space and the time and the patience to construct what I saw in our grocery store as a child.

Later a delicatessen store was opened in a building which by that time had been constructed on California Avenue at Eighteenth Street, just a block from our house. This proved a very helpful resource in an emergency, and I was often sent there to buy a small quantity of something that might be needed in a hurry. This store was kept by a dapper young man with a pretty blonde wife (they were both Germans), and their twin baby boys. After a time the man disappeared, and his wife said that his brother, who had a store "in the country," had broken his arm and that her husband had gone to help him out. But time ran on, as time will, and he did not return. Finally she realized that she must tell the truth. One evening, when I happened to be alone with her in the shop, I asked her, in my best grown-up manner, whether Mr. D—— was not back yet, to which she replied (she

36

was cutting some cheese for me at the time), sadly but not at all sentimentally or self-pityingly, "No, he is not coming back. He has left me." I was too young to express sympathy or anything except blank astonishment, but I ran home very quickly with the news (by this time the cheese was incidental). The pretty blonde wife soon sold the shop and went with her children to live with her parents, who had a store on Ogden Avenue, not far from the viaduct. There she used to work, and I would see her and speak to her sometimes, looking dreadfully worn, I thought, when one of my innumerable walks would take me in that direction. We never learned anything more concerning what had really become of the husband or what was the reason for his defection.

I spoke a while back of my morbid and exaggerated horror of suicide and indicated that I had come by it honestly. I have no idea whether statistics would support the idea that Czechs are more given to self-destruction than other races (this accusation has been brought against many peoples, and one of the slang terms for suicide is "the Dutch act"), but I do know that anybody brought up where I was could have found no difficulty in believing it. I can recall four suicides in the immediate neighborhood, though I think one of them actually occurred after we had moved out of it. Two were men and two were women. The owner of a store I knew very well poisoned himself one day and threw the bottle out the window into the prairie next door. It was not difficult to understand why; he was the gentlest of men, and his wife was a veritable shrew. (She took to religion afterwards; I hope it did her some good.) The case was different with the other man, a German this time, whom we knew much better, for he had a good wife and a son who went to school with me, and he seemed a pleasant, well-adjusted man. I remembered him well from the Saturday afternoon when he had come over to our house to help my father do some work, and his act troubled me because it seemed so senseless and unmotivated. The two old women died earlier, and both hanged themselves. One of them I had frequently seen sitting in front of her house, with red, sunken eyes and an abstracted expression; she never looked at anybody and seemed as old as the world itself. I cannot express the horror which her act inspired in me; I even hated to pass her house afterwards.

The horror of death in a Czech neighborhood was multiplied many times by the hideous custom which still prevailed in those days of burying the dead with a brass band, which marched through the street playing lugubrious dead marches! This obscene horror nearly drove me out of my mind. William Cowper used to speculate about whether if there were music in heaven, there might not be a kind of unmusic or antimusic in hell, as harrowing as music is pleasurable. I am sure there is, and I am sure too that I heard it on the streets of Chicago. From another point of view, one might say too that a Bohemian funeral in those days was an anti-circus parade.

Even without the brass band, however, the regalia of death in those days were hideous, and to a sensitive person, well-nigh unendurable, and the cemetery bell, which tolled once for every carriage entering the gates in a funeral procession, was very nearly as bad as the brass band.

I have already said that my grandmother died when I was nine, and within five years there were three other funerals in the family. On each occasion the women of the family draped themselves in black with long mourning veils of quite unspeakable hideousness over their faces. I would never dream of allowing a child to look upon a corpse or attend a funeral (if I could help it, I would never allow a funeral to be held), but nobody thought of protecting me. You did not, in those days, adjust yourself to your loss as *best* you could; instead you made the *worst* that could possibly be made of it, using every means at your disposal to keep your grief fresh, and feeling guilty in the precise ratio of your ability to return to normal activities and a normal outlook. To assist in developing all this virtuous misery to the highest possible degree, you avoided all entertainment, even music, for a full year after the death had taken place. I was even expected to

38

stop going to the movies when my grandmother died, and I actually did it until almost a year had passed, at which time something came along that I very much wished to see, and my mother said I might go, which I did, but without feeling quite right about it. Children, too, were expected to grieve like adults. I knew it was expected of me, not by my mother but by some other members of the family, and precisely because I knew it was expected, I knew, too, that I could not do it, for I have never been so constituted that I can keep emotion on tap and serve it up on demand. I realize that all this sounds as if we must have been an insane family, but we were not; this is actually the way sane people behaved in the face of sorrow, not so very many years ago.

I speak of my school years in some aspects in other connections later in this book, and I do not intend to say much about them here. One of the most vivid pictures of my grade-school years that comes back to me is the image of myself descending the cement steps leading to the school basement (the walls of the entranceway were lined with a shiny brown tile brick that I have never seen anywhere else) and saying to myself that I should have to do this every day *for eight years*! From the point of view of one who had not yet lived that long, it seemed an interminable time, yet the time has passed and how many, many years more!

I had a variety of teachers—of varying merit and demerit— but the person who meant the most to me in my grade-school years was the principal of the school, W. W. Reed, who taught us our American history in the eighth grade and made a wonderful job of it. He must have been the second of my heroes, Dr. McKee being the first. Mr. Reed was a small but stocky man; I saw a good deal of him outside of class, and he was always kind and encouraging to me. Temperamentally we were almost antithetical, for he was as steady as I was quicksilverish. He was, at the time, deeply involved in the Progressive movement in Illinois, and if the Bull Moose had not died, he might very well have become a candidate for political office. I am sure he must have been very conscious of many of my deficiencies, as they were then, but un-

39

like many "strong" people, he did not try to make you over into his own image; instead he accepted you for what you were and encouraged you to make the most of what had been given you to work with. I am sorry he did not live quite long enough to read my book about his great hero Theodore Roosevelt, but I shall always be grateful to him.

My third hero was a young clergyman named Chester Carwardine. I have, perhaps, so far, given only a confused picture of my religious life. Traditionally my family was Lutheran, but the ministry of the Lutheran church in Chicago at this time was primarily a German (and Scandinavian) ministry, and they were very slow in realizing that if they did not make the language shift soon, they were going to die with the older generation. I was taught my prayers and the essential doctrines of the Christian religion as soon as I was old enough to learn anything, but although it was assumed that when the time came, I should be "confirmed," I was taken to church very rarely, and the service, being in German, was quite meaningless to me. (I never really learned German until I went to high school, and it has been kept up during my mature life mainly in connection with German opera and Lieder.) Because my grandparents spoke German while all the younger members of the family spoke English, except when they communicated with their elders, I at one time believed that German was the language spoken by all the old people in the world and that all the young ones spoke English. When I grew old, I should probably speak German too.

Under the circumstances, I might very well have concluded that God was German also, and that, as such, He had, for the present, nothing to do with me, and perhaps I should have done this if it had not been for the Sunday school. Like most Americans, I came to the Sunday school by a process of trial and error. When I reflect upon the bumbling inefficiency with which most Sunday schools are conducted, and how many people are trying to teach in them who have never even learned anything for themselves, and then pile on top of that the all too obvious deficiencies of far too many American clergymen, it often seems to me that human beings must be incurably religious, or else the church would have perished long ago. The first English-speaking Sunday school in our neighborhood was conducted by a group of Dunkers, who began modestly in a rented store. I am sure they were very worthy people, and their enterprise has prospered and survived to this day. Even then they were giving the community its first taste of what is now known as social service, and when one of their devoted workers, a young woman named Miss Manners, contracted diphtheria and died, the entire community was shocked. But the Sunday-school teacher I drew there was good for nothing, and my attendance did not continue long.

The Douglas Park Methodist Church was another matter. Here, too, I had teachers good, bad, and indifferent, some of whom took their duties very lightly and performed them irregularly, and my attendance was spotty, but when I was thirteen or fourteen, I began attending Epworth League, and it was at this time that I made my first vital contact with religion. Part of this was due to the stimulation of the League itself, which was the livest and most enthusiastic body of its kind I have ever encountered, and part of it was due to the pastor of the church, Chester Carwardine. What I should think of his sermons now (he died young, of tuberculosis), I have no idea, but they were just what I needed then. He was zealous but he was no fanatic. His wide range of literary and historical references aided him notably in establishing a vital contact with such a person as myself, and his breezy informality and lack of all "holier-than-thou" pretenses was a welcome relief after what I had hitherto associated with clergymen. A product of Garrett Biblical Institute at Northwestern University, he was no fundamentalist, and thus he saved me from the whole dismal (and grotesquely misnamed) "conflict between religion and science" which was still disturbing many Americans in those days, long after Europeans had put it behind them. From him I learned that there can be no such thing as a conflict between religion and science, though there has undoubtedly been conflict between science and some of the erroneous ideas which ignorant men have quite arbitrarily identified with religion.

Such slight contacts with clergymen as I had had before this time had not been very happy ones. I am sure that there have been as many saints among German Lutherans as in any other communion (they are not too numerous anywhere), and I loved what my mother had told me about Pastor Klein, the beloved teacher of her childhood, but saints never set the norm. There is a story about a mother who told one of her children, "Go see what Johnny is doing and tell him to stop it." Clergymen often conduct their business upon a similar basis. One does not get far as a castigating moralist who emerges from the sacristy with the air of a Moses descending from the Mount to encounter a congregation prostrated before the Golden Calf, and I heard with horror of a clergyman known to the family whose notion of comforting a most worthy and faithful member of his congregation in her bereavement had been to punctuate his discourse at her drunken husband's funeral with a frequently reiterated "Der Mensch ist nicht zum fressen und saufen in der Welt gekommen!" Later, when she had to support herself by taking in washing and solicited his business, knowing that the woman he employed was not a member of his congregation, he told her that he could not support every washwoman in Chicago. I have no reason to suppose that the Lutheran pastor under whom I sat for catechetical instruction would have been capable of such brutality, nor have I any complaint as to his relations with me, but I felt something distant and disapproving in him for all that, and there was a barrier between us that was never crossed. I suppose the basic difference was that we were simply the products of different cultures.

The bright young people of today have come to think of midwestern Methodist culture of the early twentieth century as a very narrow thing. I can only report that for me it was nothing of the kind; on the contrary, it was a tremendously stimulating and broadening influence, under which, for the first time, I began to develop what could reasonably be described as a world-vision. The emphasis was never negative but positive. If there were certain things you did not do, this was not a deprivation: you did not wish to do them or you avoided them because they got in the way of something you wanted more. There was work waiting to be done in the world, and you were going to help to do it, and enjoy yourself greatly in the process too.

Let me add a special note for the benefit of one of my one-time neighbors in Evanston, Illinois, the Women's Christian Temperance Union. (In Oak Park, I was to attend for a time a church named for their founder, Frances E. Willard.) In my childhood one of the Union's great propaganda weapons was the speaking contest. They put one on at the Douglas Park Church in which five or six girls held forth on the alcohol problem. I do not recall that any sentimental appeal was made—there was nothing like the "Father, dear father, come home with me now" of the *Ten Nights in a Barroom* school. As a matter of fact, the approach was rather coldly scientific, taking the form of a definition and description of what alcoholism costs in health, in wealth, and in the destruction of human beings who are otherwise quite as good and could be quite as useful as anybody else. That night I made up my mind that I would never drink alcohol, and in the increasingly drunken country in which I have had to live ever since, I have found no reason to change my mind. And if you think this contradicts what I have said about Douglas Park Church being for me a liberalizing influence, may I respectfully suggest that you take your *Spoon River Anthology* down from the shelf and read the piece called "Jacob Godbey." Masters wrote that one just for you.

If I were growing up in the Lutheran church today, I think my experience might be very different than it was then, especially if the particular church involved was not connected, as mine was, with the (then, at any rate) extremely reactionary Missouri Synod. For one thing, the magnificent Lutheran church music now impresses me much more than it did then when I was in my Gospel hymns period. I also think the Lutheran church has a basic sobriety which has helped it to avoid some of the sleazy vagaries which, in these hysterical days, have in many churches replaced the old outmoded fundamentalism without improving upon it.

I was not formally of the Methodist persuasion for a very long period, and I have had other denominational affiliations since, for I have always regarded denominationalism as Theodore Roosevelt regarded the tariff—"purely a matter of expediency." Nevertheless, the contribution which Methodist culture made to my development was an important one, and I should be ungrateful not to remember it. Perhaps it was fitting that I should spend the crowning years of my teaching career at Boston University, an institution founded by the Methodist church.

So far in these pages, I have been concerned largely with the setting or framework of my yesterdays. But the reader will already have perceived that for me the world within was always much more important than the world without. The rest of this book will be largely devoted to exploring that inner world in its various phases.

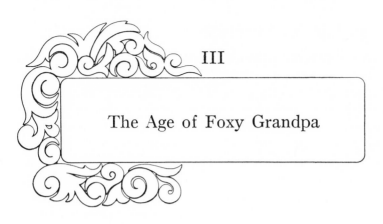

III

The Age of Foxy Grandpa

I AM SURE that if I ever had any claim to be considered an intellectual, I must forfeit it with the admission that my first vital contact with the world of art was made through the comic strip. The conclusion does not interest me very much, but I am inclined to question the premise. I made my contact on the level where a child lives. I reached out toward something that lay within the range of my comprehension, and I embraced it because I loved it and not because somebody told me it was the thing to do. Beginning thus, I may have missed something, but I believe that I also gained much.

In the very early days, which is all I am concerned with here, my comics were the Hearst comics (available to me in the Chicago Sunday *Examiner*) and the New York *Herald* comics, which I pored over in the paper my aunt took, the Chicago *Record-Herald*. Our daily paper was the *Daily News*, the top half of whose back page was devoted to comics, but the only one of these I can remember is R. W. Taylor's "Brainy Bowers," which, I learn from Stephen Becker's excellent *Comic Art in America*,[1] ran from 1902 to 1908. This was a tramp strip. Brainy Bowers

---

[1] Simon and Schuster, 1959.

As Far As Yesterday

was a squat, paunchy tramp, with a queer pointed hat, who was always badly in need of a shave, and he had a stupid, comparatively innocent sidekick named Drowsy Dugan, a beanpole sort of character, with puffy cheeks and a droopy mustache, who was always being led into scrapes and then left to hold the bag by his more crafty companion. The *News* cartoonists always celebrated a holiday by devoting the entire space available to comics the night before to one large picture in which all the comic characters appearing in the paper were shown engaged together in some activity appropriate to the season. These pictures I found quite enchanting and would look forward to them eagerly as a holiday drew near.[2]

But it was the Sunday supplement (the "colored sheet" was my name for it) which was really the thing. The *Examiner* had "The Katzenjammer Kids," "Happy Hooligan," "Foxy Grandpa," and "Little Jimmy." The *Record-Herald* brought me "Buster Brown" and "Little Nemo in Slumberland," and, for a little while, Walt MacDougall's "Strange Visitors from the Land of Oz," which was not really a comic strip. At an earlier date MacDougall had done a boy strip called "Fatty Felix" which I can just barely remember; indeed my remembrance of it is so vague that it seems to belong to another life.

Small boys and their mischievous—in the case of the Katzenjammer Kids, almost diabolical—ways were the stock-in-trade of

[2] Co-operative enterprises of this kind were not unusual in the early comic strip, as Becker makes clear; see on p. 20 of *Comic Art in America* the reproduction of a 1902 page in which the Katzenjammer Kids and their mother (Dirks), Foxy Grandpa and his boys (Schultze), Happy Hooligan, Gloomy Gus, Alphonse and Gaston (Opper), and Tumble Tom (Swinnerton) share an airship misadventure. Opper, of course, ultimately syncretized his own strips. Originally Happy Hooligan, Alphonse and Gaston, and the mule Maud ("And Her Name Was Maud"), who invariably finished by kicking the old farmer Si out of the last panel, each had their own show. Later the mule and the Frenchmen appeared, when they were used at all, in the Hooligan supporting cast. Considering how little range of action she was permitted (I think she never talked), Maud was a surprisingly vivid folklore animal, and even after all these years one still sometimes hears people who allow themselves to be hamstrung by an absurd and senseless over-politeness described as "a regular Alphonse and Gaston."

the early comics, thus suggesting that they must have been aimed, in the beginning, almost wholly at a juvenile audience. "The Katzenjammer Kids" itself, which began on December 12, 1897, and has therefore now been appearing for more than seventy years, derived from the *Max and Moritz* of the German Wilhelm Busch, which Hearst had first encountered on a boyhood trip to Europe.[3] I have already suggested that Hans and Fritz are more demonic than human; perhaps they descend from tricksy, malevolent German kobolds. Certainly they have never been realistically conceived, and probably it is this circumstance which has saved them from becoming a corrupting influence in spite of the generous admixture of sadism and cruelty that has always appeared in the strip. The devices they employ to exercise their deviltry would tax the resources of the Disney studio, and though everybody except Mamma is forever taking punishment, nobody ever seems to be hurt. In this sense, I suppose the strip brings us the same sense of exhilaration as the old slapstick comedy, perhaps proceeding from a refreshing feeling that the characters are superior to the ills of actual life.

The historians say that there were *three* Katzenjammer kids in the first strip published, but the third was dropped immediately. This supererogatory Katzenjammer was, of course, before my time, and I have seen the "thin and nervous" Mrs. Katzenjammer of whom Coulton Waugh speaks only in the picture which he reproduces on page ten of *The Comics*; as he wittily remarks, she had not yet "arrived at that complacent acceptance of the astonishing evil resident in her sons which allowed her, later, to swell to such widely cheerful proportions." I can, however, proudly claim to have got in early enough in the show to know that the Captain is not Mrs. Katzenjammer's husband nor the father of the kids, as many youngsters believe, but merely a boarder with an abnormal appetite for punishment. It seems to me that I can vaguely remember a Katzenjammer father, but I may be thinking

---

[3] *Max and Moritz* may now be savored by Katzenjammer connoisseurs and others in an attractive Dover paperback of that title, with text in both German and English.

47

of the grandfather.[4] Sometimes I think I can remember when the Captain first arrived on the scene, but I am not sure of this either, though I do know that I was present when the Inspector appeared. I also remember very clearly when the Katzenjammers set out on their first voyage. A good many people seem to be under the impression that they always lived on a cannibal isle and associated with pirates and other questionable characters, but this is not true. They once inhabited a normal American (or German-American)[5] home—or one as normal at least as a home with such children in it could be expected to be.

In a way, it may seem odd that the Katzenjammers should have manifested much greater survival value than the other "kid"-strips; to use an expression which is much in favor just now, one would think it might have been easier for children to "identify" with the youngsters who appeared in any of the others. But perhaps we did not wish to "identify" but only to be taken out of ourselves.

[4] The grandfather may be seen in an 1898 cartoon reproduced by Becker, p. 17. Martin Sheridan, *Comics and Their Creators* (Hale, Cushman & Flint, 1942), reproduces, unfortunately on an ineffectively small scale, a brilliant cartoon of much later date which shows how desolated the Kids were when, on one occasion, "their" Captain decided he had had enough and moved to clear out (Mamma, of course, won him back). This is one of the few occasions on which the Kids ever showed any true human feeling. As all devotees of the comics know, since 1913 there have been two Katzenjammer strips—"The Captain and the Kids," which is still signed Rudolph Dirks, but which has, alas! now gone "modern" in a completely idiotic way and completely lost its character, and "The Katzenjammer Kids," long drawn by H. H. Knerr and now signed by Joe Musial. The explanation goes back to a lawsuit occasioned by Dirks's desire to leave Hearst for the *World*, which resulted in the fantastic decision that he might continue to use his characters elsewhere but that Hearst retained the title to the name "Katzenjammer"! This story has been told in detail by both Becker and Sheridan and also by Coulton Waugh in *The Comics* (Macmillan, 1947) and need not be repeated here in detail. Let it also be recorded that during the insanity of 1917–18 there were papers which used the name "The Shenanigan Kids"! There was a great deal of "stealing" of popular cartoonists in the early days, and many passed freely back and forth between Hearst and his competitors. There was a time when there were two Buster Browns, with one of whom R. F. Outcault had nothing to do, and when "Little Nemo" went to Hearst, the name was changed to "In The Land of Wonderful Dreams."

[5] The wonderful German "brogue" of the Katzenjammers is, of course, an important element in their appeal.

48

The Age of Foxy Grandpa

The more "normal"—naughty but not devilish—children included Buster Brown and Foxy Grandpa's (nameless) "Boys." Swinnerton's Little Jimmy was more thoughtless and absent-minded than mischievous. All these children inhabited middle-class American homes—upper middle-class in Buster Brown's case at least, since here there were Irish servants who were sometimes drawn into the fun.

I do not recall that Swinnerton ever got more than half a page for "Little Jimmy," but instead of using only the six panels which were customary in this space, he sometimes used as many as fifteen.[6] His basic idea, as I recall it, was always about the same: the wide-grinned Jimmy, with his funny round little hat, would be sent on an errand, on which he would dawdle and get into trouble from which his lean, mustachioed father would have to retrieve him, and for which he would be punished. To shift from Jimmy's adventures to his irate father at home, Swinnerton always used a narrow panel, reading "And in the Mean Time," with a hand pointing to the next picture; it was he who taught me—and I should think thousands of my contemporaries—the meaning of this expression.[7] Foxy Grandpa's boys need not be discussed here, for they were only foils to their grandfather. But Buster Brown and his dog Tige and his pretty cousin Mary Jane, the only girl I can recall in any of the early "kid"-strips, had a larger influence; in a way, Buster has never died, for Buster Brown hosiery is still made and sold, and his picture used to advertise it, with Tige pulling on a stocking to show how strong it is. In my time, however, his influence on fashions was much wider; every genteel little boy in America had his "Buster Brown suit" for dressed-up occasions; if I must tell the terrible truth, I had one myself and was photographed in it.

[6] Waugh gives a good "Little Jimmy" complete on his p. 13.

[7] Swinnerton, too, was one of the real pioneers; see his "Journal Tigers" of 1897 in Becker, p. 6. He was very fond of drawing little tigers, one of whom, the flirtatious "Mr. Jack," whose actions my mother considered unpleasantly risqué, once had a continuing strip. After moving to Arizona, Swinnerton acquired more reputation as a serious painter than I suppose ever came to any other of the American cartooning kings.

As Far As Yesterday

What Buster did was genteel enough compared to the pranks of the Katzenjammers, but this represented a kind of reformation of manners on his creator R. F. Outcault's part. Outcault had started very early, and his first famous creation, the Yellow Kid of 1896, was distinctly slummy, representing a somewhat startling eruption of low life into the genteel homes of the period.[8] In retrospect, it is hard to understand his full impact, for there was nothing to him except his yellow, nightgown-like garment, reaching clear to his bare feet, and surmounted by a bald head, decorated only with enormous ears, the countenance sometimes smiling, sometimes prematurely worn and aged, and he often appeared as the focusing-point in a large, complicated drawing, involving a variety of figures and requiring as careful study as those of Nast and the other great political cartoonists of days gone by.

Buster, like Little Nemo, had the advantage of always having a full page at his disposal (most of the Hearst cartoons got only half a page most of the time, awaiting their "turns" for the twelve-panel front page, which was never divided). Outcault's trade-mark was his last panel, which always consisted of Buster (often with a pillow tied to his sore backside to testify to the effects of the spanking he had just received), attended by Tige, and standing beside a sermonizing proclamation headed "RESOLVED" in which he summed up the moral of his adventure. He never seemed to profit by this sermonizing, but he was very good at it, and Outcault sometimes frankly used it to express his own concerns.[9] In "Buster Brown Goes Shooting," for example, a 1905 strip reproduced by Thomas Craven in his *Cartoon Cavalcade*,[10] Outcault attacks Theodore Roosevelt's hunting activities.

[8] "Yellow Kid" cartoons are reproduced in all three of the histories of the comics which I have listed—Sheridan, Waugh, and Becker; see also Thomas Craven, *Cartoon Cavalcade* (Simon and Schuster, 1943), 22.

[9] This device descends directly from the Yellow Kid, the blank front of whose garment was often covered with lettering.

[10] Pp. 42–43.

50

The Age of Foxy Grandpa

Here Buster goes out into the fields with a gun, though carefully stipulating that he does not wish to kill anything, and despite the warning of Tige, who talked as freely as the human characters, and who, like Jiminy Cricket in Disney's *Pinocchio* at a much later date, was always a wise, though frustrated, conscience to the erring boy, shoots at a hornet's nest, with results which, except that a ram is brought into the last panels to reinforce the angry hornets themselves, can hardly have been a great surprise to any reader. At the end a very dilapidated Buster points to

RESOLVED!

THAT I DIDN'T GET HALF AS BAD A

DOSE AS I SHOULD HAVE GOT. THOSE

WHO DELIBERATELY SHOOT AN INNOCENT

AND INOFFENSIVE CREATURE ARE COWARDS

AND SINNERS. BUT THE IDEA OF A PRESIDENT

GOING OUT ARMED WITH A GUN AND A CAMERA

AND A PRESS AGENT TO SHOOT HELPLESS &

UNARMED ANIMALS WHO WOULD HAVE

VOTED FOR HIM IF THEY HAD HAD A VOTE.

THEY NEED HIS PROTECTION MORE THAN

ANY ONE ELSE. IS IT KIND OR JUST?

CAN A GREAT MAN DESTROY THE WORKS

OF HIS CREATOR, AND TAKE A LIFE WHICH

HE CANT REPLACE? JUST TO GET HIS PICTURE

IN THE PAPERS FOR SMALL BOYS TO LOOK

AT—OH, WELL, I CANT HELP IT. BUT DONT

LET US KILL THINGS BOYS—NOT EVEN TIME.

BUSTER BROWN[11]

[11] I have a collection of Buster Brown cartoons, *Buster Brown on His Travels* (Cupples & Leon Company, 1910), in which Buster goes, among other places, to Africa, where he puts on a T. R. mask and frightens the animals. These cartoons are not signed by Outcault and must have appeared in the *Herald* while he was working for Hearst. The panels vary in size more than was customary in those days, tending toward a generous expenditure of space, and the drawing of the

As Far As Yesterday

I often think that though I have been in many ways a very childlike adult, I must have been a very old child, for I did not give my heart to any of the children I have named. In reading "Little Nemo in Slumberland," I was, I think, normal in being less interested in the dreamer than in what he dreamed. But believe it or not, my favorite character in "The Katzenjammer Kids" was Mamma, and my great heroes, both adults, were Foxy Grandpa and Happy Hooligan.

Hooligan, if I may judge by such cartoons as are still available for my inspection, has now faded for me, had begun to fade, indeed, before I was out of my childhood, though many of the political cartoons by his creator, Frederick Burr Opper ("F. Opper") still seem quite brilliant. But when I was six or seven, I gave the wide-mouthed, long-lipped tramp, with his patched trousers, big feet, and tomato can hat, an affection which was almost adoration. Only for me what he wore on his head was not a tomato can; it was his "crown"! Dr. McKee was, as I have sufficiently proclaimed elsewhere in this volume, one of the persons I have loved most in this world, but I can still recover the anger I felt the day he inadvertently told me that Happy Hooligan was wearing a tomato can! What a wanton degradation of a gallant hero! Having discovered the chink in my armor by chance, the doctor mischievously went on to bait me, and I think it was on the same occasion that he strained the tie between us by insisting

---

jungle animals in the strip I have described is very fine. When Outcault crossed the Atlantic in 1904, he did a beautiful shipboard drawing of Buster and Tige—

RESOLVED!
THAT THIS IS THE BEST
CROWD THE OLD
KRONPRINZ EVER
CARRIED ACROSS.
YES HONEST!
BUSTER BROWN

Bearing the signatures of Charles M. Schwab, Fritzi Scheff, and other distinguished passengers, as well as Outcault's own, this drawing was auctioned off for charity and knocked down to Schwab for a substantial sum. It is now in my collection.

52

that a gorgeous brown ornament which I especially loved on our Christmas tree was a turnip!

Actually, the real misrepresentation is to speak of Hooligan as a tramp at all. For though his name seems to suggest it, and though he never seemed to have anything to do, he was as far removed as he could possibly have been from any of the associations which the word "tramp" carries. He was the Don Quixote of the comic strip; he was a saint in motley; he was the Fool in Christ. He roamed the world, rushing flat-footedly to the rescue of every creature in trouble ("I'll help youse") and never incurring anything but punishment as his reward. With the best meaning, he incurred the worst. Yes, he was stupid, but goodness is better than wisdom, and as I look back upon him now, I think that a child could have had a worse introduction to the heroes of fiction. I had a picture of him on a post card which I cherished as tenderly as, at a later date, I ever cherished the image of a favorite actress. And one morning in 1906, Opper really went to town with a head drawing across the page showing Happy's Father, Sister Rosanna, Cousin Hannibal, Niece Florinda, Uncle Absalom, and Cousin Bedelia's Baby, all with the same foolish grins and tomato can hats, and each, if possible, more fantastically rigged out than all the rest. That day the Spirit of Beauty really did break her blossoms about my chamber![12]

So far as I know, the spirit of Happy Hooligan was recaptured in the modern comic strip only by Denny Dimwit, who, for a short time in the early fifties, took over the Sunday panels of Branner's "Winnie Winkle." The name was never changed, the connection being made through making Denny a playmate of Winnie's little brother Perry, but as time went on, the other boys tended to drop out, and Denny and his father, who was as ragged, ugly, and gentle as he was, increasingly took over. Denny seemed for a time to be catching on; at least he got far enough so that there were Denny Dimwit dolls in the stores at Christmas time,

---

[12] I never thought of this picture for half a century; then Stephen Becker reprinted it on p. 18 of his book, and all the years melted away.

alongside Mickey Mouse and Donald Duck; then suddenly, and without any explanation, he was dropped, and the Sunday panels thereafter devoted themselves to the completely boring adventures of some young adults in whom I cannot believe anybody ever felt the slightest interest.

Foxy Grandpa could not well have been more different from Happy Hooligan. I do not mean that he was not "good," but he inherited all the immemorial tricks of the Clever Man, and he was far too "foxy" to be a saint. His two grandsons, exact duplicates of each other, were always perfectly dressed in the stiff boys' clothes of the period, with "waists," jackets, tight knee pants, long, uncomfortable-looking stockings, and collar and tie, and they had no function except to play tricks on their grandfather and invariably be worsted by him.

When they removed a plank by which he had expected to cross a stream, he simply floated over in his umbrella. When, after a ball game, they hauled sandwiches out of their pockets and devoured them with all the greater relish because he must look on, he simply drew a "nice juicy blackberry jam sandwich" out of the lower half of his "sectional dairy lunch bat." When he napped—or feigned napping—and they stole his rod while he was fishing, he used his "collapsible fishing pole walking stick" instead. When they employed a scaffold to reach the pitcher of lemonade he had set in the window, he slyly tipped it and dumped them and the lemonade in the rain barrel. When they "frightened" him in the woods by growling like bears in a hollow log, he "captured" the bear by upending the log and pouring water into it.

At midnight, on December 31, 1905, they roused him from sleep, while a charming little moon illuminated the snow-covered landscape glimpsed through the window, by blowing their horns and then rushing back to bed to feign sleep themselves, but Foxy Grandpa frightened them much more by exploding a cannon cracker beside their bed. The strip must have been at its best in 1905, and when the boys waited by the fireplace on

54

The Age of Foxy Grandpa

Christmas Eve to catch Santa Claus coming down the chimney, they supposed they were going to catch their grandfather, but what they got instead was a dummy in a Santa Claus suit and wearing a pumpkin head. Because it was Christmas, the youngsters could not be left, this time, on a note of defeat or disillusionment. So Foxy arrived with a pair of shears to cut the dummy open and show that he was stuffed with toys. "Oh, look boys! Santa Claus's little joke is not so bad after all."

This may not sound like much as I tell it (I do not believe "Foxy Grandpa" ever had more than six panels, filling half a page), but the artist drew charmingly, and his work had an air of sunshine about it which I have never seen approached in any other strip. His name was Carl Emil Schultze, but he signed his drawings "Bunny" and decorated the signature with a charming, varying little sketch of a white rabbit. Schultze must have taken great pride in his drawings, for he was the only prominent comic artist who refused to break into them with "balloons"; in "Foxy Grandpa" the dialogue was neatly typeset under each panel. His dialogue, however, was Schultze's weakest feature and was generally genteelly stilted in the extreme.

Schultze did not arrive at his clean-limned figures and charming backgrounds without experimentation; I have seen early Foxy Grandpas in which the drawing is crabbed in comparison with what he later achieved. In the early days, too, Grandpa seems to have been devoted to the weed; this later dropped out altogether.

I have already said that there was originally a third Katzenjammer Kid. In a sense, there was also a second Foxy Grandpa, though I never saw him in the paper myself. And thereby hangs a tale.

One of the best-remembered nights of my childhood is that of a Saturday in 1909 when my parents took me to see an aunt who had just presented me with a new cousin. His older brother, a boy just a year younger than I, with whom I often played, entertained me, while my elders were engaged with more important matters, by showing me a cartoon book called *Foxy Grandpa and Uncle Alex.*

Uncle Alex behaved just like Foxy Grandpa, but he was taller and much leaner and he always seemed to be in action. I have rarely been more enthralled by anything than I was that night by those cartoons, and I have never ceased to hope that someday I might come across them again.

A few years ago, I almost, if not quite, made it, when I sent for the only Foxy Grandpa book listed in the card catalogue of the New York Public Library. It was not *Foxy Grandpa and Uncle Alex* but a miscellaneous early collection, but it did contain some Uncle Alex cartoons, this being the first and only time I had seen him since that night in 1909. I was delighted to encounter him again, though I cannot honestly say that I found him quite so enthralling as upon our first meeting.

It is easy to understand why he was dropped. Grandpa himself was more than a match for the boys; to have him aided and abetted by another adult gave an unpleasant impression of stacking the cards. Moreover, Uncle Alex's continued presence in the strip must have made for a divided unity and taken some of the spotlight off Foxy Grandpa himself.[13]

Winsor McCay's "Little Nemo in Slumberland" began in 1905, ran for a decade, was resurrected from 1924 to 1927, and reprinted in part in 1947 under the supervision of the artist's son, himself Little Nemo's original. It still inspires a nostalgic affection in the *aficionado* of the comic strip which has never been awakened to the same degree by any other work except George Herriman's "Krazy Kat." It was not McCay's only creation by any means (his *Gertie the Dinosaur* was, in 1909, one of the early "animated cartoons" on the screen), but surely there had been nothing in the sadistic "Dreams of a Rarebit Fiend" to prepare anybody for the gentle whimsy and fantasy of "Little Nemo."

[13] "Foxy Grandpa" has been neglected by all historians of the comics, but see the pictures in Becker, p. 20, and Craven, p. 45. John T. McCutcheon gives some personal glimpses of Schultze in his autobiography, *Drawn from Memory* (Bobbs-Merrill, 1950).

56

The Age of Foxy Grandpa

Though his dreams were sometimes terrifying, they were very different in character from those of his predecessor.

Of course "Little Nemo in Slumberland" was in no genuine sense a "comic." It represented, instead, one of the earliest attempts to break away from the slapstick and shenanigans that the first artists of the comic strip had taken as their province, but instead of moving toward the "soap opera" which most later rebels have favored (Harold Foster's "Prince Valiant" being the most conspicuous exception), it moved instead into fantasy. "Little Nemo" descended, as has often been pointed out, from children's illustrated storybooks, and it took its boy hero (who always woke up in the diminutive last panel) through a series of adventures in which this world and fairyland freely intermingled. Except for Herriman later, no other comic-strip artist ever divided his pages so boldly, unevenly, and imaginatively as McCay did, few have ever drawn so brilliantly, and I very much doubt that any other ever used color so creatively. The strip was full of wonderful buildings and wonderful animals, and there was almost nothing in the way of backgrounds that McCay could not supply.

His weakness, if he had one, was in his characters. Nemo himself was a lay figure, and the cigar-smoking, green-faced Flip, if vivid, was not lovable, though the gentle little Impy, who looked like a comic-opera cannibal, was. I think I myself liked McCay best when he stayed closest to human—and childish—experience, as in the simple but lovely strip in which Nemo dreams that he is putting his Noah's Ark animals away when they come to life and crowd out of the Ark into his room, growing bigger and bigger and finally quite overwhelming him, so that he wakes up in terror. Almost equally delightful was the dream in which the legs of his bed grew by stages as tall as a skyscraper, taking him out for a ride through New York, until at last they got themselves entangled in a church steeple and dumped him out, so that this time, in the last panel, he woke up on the floor.[14] Not only can

14 Both these examples are included in *Little Nemo in Slumberland*, by Winsor

one almost believe an imaginative child to have had such dreams as these, but the story-line here is simple enough to be comfortably embraced in a page of cartooning; this was not true of McCay's more grandiose conceptions, which ran on, consequently, from one week to the next, often spilling off the page and losing concentrated force and impact.

I do not propose to speak at length of any other comics, not even of "Krazy Kat." Ring Lardner used to say that Mary Garden had "fixed" her great roles so that nobody else could sing them. Herriman "fixed" "Krazy Kat" too; other cartoons have been carried on by other hands besides those of their creators, but when Herriman died in 1944, the possibility of anybody else taking over "Krazy" was not even considered. By the same token, I would say that Gilbert Seldes has written so well about the Kat[15] that it becomes unnecessary for anybody else to emulate him. About all I have to add here to what has been written elsewhere is that I am happy to be able to remember Krazy's humble origins in the Herriman strip which preceded it in the Hearst papers, "The Family Upstairs," below whose panels a mouse and a cat engaged in never-ending warfare. Everything Seldes and others have said about "Krazy Kat" at its best is deserved—Herriman created a country and a mythology of his own—though I think it must be admitted that it represents the kind of cartoon which requires inspiration for its full effectiveness, and that every time the clock strikes it does not strike twelve. Parenthetically I may add that I think the same thing must be said today of the only

McCay, with an Introduction by August Derleth (McCay Features Syndicate, 1945). The use of New York City background in the bed-walking strip and one other in this collection shows how effectively McCay could assimilate the American scene when he chose, and there is another cartoon showing Niagara Falls which must have been beautiful in the original colors. All the reproductions in the little book I speak of are in black-and-white, but the reader can get some idea of how enchanting McCay's use of color could be by looking at the plate facing p. 16 in Waugh.

[15] In *The Seven Lively Arts* (Harpers, 1924), reprinted in a revised edition, without the illustrations, by Sagamore Press in 1957. An extensive, though not ideally-edited, collection of the cartoons is available in *Krazy Kat*, by George Herriman, with an Introduction by E. E. Cummings (Holt, 1946).

contemporary comic strip for which I can pretend to care very much, Charles Schulz's "Peanuts," which can be either wonderfully penetrating or completely flat. It is interesting that this most sophisticated comic, so much admired by the intelligentsia, should, in a sense, represent a return to the "kid"-stuff with which the comic strip began, and which most of the dull cartoonists of today have abandoned. But what a difference in the approach and method of treatment![16]

Of course I looked at a great many other comics in my youth, but those of which I have spoken were the ones which gave me most. I enjoyed "Mutt and Jeff" in the daily *American,* remained faithful to them for a number of years, and still read them when a paper in which they are contained comes in my way, but I was always conscious of a certain limitation in their appeal. It seems doubtful that anybody can ever really have been drawn to Mutt. Jeff is another story, but though Jeff is sometimes as "foxy" as Foxy Grandpa, his "foxiness" is of a decidedly more grubby variety. The farthest I ever descended as a child was to two adventure strips which were no doubt intended as burlesques of popular melodrama, but which, at the time, I took dead seriously —"Hairbreadth Harry," by Charles W. Kahles, which began in 1906 in the Philadelphia *Press,* and which I encountered in Chicago in the Sunday *Record-Herald,* and Harry Hirshfield's "Desperate Desmond" in the Hearst papers, beginning in 1910. Perhaps "Desperate Desmond" was to the American comic strip

[16] Both "Krazy Kat" and "Peanuts" can do with explication, at least for those who do not read them faithfully day by day. Schulz's principal explicator is Robert L. Short, *The Gospel According to Peanuts* (John Knox Press, 1964). This is a perfectly serious religious work, and I do not believe it ever forces the note, yet one might be reasonably familiar with the cartoon without suspecting very much of it. I am sorry to have to add, ungraciously, that I think it a pity that the actual drawing in "Peanuts" should be so surpassingly ugly. But I should like to drop a tear in passing over the demise of "King Aroo," the only cartoon creation of recent years worthy in any sense of comparison with "Krazy Kat," which ran through a brief career roughly contemporaneous with that of Denny Dimwit, and which, like him, was then brutally murdered without so much as an obituary. Fortunately one collected volume survives: *King Aroo,* by Jack Kent, with an introduction by Gilbert Seldes (Doubleday, 1953).

what Theda Bara was to be to the movies. The hero in this strip was named Claude Eclair and the heroine was Rosamond. In "Hairbreadth Harry" the villain was called Rudolph, and the heroine was Belinda the Beautiful Boiler Maker. That name was, I still think, an inspiration, but I doubt Kahles ever reached quite as high again. Of all the cliff-hanging adventures he devised I can remember only one. One Sunday, Harry, pursued by Rudolph and his myrmidons, approached a precipice. On its edge grew a tree from whose branches a large serpent was hanging. The dauntless Harry grasped the serpent's neck, swung himself over the precipice, and Rudolph was foiled again. But because I feared and hated snakes above everything else in the world, I for some reason took this as a personal affront. I could hardly have been more aggrieved if somebody had struck me in the face, and I swore that I should never, no, never look at "Hairbreadth Harry" again! I have often wondered whether Charlie Chaplin was influenced by this when, in his last Keystone, *His Prehistoric Past* (1914), he let himself down over a cliff by a snake.

The big change in the comics began in the early twenties, which was also the time that the Chicago *Tribune*–New York *News* syndicate began to secure the pre-eminence in the field which it long maintained. Despite "Old Doc Yak," who was Sidney Smith's hero before "The Gumps," I think it may be said that in general *Tribune* comics were less fantastic and imaginative, more domestic and down-to-earth than the Hearst comics, and if the change of which I am speaking can be nailed down to a date, it must be Valentine's Day in the year 1921. Frank King's "Gasoline Alley" had been running since August 24, 1919. At first it was a single panel showing the men of the neighborhood fussing over their cars, and this did not interest me at all. But on the date I speak of a foundling baby was left on Walt Wallet's doorstep. And that baby became Skeezix, the first child in the comics to grow up and have descendants.

In a world in which the Katzenjammer Kids still had the same age they had attained in 1897, this was creative cartooning. Unimaginative people felt that it was superior in kind to what Dirks had achieved, which of course is nonsense; art which mirrors life is not as such superior to art which transcends life. Nor was it altogether revolutionary, for most comic-strip characters still retain perpetually the age at which we first meet them. But it *was* an interesting novelty, and it presaged a whole series of new developments which, at that particular time, interested many more people more deeply than anything any of the old-time cartoonists could have provided would have interested them. For many years thereafter, important successive events in the life of the Wallet family were followed as avidly as if they had been actual news events. I know no parallel in the "serious" art of our time except when the last of Galsworthy's Forsyte novels, *Swan Song*, appeared, and a London paper headlined

DEATH OF SOAMES FORSYTE.

The new development interested me too, and I continued my exploration of "Gasoline Alley" for many years, though I have now given it up. But I never passed on to the other strips through which the comics ceased to be comics. I have never liked serials, and I said good-by to all that when I outgrew "Desperate Desmond." I have always found "Little Orphan Annie," "Dick Tracy," and "Li'l Abner" quite unreadable, and I certainly would not try to read any of them except for money. "Pogo," of course, stands on a higher level. The drawing is attractive, the text is literate, and the informing point of view is intelligent and humane. I have often thought that I "ought" to read "Pogo." But when I have tried I have rarely felt that it was worth the effort involved.[17]

This does not mean that I demand a belly-laugh per minute

[17] I have, of course, said nothing of that great chief of all cartoonists of the nostalgic school, John T. McCutcheon, whose works are not exactly "comics," for which I would refer the reader to *John McCutcheon's Book*, edited by Franklin J. Meine and John Merryweather, with an Introduction by Vincent Starrett, which was published by the Caxton Club of Chicago in 1948 in a magnificent limited edition designed by Bruce Rogers.

while reading the comics. As a matter of fact, I doubt that I often laughed while reading about Foxy Grandpa, Buster Brown, or Happy Hooligan. These amazing creatures occupied a wonder world, and I explored it with delight.

One word more. Most of the Sunday strips of the first generation of the comics were collected and republished in book form. Since they were reprinted in the actual size in which they had appeared in the papers, each book, bound in stiff cardboard covers, was half the size of a newspaper page and sold for about sixty cents. Some of these books were brought out by standard publishers; the respected Frederick A. Stokes Company carried I know not how many "Foxy Grandpa" and "Buster Brown" titles for many years. Now all these books are very difficult to find; I can only conclude that, being bought for children, they were literally read to pieces. I myself am the proud possessor of the Buster Brown book I have already described and of a much more cherished fragment of a "Foxy Grandpa," but I have not encountered anything new for many years. Only the other day, a very intelligent bookseller of my acquaintance, a contemporary of my own, told me that he had never heard of these books, and not long after he proved it by offering me something utterly unrelated to them with an inquiry as to whether that was what I was talking about. It is sad to think of any man wasting his life as that man must have wasted his.

62

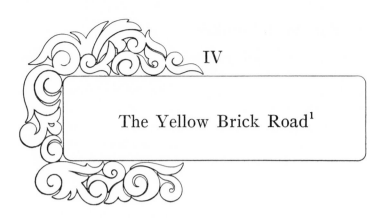

IV

The Yellow Brick Road[1]

I ACQUIRED MY FIRST BOOK when I was nine months old. It was the engaging chronicle of the *Three Little Kittens Who Lost Their Mittens,* and it was purchased for me by my grandmother while she, my mother, and I were on a shopping tour in a Chicago department store. I am told that I clasped it to my small person with both arms and exclaimed rapturously, "My kitty mamma!" I had managed to join two of my ruling passions—books and cats —at a very tender age. I wish I still had that book. I would give it a place of honor on the shelf that holds Carl Van Vechten's *The Tiger in the House,* Agnes Repplier's *The Fireside Sphinx,* and so much besides.

Yet my childhood was much less bookish than it ought to have been. Except for Dickens' novels, we had few books in our house, and the Dickens was printed in a type which made it very unattractive to a small boy. The school library was very small also, and there was no branch of the Chicago Public Library near

1 Much of the material about L. Frank Baum and the Oz books in this chapter is taken from the pioneering critical essay on the subject, my *Utopia Americana,* "University of Washington Chapbooks," No. 28, Edited by Glenn Hughes (University of Washington Book Store, 1929). Copyright, 1929, by Edward Wagenknecht; copyright renewed, 1957, by Edward Wagenknecht.

63

where I lived. I never had a public library to revel in until we moved to Oak Park when I was fifteen, and I could hardly exaggerate the delight I took in the Oak Park Public Library, then housed in the charming old Scoville Institute, next door to the First Congregational Church, and with all its stacks open to the public. Except for the University of Chicago, I am sure it was the greatest intellectual influence that ever came into my life. Was the Scoville Institute always bathed in sunshine? It cannot possibly have been, but that is the way I always remember it.

Coming back now to the books of my childhood, it is amazing how little I made do and how far I stretched it. I had Grimm and Andersen at first hand, but not in good editions, and a good deal of what I ought to have had in more standard aspects came to me first in the form of curt summaries in school readers and as films. (For in those days practically all the great stories of the world were retold in one-reelers.) I was a little too late for the McGuffey readers (which have never since been equaled), and I never got very excited about the Jones readers which were standard in Chicago schools when I was a boy, but some of the supplementary readers interested me much more. I wonder how many people today remember Eulalie Osgood Grover's *The Sunbonnet Babies' Primer*. In its time it captured America, and the two little girls themselves (their faces were never shown) became almost as standard an item in popular art as was later to be supplied by Rose O'Neill's Kewpies. Despite my dislike of dolls, I was, inconsistently, very fond of them.

My first encounter with the Greek myths I made in second grade, in a little book called *In Mythland*. For many years I remembered it lovingly; finally I came across a copy of it at a church rummage sale and bought it and took it home. Alas! there was nothing there, for the great stories had been reduced to the level of "John has a ball. Tom has a kite," and it was impossible for me to understand how this book had once opened a whole world to me. But there was another more advanced book called *Four Old Greeks*, from which my second-grade teacher read

64

aloud the story of Hercules and the story of the Trojan War, and in the third grade we supplemented our regular text with Baldwin's *Third Reader*, through which a rather phenomenal number of great stories first came to me. I still have that book, and I am still grateful to its compiler.

The amount of affection that I was capable of lavishing upon such books as these seems wonderful to me today; it shows how starved I was. It was an event when my mother and I went downtown one Saturday morning to an educational supply house and bought my very own copy of Baldwin, as we had previously bought a geographical reader called *Around the World,* to which my attachment now seems somewhat less reasonable. In eighth grade we had *Treasure Island* and *A Christmas Carol* and *The Merchant of Venice*, and these were events every one, but there were not enough of them. I ought to have had much more, and I am ashamed not to have gone out and dug it up for myself.

Yet I suppose the very greatest reading pleasures of my childhood were less standard, as I think they always must be, for while a child needs guidance in his reading, he also needs to be left to make discoveries for himself. *The Roosevelt Bears,* by Seymour Eaton, enthralled me, first when they appeared on Saturdays in the Chicago *Daily News*, and later in book form with really gorgeous illustrations. In one episode they visit Harvard and read Emerson. I am sure this was the first time I ever heard of either, and I suppose they both came into my life, therefore, with a certain aura of intellectual grandeur attached to them which I have never really been able to associate with anything else that I encountered at a later stage. There was also a book called *Yama Yama Land,* by Grace Duffie Boylan (for some reason or other, it does not seem to be in the Library of Congress catalogue, and I unfortunately gave my copy away to a little girl in a moment of misguided generosity). It was popular at the time on the stage as well as between covers, and Bessie McCoy as the "Yama Yama Girl" won many hearts besides that of Richard Harding Davis. But it never meant as much to me as another, less well-known book which I still have—*Zauberlinda, The Wise Witch*, by Eva Katherine Gibson, which combined western Americana with Germanic fairy-lore. I had read this book in a borrowed copy before I owned a copy of my own, but one day, when I came home from school for lunch, my mother had a *Zauberlinda* for me beside my plate. If somebody were to give me a Gutenberg Bible now, it could not thrill me as that book did then. I always enjoyed the noon lunches at which I shared the morning's doings with my mother, but when I think of them now, my mind always goes first to the one which was graced by *Zauberlinda*, which was Monday, October 19, 1908, as my mother's writing on the flyleaf of the book still informs me.

I have got rid of all my multitudinous Algers too; if I still had them, they would be worth considerably more than the average of nineteen cents each which I paid for them case-bound. But though I do not wish to take up a superior attitude toward this writer, who gave me so much pleasure as a boy, I do think I read too much of him, so that he held me too long and perhaps kept me away from other things that I ought to have been reading. When I was in sixth grade I had a teacher who was very sure of this, and who encouraged me to read "good" books. My uncle had already tried to introduce me to Mark Twain, but unfortunately he began with *Huckleberry Finn*, which, though I read it with pleasure, I was not really prepared for; I ought to have had *Tom Sawyer*. I still remember the day I bought *Evangeline* in "The Riverside Literature Series" at the school bookstore, which must have been the first time I ever saw the Houghton Mifflin Piper; now, under Miss Bergner's prodding, my mother and I went downtown one Saturday morning and bought the "Household Edition" of Longfellow's *Poems*, the first standard hardcover book I had ever bought. It is interesting to remember that I never read it straight through until I was preparing to write my book on Longfellow about forty years later.

I suppose *Yama Yama Land* and *Zauberlinda* were both imitations of L. Frank Baum's *The Wizard of Oz*, and this brings me

66

at long last to the principal subject of this chapter. For Oz was the true wonderland of my childhood, and whatever else I missed, I am glad that I had this.

Librarians and authorities on children's books have long been more than a little myopic about the Oz books; incredible as it seems, they are not even mentioned in the authoritative *Critical History of Children's Literature*[2] which is such an excellent book in so many ways. In this year of grace, this prejudice seems to be melting away, at least so far as Baum's own work, and more particularly the earlier volumes in the Oz series, are concerned. Collectors, of course, never pay much attention to the critics, and first-edition copies of Baum's books have long commanded high prices which are continually climbing higher. Vincent Starrett gave *The Wizard of Oz* a chapter in his *Best Loved Books of the Twentieth Century*,[3] and David Dempsey contributed a discussion of "The Wizardry of L. Frank Baum" to William Targ's *Bibliophile in the Nursery*.[4] In 1956 the Columbia University Libraries observed Baum's centenary with an exhibition of his own writings and the writings of others about him,[5] and in 1960, when a standard review published a more than ordinarily insane piece of Freudian balderdash called "The Utopia of Oz," he began to pay the toll which is nowadays customarily exacted of every writer who has the misfortune to attract the attention of one of those critics whose swooning admiration of their own subtlety proves too much for their common sense.[6]

[2] By Cornelia Meigs, Anne Eaton, Elizabeth Nesbitt, and Ruth Hill Viguers (Macmillan, 1953).

[3] This was first serialized in the Sunday book section of the Chicago *Tribune*, then published in paperback by Bantam Books, 1955. Actually *The Wizard of Oz* does not quite qualify under the Starrett title. It was published in May, 1900, when the nineteenth century still had a little more than six months to go.

[4] World Publishing Company, 1957.

[5] See the catalogue, *Exhibition of Books by L. Frank Baum* (Columbia University Libraries, 1956), and Roland Baughman's article, "L. Frank Baum of the 'Oz Books,'" *Columbia University Columns*, Vol. IV (1955), 15–35. Both these items are important bibliographically; so is the December, 1962, number (Vol. XIII, No. 4) of *The American Book Collector*, to which a number of "authorities" on Oz, including the present writer, contributed.

[6] *Georgia Review*, Vol. XIV, 275–91. The writer is S. J. Sackett.

Baum has acquired an authorized biography[7] and a journal, *The Baum Bugle*.[8] In 1967 the Book-of-the-Month Club arranged with Dover Books for special editions of both *The Wizard of Oz* and *The Land of Oz* and took the two center pages of *The New York Times Book Review* to offer them, together with an LP record taken from the sound track of the Judy Garland film, to those wishing to take out a trial subscription.

Baum discovered Oz more or less casually and accidentally, nor did he, at the outset, have any idea what a gold mine he had struck. He had published in 1897 a book called *Mother Goose in Prose*, which is a volume of charming stories inspired by the historic jingles, the general idea being to tell that part of the story which Mother Goose did not tell. The book is excellent in its way and can be read along with Sarah Addington's later stories about the Mother Goose characters, *The Boy That Lived in Pudding Lane* and the others. But unlike *The Wizard of Oz*, *Mother Goose in Prose* is in no sense American in its inspiration; the author's fancy plays about and utilizes and transforms what he has read about, not what he has seen. And the same thing might be said about some of the later Baum books—*The Life and Adventures of Santa Claus, The Enchanted Island of Yew, The Magical Monarch of Mo, John Dough and the Cherub,* and *Queen Zixi of Ix, or The Story of the Magic Cloak*. Of course this is not to say that these works are inferior as literature. For my money, *John Dough* and *Zixi* rank with the very best of the Oz books, and nothing could persuade me that *Zixi* is not one of the best fairy tales ever written by anybody. (Frank Joslyn Baum, the writer's son, once told me that he agreed with me about this.) It is a strange commentary on the hazards of success in literature that though all the Oz books—good, bad, and indifferent—by Baum and other writers, should have been always available,

[7] Frank Joslyn Baum and Russell P. MacFall, *To Please a Child* (Reilly & Lee, 1961).

[8] Published by the International Wizard of Oz Club, with headquarters at 1620 First Avenue South, Escanaba, Michigan, 49829.

John Dough and *Zixi* have long been out of print in America.[9]

When he finished *The Wizard of Oz*, Baum had no idea that he had embarked upon a series. The next year he came out with the quite unrelated *Dot and Tot in Merryland*, which is set in a candy country, ruled over by a doll, and which, to me at least, is not one of his most interesting stories. Indeed the idea for an Oz series originated not with Baum but with the children who deluged him with letters, begging him to tell them what became of the Scarecrow, the Tin Woodman, and others after Dorothy had returned to Kansas. He did not yield to this pressure for four years; then, in 1904, he published *The Land of Oz: A Sequel to "The Wizard of Oz."* Presumably that was still to be the end of it. But he had not re-introduced Dorothy into Oz, and he now had Ozma on his hands as well. Still, it was not until 1907 that the third Oz book, *Ozma of Oz*, appeared. At last he had caught the message, and the next three years produced in succession *Dorothy and the Wizard in Oz*, *The Road to Oz*, and *The Emerald City of Oz*. And now untold thousands of American children looked forward each Christmas to finding a new Oz book under the Christmas tree.

Then, in 1910, Baum once more rebelled. He had a great many stories quite unrelated to Oz in his mind that he wanted to write; he probably feared, also, that if he continued to cultivate the one field, the stream of his fancy would finally run pretty thin. Certainly *The Road to Oz* is the least impressive of the first six Oz books, though a very strong recovery was signalized by *The Emerald City of Oz*. It was in that work, however, that Baum invented an elaborate fiction about how the Land of Oz had been made invisible and cut off from communication with the rest of the world, and himself, as Royal Historian of Oz, thus incapacitated from securing further information concerning it. I can still remember how sad this announcement made me.

[9] The Opium Press in Hong Kong (surely a name for a publisher of children's books which would be rejected as too absurd for either the comic strip or slapstick comedy) has recently brought out a small edition of *John Dough and the Cherub* with very Chinese-looking illustrations.

As Far As Yesterday

I ought to have known better, and so should he. The imaginations of Baum's readers were Baum-nurtured; they had seen far too many difficulties surmounted to consider any such obstacle final. Until 1913 Baum went on writing some of the other stories he desired to write. Naturally they were much less successful commercially than his Oz books. Then, in 1913, wireless re-established communication with Oz (reality was catching up with fairyland), and Baum delighted a huge audience with *The Patchwork Girl of Oz*, which was so successful that he promised the children of America that he would go on writing books about Oz as long as they cared to read them. He lived long enough to produce seven more of them, one each year, until he died in 1919.

In *The Royal Book of Oz*,[10] the Scarecrow, having gone out to look for his family tree, inadvertently slides down the bean pole and lands in a mysterious kingdom where, very uncomfortably for himself, he is regarded as the incarnation of a long-lost Emperor. Making the best of a bad situation, the Scarecrow gathers the fifteen little princes together and tries to amuse them. They

[10] As all devotees of Oz know, Oz books have been written since Baum's death by Ruth Plumly Thompson, Jack Snow, Rachel R. Cosgrove, and (in collaboration) Eloise Jarvis McGraw and Laureen McGraw Wagner. From 1921 until she decided she had had enough in 1940, Miss Thompson was officially "Royal Historian of Oz," producing nineteen books as against Baum's fourteen. (*The Royal Book of Oz* was published as "by L. Frank Baum, enlarged and edited by Ruth Plumly Thompson," but actually it was wholly hers.) Since she stopped writing Oz books, the field has been pretty well open, though Jack Snow would probably have pre-empted it if he had lived. At this writing, the latest Oz book is *Merry Go Round in Oz*, by McGraw and Wagner. Actually, Mrs. Wagner had the idea, but her mother did all the writing. Mrs. McGraw is an accomplished writer, as her other publications have shown, and *Merry Go Round in Oz* is probably the best written of all the Oz books, including Baum's. It does not seem to me very "Ozzy" however, and I question the wisdom of bringing in so much material from other literary sources and blending so many traditions as has here been attempted. About Miss Thompson's work, all I can say is that though many Oz fans admire it, I have never been able to care much for it myself, which, I am sure, is much more of a loss to me than it could possibly be to her. I have often thought, indeed, that Baum's reputation might stand higher than it does if the series had not been continued by other writers whose efforts are often carelessly confused with his own. Russel B. Nye makes as good a case as can be made for Miss Thompson in his article "Ruth Plumly Thompson: An Appreciation," *Baum Bugle* (Autumn, 1965). For an encyclopedic treatment of all the Oz books up to the date of its publication, see Jack Snow, *Who's Who in Oz* (Reilly & Lee, 1954).

are very literal-minded children, however, and he does not succeed very well. For example, when he tries to tell them of the wonders of the Land of Oz, the oldest prince immediately flips out a map, and not being able to find the Land of Oz therein, at once announces serenely that he does not believe there is such a place. Well, I once knew a boy who started to read Pyle's *Men of Iron* and threw it aside in disgust when he learned that it was a romantic story of knights and knighthood. He had expected a story about the Gary, Indiana steel mills.

Now this is the kind of child that Baum did not believe in nor write for. He used to say that his stories were intended for everybody whose heart was young, no matter what his physical age might be. In the Preface to *The Magical Monarch of Mo* he addressed the children as follows:

> These stories are not true; they could not be true and be so marvelous. No one is expected to believe them; they were meant to excite laughter and to gladden the heart.
>
> Perhaps some of those big, grown-up people will poke fun at us —at you for reading these nonsense tales of the Magical Monarch, and at me for writing them. Never mind. Many of the big folk are still children—even as you and I. We can not measure a child by the standard of size or age. The big folk who are children will be our comrades; the others we need not consider at all, for they are self-exiled from our domain.

I have said that Baum wrote *American* fairy tales. By this I do not mean that he has used no European materials. Had this been the case, his output could hardly have been recognized as wonder tales at all. The greatest villain in all the Oz books is the Nome King (the *G* was omitted to make it easier for the children to pronounce the word!), ruler of an underground nation of elves, as old as fairy lore itself. Again, we have Polychrome, the Rainbow's daughter, surely a character with nothing distinctively American about her, and in *Dorothy and the Wizard in Oz* there is a thrilling fight with gargoyles, taken straight off the medieval cathedrals.

As Far As Yesterday

These, however, are not the distinctively "Ozzy" characters. In *The Wizard of Oz*, Dorothy finds the Scarecrow, newly made, with a pole up his back, in what seems very like an American cornfield. She lifts him down, and they follow the Yellow Brick Road to the Emerald City, where Dorothy plans to ask the Wizard of Oz to send her home to Kansas, while the Scarecrow wants brains instead of straw in the painted sack that serves him for a head. The next addition to their party is the Tin Woodman, whom they find badly rusted in the woods, and who cannot go along with them until they have oiled his joints so that he may walk. The Tin Woodman was once a man of flesh and blood, one Nick Chopper, in love with a pretty Munchkin girl. But a wicked witch enchanted his ax, so that as he was working in the forest he gradually cut himself to pieces. Fortunately he had among his friends a very wonderful tinsmith, who, as soon as any part of Nick's body had been cut off, would replace it with tin, until at last the man was all tin and as good as new. Only one thing was lacking: he no longer had a heart, and consequently he did not care whether he married the pretty Munchkin girl or not. The Tin Woodman therefore goes along with Dorothy and the Scarecrow to the Emerald City in the hope that the Wizard may give him a heart. Now who but a citizen of a country as heavily mechanized as the United States could ever have dreamed of such a creature as that?

Other, similar characters were introduced in later volumes. In *The Land of Oz* we met Jack Pumpkinhead, the Sawhorse, the Woggle Bug, and the Gump. Mr. H. M. Woggle Bug, T.E. is the aristocrat of the Oz books. Once he was an ordinary bug who happened to dwell in a schoolroom. Here he drank eagerly of the fountain of knowledge: hence the "T.E." after his name, which means "Thoroughly Educated."[11] One day, in the course of a natural-science lecture, the professor noticed the bug, and, by means of a magic lantern, threw him upon the screen in a highly

[11] Baum was anti-intellectual in his dislike of classical music and his mistrust of higher education.

72

magnified state ("H.M."). In this condition, the creature managed to make his escape, after which he became the most learned man in the Land of Oz. Jack Pumpkinhead was a Halloween prank, a body of wood with a pumpkin on top of it, brought to life by means of a magic powder. At first Baum apparently believed that when Jack's head spoiled that would be the end of him, but when fully embarked upon the Oz series, he decided that the Pumpkinhead was much too good to lose; accordingly he made him a farmer engaged in raising pumpkins. The upper part of Jack Pumpkinhead has died and been buried several times but he is still very much alive. The Gump is simply a crude sort of flying machine, made out of sofas, palm leaves, etc., with a stuffed head on the front to give it a sense of direction. The Sawhorse was intended originally simply for sawing wood, but once Tip had brought him to life with the magic powder, he was of course much better than a flesh and blood horse, for he did not need to eat, and he never tired. No wonder that he became the favorite steed of the Princess Ozma.

In *Ozma of Oz* we meet still another amazing creature, Tik-Tok, a marvelous machine man. Unfortunately he runs down every now and then and stands helpless waiting for somebody to wind him up again, but when he is correctly wound up, he is as good a man as any.

Later volumes introduce the Woozy, a strange animal with all square surfaces, the Ork, an ostrichlike creature, who flies by means of a tail which is attached to its body like the propeller of an airplane, and a marvelous, magical Teddy bear. Again, we have rubber mountains, submarines, sinking palaces, a vegetable kingdom, a country whose inhabitants are kitchen utensils, and a city inhabited by various kinds of bakery goods.

The use of machinery in the Oz books is also distinctly American. In general, magic may be said to inhere not in persons but in things, and whoever possesses the magical instrument can perform the magical feat. The forces of nature, as we know them in America, often serve as means of conveyance. In *The Wizard of*

As Far As Yesterday

Oz it is a Kansas "cyclone," as Baum calls it, though he describes it as behaving like a tornado, which carries Dorothy and her house over the Deadly Desert and deposits them in the Land of Oz. In *Ozma of Oz* Dorothy is shipwrecked. In *Dorothy and the Wizard in Oz* a California earthquake carries the girl down into the center of the earth, from which she finally makes her way to Ozma's country. In *The Scarecrow of Oz* Trot and Cap'n Bill are sucked into a whirlpool. And in *The Road to Oz* the Wizard sends people home from Ozma's birthday party in soap bubbles!

Indeed, the United States is very well represented in Oz. Dorothy, of course, hails from Kansas; the Shaggy Man came from Colorado; Betsy Bobbin's home was in Oklahoma. The Wizard himself is a native of Omaha, where he was connected with Bailum and Barney's Consolidated Shows. On exhibition days he used to go up in a balloon to attract the crowds, and once, losing control of his balloon, he was carried to the Land of Oz. Though the Wizard was a good ruler, his pretended magic was all imposture, as Dorothy learned when she wanted him to send her home to Kansas. Not until late in his career, when he became a pupil of Glinda the Good did the Wizard learn any real magic.

Now what is the significance of all this? Not, I think, that American magic is better than old-world magic, but simply that Baum enlarged the resources of fairyland. He did not destroy European magic; he simply added to it. And he did one thing more. He taught American children to look for wonder in the world around them and to realize that even smoke and steel can be transformed to wonder if the vision is there. In *Tik-Tok of Oz* the Shaggy Man explains all these things to Betsy Bobbin:

> "All the magic isn't in fairyland. . . . There's lots of magic in all Nature, and you may see it as well in the United States, where you and I once lived, as you can here."
>
> "I never did," she replied.
>
> "Because you were so used to it all that you didn't realize it was magic. Is anything more wonderful than to see a flower grow and blossom, or to get light out of the electricity in the air? The cows

that manufacture milk for us must have machinery fully as remarkable as that in Tik-Tok's copper body. . . . "

This seems to me significant and important. It is not healthy for children to feel that romance belongs only to the past, and that everything in their own country is drab, uninteresting, and businesslike. For, after all, we do grow to resemble our dreams, and if we are dull, unimaginative children, what shall we be as adults? Baum's work was significant because it pointed in the right direction: he has helped to teach three generations how to find wonder in contemporary American life.

I have spoken of the Land of Oz as an American utopia. By this I do not mean that the Oz books are full of social criticism. Yet the utopia element in them is strong, and if the children do not forget it all by the time they grow up, perhaps it is not too fantastic to imagine that it may do some good. It would not be a bad thing if American lawmakers and executives were to imbibe a few of the ideals which actuate the lovely girl ruler of the Emerald City—Ozma of Oz.

Perhaps the best brief description of Oz as utopia occurs in *The Emerald City of Oz*:

> The Emerald City is built all of beautiful marbles in which are set a profusion of emeralds, every one exquisitely cut and of very great size. There are other jewels used in the decorations inside the houses and palaces, such as rubies, diamonds, sapphires, amethysts and turquoises. But in the streets and upon the outside of the buildings only emeralds appear, from which circumstance the place is named the Emerald City of Oz. It had nine thousand, six hundred and fifty-four buildings, in which lived fifty-seven thousand three hundred and eighteen people, up to the time my story opens.
>
> All the surrounding country, extending to the borders of the desert which enclosed it upon every side, was full of pretty and comfortable farmhouses, in which resided those inhabitants of Oz who preferred country to city life.
>
> Altogether there were more than half a million people in the Land of Oz—although some of them, as you will soon learn, were not made

of flesh and blood as we are—and every inhabitant of that favored country was happy and prosperous.

No disease of any sort was ever known among the Ozites, and so no one ever died unless he met with an accident that prevented him from living. This happened very seldom, indeed. There were no poor people in Oz, because there was no such thing as money, and all property of every sort belonged to the Ruler. The people were her children, and she cared for them. Each person was given freely by his neighbors whatever he required for his use, which is as much as any one may reasonably desire. Some tilled the lands and raised great crops of grain, which was divided equally among the entire population so that all had enough. There were many tailors and dressmakers and shoemakers and the like, who made things that any who desired them might wear. Likewise there were jewelers who made ornaments for the person, which pleased and beautified the people, and these ornaments also were free to those who asked for them. Each man and woman, no matter what he or she produced for the good of the community, was supplied by the neighbors with food and clothing and a house and furniture and ornaments and games. If by chance the supply ever ran short, more was taken from the great storehouses of the Ruler, which were afterwards filled up again when there was more of any article than the people needed.

Every one worked half the time and played half the time, and the people enjoyed the work as much as they did the play, because it is good to be occupied and have something to do. There were no cruel overseers set to watch them, and no one to rebuke them or to find fault with them. So each one was proud to do all he could for his friends and neighbors, and was glad when they would accept the things he produced.

Much fuller command over nature exists in Oz than in any real country yet known. Animals can talk and mingle with human beings on terms of equality. Even insects are considerate and kindly; if a mosquito alights on you, you do not kill it, but simply politely request it to move on, and it complies. Many of the inhabitants of Oz, not being made of flesh and blood, do not need food, drink, sleep, or clothes. Those who feel that misery and maladjustment are necessary to interest either in literature or in

76

life may perhaps find support in the Oz books, for the country is so peaceful around the Emerald City that it is difficult to find adventure there. Consequently most of the Oz books take us off to obscure corners of the Land of Oz, which have not yet been civilized, and where the girl ruler's sway is only nominal.

Finally, there is no army in Oz. Ozma refuses to fight, even when her kingdom is in danger of invasion by the Nome King and his allies. "No one has the right to destroy any living creatures, however evil they may be, or to hurt them or make them unhappy. I will not fight—even to save my kingdom."

I am not sure that the children understand all the humor and satire in the Oz books. It will be remembered that in *The Wizard of Oz*, Dorothy, the Scarecrow, and the Tin Woodman travel to the Wizard because they desire, respectively, to get home to Kansas, to acquire some brains, and to receive a heart. The fourth member of the part is the Cowardly Lion, who wants the Wizard to give him courage. Though the Lion is a most ferocious fighter, he is much concerned because whenever he faces danger he is afraid. He trembles desperately, pitches in to do his best, and comes out victorious. Yet he knows that the king of beasts should not be a coward. So the Lion goes to the Wizard of Oz in search of courage.

Baum makes the entire journey a commentary on the text "Man does not live by bread alone but principally by catch-words." When danger arises, it is the Lion who protects the party. When a difficult problem arises, the Scarecrow solves it. Once the Tin Woodman accidentally steps on a beetle and kills it. Greatly distressed over his clumsiness, he weeps bitter tears, which run down his tin cheeks and rust the hinges of his jaw, so that the next time Dorothy speaks to him, he is unable to answer her until after she has taken the oilcan from her basket and oiled him up again. After he has a heart, he explains, he will not need to be so careful: his heart will tell him when he is doing wrong. But at present ceaseless vigilance is necessary to ensure his living a halfway decent life. The point of course is that all these creatures already possess what they are seeking. But because they lack the name, the reality of the situation eludes them.

When they arrive at the Emerald City, it is easy for the Wizard to satisfy the Scarecrow, the Tin Woodman, and the Cowardly Lion. The Lion eats a dish of porridge called courage and never trembles again. A silk heart stuffed with sawdust serves the Tin Woodman quite as well as a heart of flesh and blood, especially since the Wizard assures him that it is a very kind heart. The Scarecrow's brains are a judicious mixture of bran with needles and pins, and whenever one of the metal ingredients comes sticking through the sack which forms his head, he feels particularly sharp. But Dorothy wants to get home to Kansas, and Kansas does not lie within herself. That is a different kind of problem, and here is where the fake Wizard meets his downfall.

There are numerous other examples of satire. The absurd conceit of the Scarecrow after he gets his brains and the outrageous sentimentality of the Tin Woodman after he has acquired his heart are notorious and delightful. The Donkeys of Dunkiton think that donkeys are the wisest and most beautiful of all creatures. The worrying fraternity are made fun of in the Flutterbudget incident in *The Emerald City of Oz*.

Sometimes the satire cuts deeper, as in the achievement of the Woggle Bug, who has reduced all knowledge to pills, so that the students in his college will not need to waste any of their valuable time studying but are free to devote it all to such important things as football and other outdoor sports. Finally, even magic itself is made fun of. In *The Magic of Oz* Baum gives the world a formula for producing transformations. You simply pronounce aloud the word PYRZQXGL.

When I was a child, I heard much of the many letters the children wrote Mr. Baum and of his pride in them. I always intended to add one to that mighty collection, yet somehow I never did it until 1919. Then, no longer a child, I wrote to tell the magician of my childhood days what his books had meant to me. And thus he wrote in reply, exactly two months to the day before he died:

The Yellow Brick Road

March 6th, 1919

DEAR MR. WAGENKNECHT:

Your good letter was received some time ago. I thoroughly appreciated your writing me, and hoped to have answered it before. But with heart trouble we are inclined to be lazy, and time glides by without accomplishing all we would like to. I am very glad my books have given you pleasure, both in your childhood days and also now you are older. I have quite a few readers of mature years, who being children at heart still enjoy my tales. Received a letter from a church of England clergyman lately, telling me what a comfort my books were to him. When tired and discouraged with this war-torn world, he could let himself be taken to Oz, and for a time forget all else. It is things like your letter and his as well as the children's letters that make one feel they have done a bit to brighten up a few lives.

I am writing a little each day, and will have a new book ready for fall trade.

Thank you for writing me. It helps.

Ozily yours,

L. FRANK BAUM

So at the end the gentle, tired magician still believed in the goodness of the world that he had made.

There are some rough spots in our American utopia, but there is no denying its authenticity. It would be an easy thing to make the history of Oz a somewhat more highly finished record, but the chances are nine out of ten that you would at the same time make it somewhat less American. Someday we may have better American fairy tales, but that will not be until America is a better country.

79

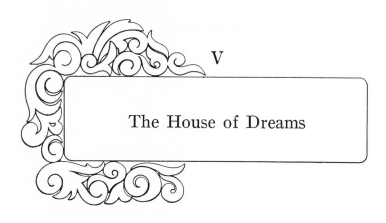

V

The House of Dreams

IT WAS A SUNDAY AFTERNOON, and my mother and I had had our usual walk through the park to the home of my aunts. But when we arrived we found them coated and hatted, prepared immediately to bundle us off again. For *Little Red Riding Hood* was being played at the People's Theater on the West Side, and my aunts were strongly of the opinion that they would not be doing their duty by me unless they gave me an opportunity to see it.

The idea seemed foolproof, but somehow or other it did not work out. I do not know how old I was (except that I must have been very small), and I have no idea why I behaved so badly, unless it was that having prepared for one kind of afternoon, I could not quickly adjust myself to something else (such shifts are still difficult for me). I comfort myself with the reflection that Sir Walter Scott, too, was disappointed upon his first visit to the theater. His play was *As You Like It*, and as soon as Oliver and Orlando got fairly launched upon their quarrel, little Walter shared their distress. "Ain't they brothers?" he cried aloud. But when I remember how soon the theater was to become one of my ruling passions, and how much money I was to spend on it—

sometimes, I fear, to the secret disapproval of those same aunts who tried thus, prematurely as it proved, to introduce me to its intoxications—it still seems to me that Thespis and I experienced an almost unbelievably maladroit introduction.

Of the play itself I remember nothing except one scene that could not possibly have been in it. I can still see the Wolf meeting Little Red Riding Hood in the forest, but as I see him, the Wolf has no shaggy hide. He is simply a man running on all fours, as we used to do when we acted Red Riding Hood at school. Obviously the play could not have been presented in this manner. So the one thing I remember didn't happen at all.

What did happen was that I was possessed by the imp of the perverse if any child was ever taken over by him. Nothing was right. I hated the play. I hated the theater. I hated everything and everybody around me, and I wanted to go home. A lady who sat near us tried to save the day. And for the moment it seemed—and my mother must certainly have hoped—that she might succeed. For she had some kind of program or folder which was illustrated with the most charming little woodcuts I ever saw in my life. I don't know what they were or what they portrayed, but how I wish I might see them again. Even at the time I knew I loved them, but I didn't want to love them. I wanted to tear them up. I didn't tear them up. Instead I gave them back to the lady. But I still wanted to go home. And at last we went—I do not know how long before the performance ended. And then I was sorry that we hadn't stayed, sorry for what I had missed, and sorry for what I had done to my mother and my aunts, to say nothing of some vaguely apprehended beauty at the heart of things.

I do not know how long my mother waited before she tried it again. And I don't know either whether she thought my critical faculties were budding prematurely, or what her motive may have been, but this time she chose a much more expensive theater and a much better show. This was *Way Down East*, making one of its perennial visits to McVicker's. And that day, in that theater and through that play, I entered the portals of the House of Dreams.

It is all vague and shadowy in my mind now. I am sure I did not understand the story, and I have no recollection of the actress who played Anna Moore. But I do remember Kate and the old gossip Martha, each in one moment in the Bartlett kitchen. I see Kate pressing a bouquet of red roses against her blue dress, and I see old Martha showing her startling plaid stockings as she sat down to the Bartlett table. These things and one more. Toward the end of the play, a procession of supposedly naked boys passed before the curtain. They had been in swimming—illegitimately, of course—and their clothes had been stolen, and now each had only a barrel to cover him. Or was that later, in *The Old Homestead*? At any rate, one of the boys stumbled and fell—or threatened to fall—with the promise of startling disclosures. Of course the "accident" was part of the show, but I did not know that. I had forgotten both the roses and the stockings until D. W. Griffith's *Way Down East* film came along in 1920 and brought them back to me. The film was quite good enough in itself for anybody's enchanted evening in the theater, but to me the pleasure was doubled, for I had the picture itself and also my reawakened memories of my initiation into the joys of theatergoing.

Of course I went back to McVicker's on other occasions later on. I remember one Sunday night when we attended *The Round-Up*, another hardy perennial of those days. During the performance the city was swept by a sudden blizzard, and transportation home was slow and difficult. I can still remember the glorious lightning made by the third rail on the Elevated (I did not yet have sense enough to be frightened), and I was almost exhausted plowing home through the snowdrifts from the station, but oh! I had the time of my life. And I remember *In Old Kentucky*, too, one Thanksgiving Day matinee, with the never-to-be-forgotten scene in which the heroine—heaven only knows why or for what, but who cares about that?—clung to an overhanging vine and

82

swung herself over the canyon, and of course *The Old Homestead*, and, later, Charlotte Walker, with (I suppose) William S. Hart (only I did not know who he was then) in *The Trail of the Lonesome Pine*.

Our visits to the downtown theaters were not frequent during my childhood, however, and when we went we chose the kind of thing I have been speaking of rather than the great stars. I knew their names and fame nevertheless from my diligent poring over the theater sections in the Sunday papers, and I was enthralled by the fame of Sothern and Marlowe in particular, though I never saw them until I had grown up, when they set a standard for Shakespearean acting and production which still serves me, yet if they had not emerged from their self-imposed retirement after World War I, I should have missed them altogether. Robert B. Mantell was a much less finished or intelligent actor, and his productions were much inferior, but though his virtues were all those of "inspiration" and not craft, he himself had unmistakably been touched by the divine fire, and I have often called his Lear the greatest performance I ever saw on the legitimate stage. During my last year in high school, I also saw Sir Herbert Beerbohm Tree in his productions of *King Henry VIII* and *The Merry Wives of Windsor*. As an actor, Sir Herbert seemed to me outshone by both Lyn Harding and Edith Wynne Matthison, but the splendor of his stagecraft was unbelievable; I have never seen anything to match it since.

Fortunately I did not have to wait until I had grown up to see the great magician Howard Thurston, who could make a woman float in the air, or cut her in two, or cause her to vanish from a cabinet on stage and then find her locked in the innermost of three trunks which he brought down from the ceiling of the theater, where they had been fastened on a pulley since before the beginning of the performance. He could cause water to gush abundantly from a faucet suspended in thin air, and cause doves to appear and disappear, and he could go down into the audience and pull a live rabbit out of the back of a man's coat. He also did a great many tricks with cards and scarves that actually required much more skill than his more spectacular effects, though of course I did not know that then, and he could send his souvenir cards flying out over the audience, clear up to the second balcony. When, many years later, I met him, and told him how he had thrilled me, he wanted to know why. "Did you," he asked, "suppose that I was a man with supernatural powers?" I said, "No, I don't think so. I believe I knew it was all tricks, though I enjoyed being fooled. But I believe your own personality appealed to me as much as anything you did." This was the right answer, and I could see that he was greatly pleased.

The personality combined great dignity with great charm. He was a courtly gentleman and a great showman, and he was always in complete control of the situation. I think he was the first man I ever saw in tails, and I have not seen many since who could wear them as he did. Years later I saw Blackstone, who did many of the same things Thurston did, and did them just as well. Blackstone, too, was a gifted showman, but he was not Thurston. By that time, the girls who waited on magicians and handed them their properties were wearing as little as the law allowed, which may very likely have performed the service of distracting the attention of the audience at times when it was convenient to the magician that it should be distracted. I remember once when a girl turned her back on him and walked toward the wings that Blackstone gazed after her and then winked or glanced knowingly at the audience. I do not say there was any harm in this, but it was entertainment upon a plane to which Thurston would never have dreamed of descending.

Thurston's publicity, which involved posters and buttons and cards and other souvenirs, was almost as wonderful as his show, and his standard portrait showed him with two little red devils on his shoulders whispering their secrets into his ears. But Thurston's devils were benevolent creatures, and no child could possibly have been frightened by them. Once I followed up an engagement of his at the Imperial Theater on West Madison

84

The House of Dreams

Street by collecting a considerable array of posters from the shops which had displayed them during his engagement, braving saloons and other establishments that I would never have condescended to enter under less pressing circumstances. I have never seen more colorful theater posters; I wish I had kept them.

It happens that when I finally met Thurston, I was on my first "date" with the girl I was to marry. Since he did not really have supernatural powers, he probably was not aware of this, but he still enjoyed a bit of hocus-pocus. So, after he had given me a signed photograph of himself, he put one of his good-luck pieces between our hands and went through some rigamarole which embarrassed the girl not a little, beginning with "Now when you are married. . . . " As I have often told her since, this took responsibility for everything that happened afterwards quite out of my hands.

One other thing should be remembered, and this is that in the days of my childhood the "live" theater still survived not only in every city but in every neighborhood. Many motion-picture theaters were not merely motion-picture theaters but motion-picture theaters and vaudeville theaters combined. There were hundreds of these in Chicago, and there must have been many hundreds of people appearing in them. Since the tariff was never higher than ten cents and often only five, they cannot have been very highly paid, and I suspect some of them were Chicago residents who were thus supplementing their regular income with extra evening work. If so, it must have been a grueling life.

If you attended the same theater for any length of time you encountered a number of repeaters. I remember only one name— Cecile Gordon. She was a pretty redheaded girl who sat on a wicker suitcase and sang. She had no voice, but her singing was not really the point. For she had a dog with her, and when she sang, the dog sang too, in his way, which was supposed to be funny. And, in those days, her audiences were just simple enough to find it so. But probably the fact that she was pretty and redheaded helped.

85

As Far As Yesterday

There were acrobats and soubrettes galore and tramp comedians and many teams consisting of a white man dressed to kill, often in a white suit and straw hat, with another man in blackface. They usually began with a song or a song-and-dance number and then went on to a dialogue in which the black man "fed" lines to the white man and acted as his butt. I'm afraid it was racially discriminating comedy, but in those days nobody found any harm in it.

There was little or nothing of what is now called "blue." The most daring act I remember was that of a person who sang "Mary Is a Grand Old Name." It was not the song that was daring but the way it was presented. The singer entered, a grotesque, lanky figure of a woman, in a perfect comic-valentine, "old maid" make-up, extending even to a cherry on the end of the nose, and a skirt split on one side clear to the waist. Though women were still skirted to the ground in society in those days, we had no trouble with our soubrettes in knee-length skirts nor our lady-acrobats in tights either, but a leg brazenly poked through a long skirt was something else again. The voice was a very high soprano, and you were not supposed to know there was a man before you until, at the end, the singer pulled off his wig and ran off the stage. I had never heard the word "transvestism" in those days, and if I had heard it, I should have had no idea why it was shocking, but I did know that some ladies were indignant that a mere man should have the nerve to present such a grotesque caricature of a woman.

Sometimes we got a "dramatic sketch" involving a number of players, but such acts must have been expensive and could not be expected every day. I remember one piece called "The End of the World," which was done in Yiddish dialect, with the devil as one of the characters, and another, much less fantastic, in which a waif was introduced, unrecognized, into the home of her wealthy and very haughty grandmother. The climax came when the child found her mother's photograph in the old lady's album, and I can still hear the haughty lady exclaim, "Youah

86

The House of Dreams

mothah's pickcha in my ahlbum? Ahbsuhrd!" It must have been the first time I ever heard what was later to be called "theater speech," or what the actress thought was such in any case.

A variety of shows, both more and less elaborate, were put on at the amusement parks, which were then in their heyday at Chicago. How I can ever have enjoyed shooting the chutes or riding the roller coaster is now quite beyond my power to understand, yet I did, though I never cared for this kind of thing anything like so much as I did for the shows. The boat ride called "A Trip to Venice" at White City brought me one of the rarest visions of beauty I have had in my life, for the boat passed through a series of (I suppose one would have to call them) stage sets, representing Venetian scenes, bathed under a soft golden light. Whether there was anything authentic—or even truly beautiful—about them, I have no idea, yet I have carried them in my mind across the years, though in the vaguest possible way, and with the slightest possible local denotation, and there are not many hours in my life that I should be more happy to recapture. It is such experiences as this that have caused me to be less distressed than many persons are about the dangers involved in children coming into contact with "cheap" art. The child does not really need Rembrandt or Michelangelo. All he needs is to have his imagination stimulated; he will do the rest. And a paper star cut out of cardboard may serve him as well as a diamond star from Tiffany's might serve his mother.

One night, at Riverview, I saw something I had never seen before and have never seen since—life-sized puppets. There was something rather sinister about them, for they flopped about the stage like dead things, yet at the same time there was a terrible energy in them, or at least so it seemed to a small boy who, by this time, was having considerable trouble to stay awake. For many years nobody ever believed me when I told them I had seen life-sized puppets; there never were such things, I was told. Ultimately I encountered a distinguished puppeteer. "Did I really see them," I asked him, "or did I imagine it?" "When was

As Far As Yesterday

it?" he wanted to know, and I told him as well as I could remember. "Yes," he said, "you saw them. There was one Italian troupe that used life-sized puppets, and they were touring the United States just about that time."

There was terror, too, in the amusement parks, as well as rapture. Once I even encountered it in the penny arcade, where I ran into a picture about a girl committing suicide. That was all there was to it. She swallowed poison before her protesting family and fell over dead. I can still see the old-fashioned clothes she wore and the quaint cap on her head, and I could not get the thing out of my mind for a long time. It still seems to me a queer choice of subject for entertainment purposes, especially in entertainment directed primarily toward children.

But there was a different kind of terror at the Katzenjammer Castle, which was at the Chutes, a small and short-lived amusement park on the West Side. It was a large, white building, ornamented with gorgeous, highly-colored statues of the then popular comic-strip characters. When my mother and I went in, we expected to encounter more such delights inside, or at least I did, for my mother was always able to keep her devotion to the comic strip under control. What we encountered was darkness and swaying floors and howling winds and the imminent threat of dire catastrophe, for the Katzenjammer Castle was one of the early, sadly misnamed "fun houses." I have rarely been so frightened in my life as I was that day.

The showiest attractions at the Chutes were a man who came down the shoot-the-chutes on a bicycle and jumped through a hoop of fire, and a "mermaid," called, of all things, "Helter," whose brightly-lithographed portraits, tail and all, decorated the posters on the Elevated stations. Both were pretty much "frosts." The man who jumped through the hoop looked like a bruiser, and there wasn't enough fire to scare a mouse, while as for "Helter," instead of being the gorgeous blonde creature of the posters, "she," too, was all too obviously human and male. Per-

88

haps "she" may even have been the bruiser who jumped through the hoop.

The most elaborate shows presented in the amusement parks, however, were what I should describe as motion pictures in the round. The principles of stagecraft employed must have been very much like those Steele MacKaye devised for his aborted Spectatorium at the World's Columbian Exposition in 1893, except that I should judge MacKaye did it much more elaborately and realistically. In any case I remember seeing "The Johnstown Flood" and "The Chicago Fire," but the two biggest and longest-lived attractions at Riverview were "The Battle of the *Monitor* and the *Merrimac*" and "The Creation." The latter was a really grandiose affair, presenting the Seven Days of Creation in stage spectacles accompanied by off-stage commentary, and shown in a building which had been designed especially for this show, with a gigantic angel built like a huge pillar square in the middle of the exterior and with wings extended on both sides clear across the top of the building.[1] The show was exciting throughout, and elaborately lighted, but of course everybody waited for the moment when Adam and Eve should appear. They wore what I suppose might best be described as pink union suits, and even I was knowing enough to realize that both characters were being portrayed by females.

But when all is said and done the real theatrical joys of my childhood came to me through the People's—that same People's which, at the outset, I had so rudely spurned. This marvelous institution was part of a once ambitious project called the People's Institute, situated at the corner of Van Buren and Leavitt streets. When it was in its glory, my father and mother and I

[1] Evidently "The Creation" was not peculiarly a Chicago phenomenon. See the pictures on p. 186 of Edo McCullough's *Good Old Coney Island* (Scribners, 1957) and in *American Heritage*, Vol. IX, No. 4 (June, 1958), p. 15, illustrating Peter Lyon's article, "The Master Showman of Coney Island." For Steele Mac-Kaye's Spectatorium, see A. Nicholas Vardac, *Stage to Screen* (Harvard University Press, 1949).

used to go there every Sunday afternoon and our seats in the "Family Circle," towards the rear of the main floor, cost us thirty cents each. Here I saw *The Fatal Wedding, The Heart of Chicago, Fanchon the Cricket, Old Heidelberg, Jane Eyre, Eben Holden, The Road to Yesterday, Zaza* (an unwonted excursion into the demimonde that gave the theater's much-admired leading woman, Marie Nelson, one of the acting opportunities of her life), and a great many other plays. The melodramas of the gaslight era were not, as even this brief list shows, the exclusive reliance of the house, but they were its staple. Had I come along ten years later, I should have missed most of them, and my life would have been poorer. I must have caught them about the last time they were done seriously.

Shall I ever forget the scene in *The Fatal Wedding* in which the blackhearted villainess tried in vain to poison the altogether perfect and completely virtuous but sick and poverty-stricken heroine? She was sitting in a poor, bare room in the tenements— our heroine—with nobody to care for her except her little daughter. In the course of her ministrations, the little girl prepares a draught for her mother and sets down the medicine glass for a moment on the corner of the bureau near the door. Stealthily the door opens and the villainess peers into the room. While the child's back is turned, the villainess uncorks a small bottle of poison and pours its contents into the medicine glass. The child, unaware of what has happened, picks up the glass and starts to carry it across the room to her mother, while the audience holds its breath. When she has nearly reached our heroine, she stumbles and drops the glass, spilling its contents upon the floor. How the villainess cursed! How we cheered! How our hearts revived within us! How we renewed our faith in the "somehow good"!

Other scenes travel across the screen of memory. I see Louise Lester, the character woman of the company, who later appeared on the screen in the "Calamity Jane" pictures with Warren Kerrigan, hobbling energetically across the stage through a clearing in the forest as a witchlike old woman in *Fanchon the Cricket*.

90

The House of Dreams

I hear Bertha Rochester's scream in *Jane Eyre*. I see the old man shutting up the house at the close of *Shore Acres*. I see the look of jealousy which Jinny flashed at her husband in Clyde Fitch's play, *The Girl with the Green Eyes*, which was comparatively sophisticated fare for the People's, the honeymoon scene in Rome before the Apollo Belvidere, and the heroine's attempted suicide in the last act, which upset me and invaded my dreams. But the suicide in *The Heart of Chicago* did not bother me at all, though the villain shot himself in the mouth, with the ruins of the burning city all around him, and when his head fell backwards and his mouth opened, a puff of smoke came out of it!

When the melodramas are performed nowadays, they are generally burlesqued, for the excellent reason that very few modern actors are capable of playing them in any other way. It is true that they were sometimes "hammed" even in their own time, but it should be remembered that they were also sometimes performed by very fine actors. Though they do not represent the highest type of dramatic art, there is a tradition behind them, and that tradition must be understood and recaptured before they can have a fair chance. Their authors and their actors were not trying to portray life; they were trying to enlarge it or escape from it. They were not trying to act naturally; they were trying to act artificially in the most beautiful possible way. And in what they were attempting they did not fail but succeeded. Though they generally employed only the primary colors, they dealt with large and serious matters, and they dealt with them in a large and serious way, being always on the side of the angels.

For me everything about the People's spelled romance. Even our journey thither was romantic. We changed from the Ogden Avenue to the Van Buren Street car at a corner graced by an institution which sold surgical appliances, and in whose display window two human skeletons were exhibited. As I have already suggested, my tastes in those days were very Gothic, and I never missed an opportunity to gloat over these skeletons.

Not far from the skeletons there was a store that sold "Velvet"

91

candy, the only place I knew where "Velvet" candy was sold. It was a species of molasses kisses which in itself interested me very little, but the boxes in which it came were decorated with pictures of monkeys, and my weakness for that creature has already been made clear in these pages. In the course of time I must have acquired the largest collection of "Velvet" candy boxes in the city.

Nearer to the theater there was a florist shop, some of whose displays almost rivaled stage settings themselves, and these glimpses of fairyland were not to be missed, even though I could only catch them for a moment in passing, from the moving car. But the entrance to the theater itself was another matter. There was an electric sign, one of the first I had ever seen; there were curved billboards— to this day, curved billboards, like curved windows (of which there are still a number in Boston), have always seemed to me much more enchanting than flat ones—and there was a case of fascinating photographs of the ladies and gentlemen of the company along one wall of the lobby. Next door there was the large plate-glass window of a confectionery establishment, which was almost covered with scrolls and pictures and ornamented titles advertising coming attractions. All this had been painted (I suppose) on the inside of the glass, and whoever had achieved it was an artist. I don't know whether the People's ever got round to *Romeo and Juliet* or not. I do know that I never saw it there. It was another stock company which, later, at the Imperial, gave me my first Shakespeare on the stage, and Miss Eda von Luke was my first Juliet. But the People's had it "Coming" for a long time, and many a Sunday I gazed in awe at the picture of the duel scene in which Romeo had driven his sword clear through Tybalt's body and out at the back.

Marie Nelson was the heart and soul of the company. How good an actress she was, judged by contemporary standards—if they are relevant—I cannot say, but I do know that she was a phenomenon. The People's played eleven performances a week —seven nights and four matinees—and changed the bill every

The House of Dreams

Monday night. In all these plays she enacted an astonishing variety of leading roles. I once heard Barrett H. Clark say that in 1910 there were 2,500 stock companies in America. There must have been a good many people like Marie Nelson, locally famous and nationally almost unknown. And I have an idea that a reasonable percentage of them must have achieved a very high degree of competence.

I remember her as a rather large woman—though it may be that she only looked large to a small boy—with dark red hair. I do not know whether she was beautiful, but she had strong expressive features of the kind that "carry" well over the footlights. I do know that she was always an actress of dignity and restraint. One leading man found it convenient to fall in love with her, and his affection not being returned, almost wrecked the theater. Or at least that was what contemporary gossip said. This much at least is certain, that he took to playing his love scenes with her with increasing force and passion, that the theater closed temporarily without official explanation, and that when it reopened there was a new leading man. I remember one play—many years afterwards, when I stumbled upon it again, I found that it was *A Scrap of Paper*, by Victorien Sardou—in which he was called upon to apostrophize a shawl that the adored one had worn, and I am ready to take my oath that there never was such an apostrophe in this world. Even then I knew he was doing some pretty execrable acting. Later Miss Nelson did marry another leading man, Rodney Ranous, and thereafter they were a team, on and off the stage.

One night before her marriage—so a relative of her husband's told me many years later—she woke up to find a burglar crawling into the window of her room. The next day she went downtown and bought the most vicious-looking bulldog she could find. Thereafter she was always guarded by him—at home, at the theater, and on the street and the streetcars between the two localities. In that neighborhood, where she was so well known, she attracted as much attention as movie stars at a later date, and when you encountered her on the cars she was likely to protect herself against intrusion by burying herself in the "sides" of next week's role.

Towards the end of her engagement at the People's, which must have been close to the beginning of World War I, there were changes in the management, and the organization was now known as "The Marie Nelson Players." But by this time stock companies were beginning to have hard sledding. The company also now seemed to be trying to break away from melodrama, but they were not being entirely successful in finding something to take its place. I think the last thing I saw them do was Jerome K. Jerome's play, *Miss Hobbs*.

Miss Isabelle Randolph, the ingenue of the company, was also extremely popular. She was a very young girl at the time; years later, when I was living in Oak Park, she turned up briefly as leading woman of a stock company at the Warrington Theater, and proved herself an excellent actress. In the old days we liked her as an ingenue, but when Marie Nelson was ill and she assumed the leading role in *The Road to Yesterday*, we were disappointed. But it is the way of substitutes to disappoint, and it is not always their fault. Moreover I am sure I did not understand *The Road to Yesterday* at the time. That charming old play by Beulah Marie Dix and Evelyn Greenleaf Sutherland deals with time-traveling, and it would be a long time before that became a popular exercise in literature. In later years I grew very fond of it.

Of the leading men connected with the company the most popular was Edward B. Haas, generally spoken of as "Ed" Haas. He had been connected with the company in its early days, before I became acquainted with it, and he returned after the debacle allegedly precipitated by the actor who apostrophized the shawl. In the meantime he had apparently acquired some reputation, and he—or the management—were disposed to make the most of it. His name was plastered all over the theater, and his photographs were hawked among the patrons between the acts. They bought them too, for he was a very handsome man, though perhaps somewhat heavier in style and in figure than the types that are most in favor nowadays. If Marie Nelson was my introduction to the theater, "Ed" Haas was my first prolonged exposure to the matinee-idol type.

There was a juvenile too, a comedian named Thomas B. Swift, whom the girls adored. When he was taken ill with appendicitis, they nearly broke their hearts, standing before a collection of his photographs and sighing for "Poor Tommy." Except for Frank Beal, the manager of the company, who helped out occasionally in character roles, these are the only names I recall.

For many years the People's Theater was used by a religious organization of a rather violently evangelistic type; later the building passed into the hands of some trade union or other which found the old auditorium a good place in which to hold its business meetings. During both periods, I suppose, the students of the Crane Technical High School, which is only a block away, passed and repassed its portals daily without the slightest suspicion that they had once been the gates of wonderland. Now the whole edifice has been swept away to make room for the Congress Street superhighway.

It was during the second phase—the trade-union phase—that I returned to Chicago after an absence of many years, and one night, when I was teaching a class at Lewis Institute on Madison Street, I strolled over to the old building to have a look. I went into the lobby—the cases that had held the photographs were still there, but there were no pictures in them—and I peered into the auditorium, where a single light was burning. Then I went around to the stage door.

When I got back to my office at Lewis, it occurred to me, for no particular reason, to open the phone book, and there, clear as type could make it, was listed after all these years, the name "Ranous, Marie Nelson," with a North Side number!

I wrote her a letter, which was returned by the post office, as somehow I knew it would be. I later learned, through the relative to whom I have already referred, that she had died, following an accident, only a few months before my return to Chicago. Since the old days at the People's she had experienced varying fortunes. Her husband, Rodney Ranous, had achieved permanent disability through being hit over the head every night with a rubber telephone in one of the touring companies of *The Bat*, and this had left her the sole support of the family during years when work for actors was hard to come by. From this she had been delivered by the radio serial *One Man's Family*, and her last years were spent in comfort. But through good days and bad she had remained the great lady the audiences at the People's had thought they saw in her so many years ago.

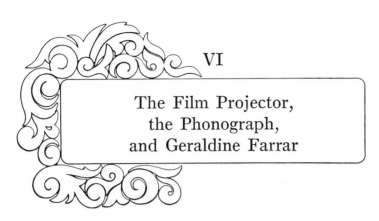

VI

The Film Projector,
the Phonograph,
and Geraldine Farrar

IT IS A CURIOUS BIT OF IRONY that a mechanical moron like myself, who has not the slightest interest in or understanding of mechanical processes, who will not ride in a plane and never learned to drive a motor car, should have been so dependent as I have been on four machines: the typewriter, the printing press, the film projector, and the phonograph. The reading and the making of books has been my work in life, and I have depended upon films and records for the lion's share of my recreation.

Young people today take all the technological wonders for granted: not only have they never known a world without films and records, but even radio broadcasting and television were there waiting for them as soon as they were ready. I do not envy them, for my generation had the excitement of discovering all these things, and for us they began as miracles.

The radio and television have never been a very important part of my life, and I do not propose to write about them. About films I could speak at great length, but I must not repeat here what I wrote in *The Movies in the Age of Innocence*. In the beginning, as I there tried to make clear, it was the simulation of

97

life itself—the sheer wonder of motion—that caught and enthralled us, and it is impossible for any youngster of today really
to understand how marvelous that was. Even those who, like
myself, actually experienced it, can no longer completely recapture the thrill, though, oddly enough, I sometimes get a suggestion of it while projecting films at home, not as I see them on the
screen but as they may be reflected in a mirror, a picture, or,
best of all, in a curiously constructed window, which multiplies
the images by two and creates the illusion of suspending them in
the atmosphere above my front yard.

For this is the astonishing thing about films—that just as many
of us were getting ready to repudiate them in their modern aspect (for all practical purposes, I myself got off the train at the
Monroe station), we were given the marvelous opportunity to
relive our lives and recapture our past through the sudden, unexpected availability of many of the old films, in eight-millimeter
copies designed for home use. So far as can now be foreseen,
motion pictures will never again mean to any generation of
young people what they meant to mine; high prices are partly to
blame, but the basic cause is the altered content of the pictures
themselves. Yet though far fewer people are seeing motion pictures *in theaters* today than was the case a generation ago, when
you take both telecasting and home-projection into consideration,
there is a very different story to tell. What we are witnessing, in
other words, is a movement of the film out of the theaters and
into libraries and homes.

If, in the days of my youth, anybody had told me that I might
someday own my own copies of the great D. W. Griffith films, I
should probably, had I believed him, have died of joy. But I
should not have believed him, any more than I should have believed him had he told me that I should be emperor of the world
and of the moon, for these were things to dream of (the films,
that is, for I never wished to rule anything), but not to possess.
When, in 1961, I reviewed all the big Griffith pictures except
Judith of Bethulia and *Hearts of the World*, which were then

98

unavailable, before writing *The Movies in the Age of Innocence*, I had not seen any of them for many years, and I did not see any of them again during the far fewer years that have passed since until I recently began to collect eight-millimeter copies. Now I can see them all any time I choose, just as I can hear a Verdi opera or reread a Dickens novel at my own fiat. And I must confess that this still seems to me something of a miracle.

But if it is wonderful to see the great Griffith films again— which, after all, I had seen many times and remembered well— it is, in a way, even more wonderful to renew acquaintance, often in films that I never saw before, with a host of persons who furnished me with the bulk of my entertainment more than half a century ago. Take, for example, John Bunny and Florence LaBadie. Bunny, the first great comic of the screen and a pan- tomimist of wonderful skill, died in 1915. Miss LaBadie died in 1917, at the age of twenty-three, as the result of injuries received in an automobile accident. A girl of great beauty and an accom- plished young screen player, she would surely have been one of the great stars if she had lived. I am sure I have never seen either of these people since they died except in 1961, when I glimpsed them both, very briefly, at Eastman House and The Museum of Modern Art. Now both have come back into my life, and I find that my reactions to them are very much the same as they were when I was a boy. This is a startling experience, and I suspect that it takes me about as close to time-traveling as I shall ever come.

It is not astonishing that persons like myself, who grew up with the old films, should be happy to renew acquaintance with them, but I confess I am surprised at the appeal which eight- millimeter collecting is evidently making to young people who were not even born when the films available were produced and who never saw most of the persons who appear in them until their images were projected upon the little home screen. Their reactions, much more than mine, prove that the old pictures have something more than a nostalgic value, and that though contemporary film makers are still under the strange impression that "movies are getting better and better," there are needs which their product does not satisfy. For many years, Lillian Gish and I stood almost alone in the conviction that the abandonment of silence and the screen technique that went with it had virtually destroyed a valuable art form; now that silent films are being made accessible again, thus increasing the number of persons who are capable of having an intelligent opinion on the subject, there may well be many more to agree with us than there used to be.

Hearts of the World and *Judith of Bethulia* were not available for reviewing when I wrote *The Movies in the Age of Innocence*. I was, therefore, obliged to describe both, in my chapter on Griffith, on the basis of my old memories of them, and I attempted no detailed consideration of either. Now that I have seen *Hearts of the World* again, not once but several times, I find that I was right in my feeling that it had done more for Lillian and Dorothy Gish than for D. W. Griffith. I think the reason for this is that while all his other big pictures were built around either a fine story or, as in the case of *Intolerance*, an idea, here he had neither, but only a contemporary world conflict, which, since the film had been made with the co-operation of the British government, had to be handled so as to adhere to the official propaganda line. The war was the central interest in the film, and the human actors did not have much to do storywise except, in one way or another, to illustrate its ebb and flow. At the time of its production, when we were all, in one way or another, involved in the passions of the time, this was enough, but its hold upon the imagination has been weakened with the passing of the years. It was not that Griffith had not been partisan before. He had, as a matter of fact, never been anything else, but hitherto, as in *The Birth of a Nation* and *Intolerance*, his partisanships, however pigheaded he might have been about some of them, had been honest partisanships; if they could not always stand up under critical examination, at least they had

100

been determined by the circumstances of his life and ancestry and rooted in his fundamental being. In *Hearts of the World*, however, he seemed more concerned with the partisanships of Georges Clemenceau, David Lloyd-George, and Woodrow Wilson than with his own. Griffith may well have quite sincerely "believed" in the Allied cause in 1917, but, as all his film work shows, he was at heart a pacifist, and even here, in a picture produced to support the bloodiest war mankind had yet achieved, he could not resist indulging from time to time in preachy subtitles (like "Does war ever really settle anything?"), directed not against the Germans but against war itself. That this was less a force for distortion than it might have been was no doubt because, at the time, we were all more or less under the impression that we were, as our head-shrinking political mentors had told us, "fighting for peace."

Judith of Bethulia was based on the story in the Old Testament Apocrypha and the poetic tragedy by Thomas Bailey Aldrich. It, too, has now been made available by Blackhawk Films, thus supplying an important hitherto missing link in the record of Griffith's development. His last film for Biograph, it was also his first "feature" (four reels), and it might be said that as *The Battle at Elderbush Gulch* (two reels) and such single-reel Civil War pictures as *The Battle* and *The Informer* foreshadowed *The Birth of a Nation*, *Intolerance* was foreshadowed in *Judith*. Its peculiar fascination derives from its standing on the threshold between the fresh and simple Biographs of Griffith's first period and the fully-developed "epics" which followed, and partaking, therefore, of the character of both. Compared with what was to come, the settings were modest and somewhat cramped (though Biograph was not alone in considering them the height of extravagance in their time) and the development a little stiff and formal; the masterly cumulative "flow" of narrative which was on its way to overwhelm the world in *Intolerance* and *The Birth of a Nation* is caught here only in course of emergence. The handling of crowds was nothing like what Griffith was afterwards

101

to accomplish: the "bacchanal" in the tent of Holofernes was unbelievably bad, and the battle scenes, impressive at the time, were soon to be overshadowed. Though he looked magnificent, Henry Walthall had almost no opportunity as Holofernes, for he was reduced almost to immobility. Blanche Sweet as Judith had richer opportunities and made the most of them; despite a tendency on the director's part to give us even this character in terms of a series of tableaux rather than in an unbroken, steadily accumulating, rising course of development, she had some excellent scenes. As Naomi, a young girl of Bethulia, Mae Marsh had all her youthful sincerity and charm, but she was given almost nothing to do. Early in the film she was captured by the besieging Assyrians and thereafter forgotten until nearly the end, when she was considerately remembered and rescued. It was almost as if she had been intended for a line of action which it was afterwards decided not to employ. Kate Bruce, as Judith's handmaid, Marah, gave, on the other hand, what must have been very nearly the performance of her career. All in all, *Judith* was a less perfect and completely integrated film than the contemporaneous *Battle at Elderbush Gulch*, but it must not be forgotten that what was attempted here was much more difficult. Atmospherically, it was thick enough to cut with a knife, and few films of any period have stimulated the imagination more.

My first encounter with the phonograph was made at Riverview through a set of earphones in a penny arcade. The record was painfully scratchy and screechy, and since what I heard was neither a good song nor a good voice, I was not enthralled. There the phonograph rested for me until 1912, when my aunt purchased the largest model of Victrola then available, and certainly the night we went to her house and I heard operatic music for the first time, including the Caruso-Tetrazzini-Amato-Journet recording of the sextette from *Lucia*, was one of the great nights of my life and one of that series of births in which the best part of every man's life consists. We are not even yet an opera-going nation, but thanks to the phonograph, we do have all the great

102

voices of the world at our command, and it is very hard for us to think our way back to a time when most Americans had never heard a great singer, and when, even among the exceptions, few got a chance to hear such a singer more than a few times during the year.[1] Of course that enchanted evening was the first of many, and I assure you that unless you have experienced it, you do not know how delightful it can be for a boy to find himself growing drowsy toward the tag-end of the evening to the strains of Massenet's "Elegie"!

I depended upon my aunt's Victrola until about 1921, when she decided that I must have one of my own and forthwith set out to help me to acquire it. I began buying records for it and storing and playing them at her house until these plans had matured, and since I was, despite all my enthrallment with singers, still basically what Sam Weller might have called a "literary cove," I started with the new Sothern and Marlowe recording of the Balcony Scene from *Romeo and Juliet*. I do not take to change quickly, and I was late in accepting the LP's—for a long time I

[1] Phonograph records are, so far as I am aware, the only commodity that has decreased in cost during our time. In the early days. Victor charged $2.00 per side for a ten-inch disc (about three minutes of music) and $3.00 per side for a twelve-inch disc (about four minutes of music), containing a solo recording by a top-flight celebrity artist, with the tariff stepped up for duets and concerted numbers, depending upon the number of performers engaged. The *Lucia* sextette was deliberately, and quite arbitrarily, tagged at $7.00, which was a good deal of money in those days, because it was designed as a prestige item, and the manufacturers believed that people would desire and prize a record which cost so much. As it turned out, they guessed right, and the contribution which this record (along with the slightly earlier recording of the same number by Caruso, Sembrich, Scotti, Journet, etc. and similar recordings of the *Rigoletto* quartette) made not only to the vogue of record-collecting but to the musical education of the American buying public can hardly be overestimated. "The Sextette," as it was generally called, made its way to every crossroads in America and was often found among the possessions of persons who owned nothing else at all comparable to it. Nowadays, however, we can buy a double-faced LP operatic recording which may play up to an hour, involving many voices and full orchestra, for $4.00 or even less. I leave it to the statisticians to figure out the percentages which exist between the relative costs of the old and the new and content myself with suggesting that the best way to combat inflation is to buy nothing but phonograph records, a suggestion which is at least as sensible as many which now find great favor in high places.

103

insisted that when I wished to hear a particular song or aria, I wished to hear just that, and not to tie myself down for an extended session with a lot of other things which perhaps I did not care to listen to just then—but I finally succumbed, and, quite undesignedly, my first LP purchase was again *Romeo and Juliet*, this time the complete Old Vic recording with Claire Bloom. Some people, apparently, are consistent in spite of themselves. They never learn, and they never forget.

This, however, is to get ahead of my story. Very few people seem to remember that some of the first celebrity records were made in Russia, and in a sense I suppose Maria Michailowa was the first queen of the phonograph. Though her person was known in this country only through a very unattractive picture in the Victor catalogue (F. W. Gaisberg says that she was "a dumpy little creature"[2]), she made a number of phenomenally successful records, and it was a poor collection indeed that did not include her Bach-Gounod "Ave Maria." Judged by the test of sales, however, I should suppose that the real queen of the early phonograph in this country was Alma Gluck, for not only did she record more selections than any other female singer, but the horn was far kinder to her velvety voice than it was to Sembrich, Eames, or Melba, for example (though Victor began with Melba by giving her a special pink label with a $5.00 price tag), and apparently nobody was ever able to accomplish much in the recording line with either Nordica or Fremstad. Was there any American of my generation, I wonder, who had not heard Gluck's "Whispering Hope" duet with Louise Homer?

Whether it was Caruso or McCormack who was the phonograph king might well be a matter of choice. Caruso, of course, was not comparable on his own ground; as Thomas Burke once remarked, he was not a man but a miracle. His fame has declined but little during the nearly fifty years that have passed since his death, and it is said that his records still earn as much money as they did during his lifetime. Francis Robinson tells us

[2] *The Music Goes Round* (Macmillan, 1942).

104

too that mail relating to him received at the Metropolitan Opera House still equals in volume the combined mail concerning all other singers, living and dead.

But if Caruso was king, then McCormack was at least crown prince. He too was a miracle in his way; his recordings were far more numerous than Caruso's, and he performed such services as a musical missionary throughout the land as no other singer has equaled. He and Lucrezia Bori were the first Victor artists to broadcast, after which they were assailed for having helped radio to destroy "the music business." "Music," retorted McCormack, "is not a business; it is an art." So it always was for him, and a consecration too, for he could turn even a simple little ballad, which would have been nothing if it had been sung by anybody else, into a rich musical experience. McCormack was a complicated human being, as most of us are, but there was true sweetness and humility and devoutness at the heart of him. "Well, Enrico," he greeted Caruso on one occasion, "how is the world's greatest tenor today?" Caruso smiled, and replied, "Since when have you been a baritone, dear John?" The measure of both men may be taken by these questions. Once, many years later, McCormack arrived in an American city to find that a tasteless local management had billed him as "The World's Greatest Tenor." The sign came down then and there. He would not submit to the indignity of such self-vaunting. "There is no 'World's Greatest Tenor,'" he declared. "The 'World's Greatest Tenor' is dead." "But, Mr. McCormack," he was asked, "is any living tenor greater than you are?" "Yes," he replied generously, "Edward Johnson is a greater tenor than I am." When McCormack was in his prime, the musical snobs were all hot on his trail, partly because he sang ballads and Irish folk songs and partly because they were irrevocably committed to the view that anything that appealed outside the ranks of the *cognoscenti* must be bad. Fortunately we have outlived such idiocy, and McCormack, who never made a bad record, now enjoys an extensive revival on LP's. "He never stooped to small or modest things," said Ernest Newman; "he invariably raised them, and with them the most unsophisticated listener, to his own high level. I never knew him, in his public or his private singing, to be guilty of a lapse of taste, of making an effect for mere effect's sake. He was a patrician artist, dignified even in apparent undress, with a respect for art that is rarely met with amid tenors. There is no one to take his place."

My own queen of the phonograph was no one I have yet mentioned however. She was Geraldine Farrar, and I still prefer her voice in its prime to any that I have heard since. I write within a week of her death, on March 11, 1967, ending our completely untroubled friendship, cultivated mainly through correspondence, of nearly forty years, and though she was eighty-five when she went away, I still feel that she left far too soon. Of course she was the first singer I started out to collect "complete." Later I did the same for McCormack. LP's as a whole encourage the collector to concentrate upon composers (I could, for example, never have developed the Richard Strauss fever which now possesses me in the days of the 78's), but for myself I still believe that in all the arts, even writing, the projection or expression of a personality is what interests me most, and I am quite in accord with Willa Cather when she writes that she derived more satisfaction from her writing than from anything she could buy except for the privilege of seeing and hearing a very few very great artists. So I still buy the records of Elisabeth Schwarzkopf, Leontyne Price, and Dietrich Fischer-Dieskau (surely the greatest singer since Caruso, and one who comes considerably closer to where I live), regardless of what they sing and whether or not I have other recordings of the same selections.

In a way, I had my most interesting experiences as a record collector with the great Bohemian soprano, Emmy Destinn. I never heard her in person, and I heard only a few of her records during her lifetime. After her death I was introduced to her in a big way by a friend who owned a large collection of her records, and for a time she almost threatened to crowd Farrar as my

106

favorite singer. Nearly all her records had disappeared from the catalogue by then, but I succeeded in accumulating a large number of them nevertheless. It was while my Destinn collecting-fever was upon me that I had two of the most interesting of my innumerable dreams. One night she entertained me at her estate in Bohemia. Again, I dreamed that I was attending one of her concerts in an actual concert hall in my city; I could even tell you where I sat. She wore a flame-colored gown with curious black shoes which turned up at the tip, like some of the shoes in the illustrations for the Oz books. What she sang I have no idea, but it was of bewildering, surpassing, overwhelming beauty, and it was utterly unlike any music I have ever heard in my waking hours, being obviously constructed upon some principle unknown to human composers. If I have ever had a dream which could make me disposed to believe that, as some claim, we get out of the real world in our dreams and enter into another plane of being, it was this one.

That Geraldine Farrar's appeal to me—and to my generation—was not wholly musical is sufficiently attested in my case by her having enthralled my imagination long before I ever heard her sing. Though it may be hard for young people to believe it today, when I was young the fame of such singers as Geraldine Farrar and Mary Garden (and such actresses as Sarah Bernhardt and Julia Marlowe) was as much a part of the world in which we lived—at least in such circles as I moved in—as that of film stars and sports celebrities became at a later period. It has been said that Miss Farrar was one of America's first "glamour girls," and that is all right, provided you will remember that though her sense of drama never permitted her to underplay a role, either on or off the stage, she was a glamour girl who was also a serious and thoroughly trained artist. At a later date, glamour girls in America became, characteristically, persons of small talent whose personalities for some reason struck a responsive chord in the hearts of their contemporaries, until finally this type, which was both artistically and humanly respectable, was succeeded by the ciphers who have nothing but a genius for publicity of the most unsavory kind, and who manage to keep their pictures in the papers without having done anything at all that could possibly cause any rational human being to have any interest in them.

But "glamour" itself is not a dirty word; on the contrary, it contributes importantly not only to the liveableness but even to the glory of life. Miss Farrar herself once pointed out that, even in the opera, there are many artists who have excellent voices and offer flawless interpretations, but whom nobody ever cares to go to see or to hear. And she asked: "What is the use of having a wonderful voice if when you step on the stage, you look like something that has been delivered by auto truck?" The auto-truck shipments have been increasing of late years in all the performing arts. Even at the Metropolitan Opera House a number of flash-in-the-pan singers have proved, since Miss Farrar left it, that whatever may be the case in less exacting forms of entertainment, you cannot have an important career in opera without a solid musical foundation. But if you would be remembered among the great singers of your time, you must have more than that: you must know how to fire the imagination and grip the heart. And this, unlike *bel canto*, is something that nobody can teach you. If you need to be taught, then you could never learn.

What Farrar offered in her prime was a heady mixture. Many years ago, a student of mine in Chicago, later a painter of considerable reputation, attended one of her concerts and became so excited that he could not go home afterwards but walked all over the city trying to work her out of his system. The foundation of the extramusical appeal was beauty, grace, and charm, but the beauty was in itself a less important element than many persons realized. There have been more beautiful women than Farrar on the operatic stage who never went anything like so far, and for us it was never so much a matter of loving her for her beauty as being enthralled by her beauty because we loved her. She was a prodigious worker, and she always gave the impression of abounding physical vitality, but this was more spiritual than

108

physical. She had a very weak, delicate throat for a singer, and she was terribly subject to attacks of bronchitis and kindred ailments, but it was not until her later autobiography, *Such Sweet Compulsion*, was published in 1938 that most of us had any idea how frail her health had really been during her later Metropolitan years. Unless she had husbanded her physical powers with great care, both on and off the stage, she would have had a very unimportant career, and whenever she allowed her ardent temperament to cause her to force her resources in order to create an effect, she always paid a price for it afterwards.

I have seen singers who slithered out upon the recital stage as if they were not quite sure whether they would be applauded or booed but rather expected the worst. Farrar always swept in like a queen come to possess her kingdom—in its way, her entrance generated as much excitement in a theater as the explosion of a cannon—and she had the gift of trailing prima donna clouds of glory from her whole operatic career on both sides of the Atlantic. Once I heard her sing a concert in a powdered wig, with her hands in a tiny fur muff, and once she wore a magnificent gown, decorated with a cascade of red roses falling from her arms. From the beginning to the end of the performance she was always in full command of the situation, and there was never any doubt in your mind that this was a festival occasion. It became that because she was present and because she chose to make it that.

Once (to digress for a moment) a very good second-string singer came to the city where I then lived to give a recital and lost her accompanist at the last minute. A friend of mine, an excellent musician, consented to play for her, but there was no time for a rehearsal. It was no fault of his that he did many things that she did not want him to do, but every time it happened, she would stop him and start over again. I have rarely lived through a more agonizing evening. The lady did not mean to be cruel; she was only stupid and lacking in imagination. Now the point I wish to make is that if such a thing had happened to Geraldine Farrar, she would have so conducted herself that nobody in the audience—no layman at any rate—would have guessed that there was anything wrong. Charles Hackett once sang a Rodolfo to her Mimi, as a last-minute replacement, perfectly familiar with the music, but ignorant of the cues because he had never sung the role on the stage. "Don't worry," said Miss Farrar. "I will give you your cues," which she did, throughout the evening, and the performance went off without a hitch. "Cara Geraldina," Martinelli once whispered to her at the beginning of a long duet in *Zaza*, "I cannot move. My suspenders have broken," and thereafter sat glued to the sofa on which he was sitting, while Farrar, on the spur of the moment, circulated all about him, inventing new endearments and fresh "business" for the whole scene. And again nothing was noticed except that, as she would say, "certain critical craniums" were moved to speculate as to why, on this particular occasion, she had chosen to play the scene so vulgarly and why Martinelli had been so unwontedly unresponsive a lover.

Unquestionably the aura of operatic glory (including even the conquest of royal personages, suitably embellished with details of their own invention by the greasy-minded) contributed much to Farrar's appeal, but to consider it in isolation would be misleading. She once told her mother that if it gave people pleasure to think her a prostitute, they would simply have to think it. "What earthly difference can it make so long as I don't have to be one?" In private life Miss Farrar was what might be called a "strong-minded" woman, who had "views" on every subject related to both the arts and the common welfare, and who never hesitated to express them. But she did not care either to dominate or to be dominated. She was much too small a woman to be called "queenly" in the usual prima donna sense; compared to most of her top-flight operatic contemporaries, she was almost girlish in her appearance (it must be remembered that her operatic career was terminated by her own fiat at the age of forty), and, as Carl Van Vechten rightly observed, she was generally excellent in what, in another branch of show business, would be

The Film Projector, etc.

called ingenue roles. ("Ach, Gott, Kind," cried her great teacher, Lilli Lehmann, when she raised the question of going on to Wagner, "du hast ja doch keine Brust!") She was "Miss," not "Madame" Farrar, and though she never went in for any nonsense which involved wrapping herself in the American flag, I am sure that her American audiences did take pride in her as a countrywoman who had stormed the operatic bastions of Europe and made a great prima donna out of the daughter of a storekeeper and baseball player from Melrose, Massachusetts. Lieder, not operatic arias, were the backbone of her concert programs, and she never presented them in what is ordinarily called a "dramatic" manner. She had her austerities too: she would never repeat a song ("the second cream puff never tastes as good as the first"), and she would not speak on the concert stage if it could possibly be avoided. The last group was always quite as standard as the first, and though she might give you "Annie Laurie," sung to her own accompaniment, as an encore, she completely avoided the semipopular ballads with which, in those days, many singers used to close.

It is interesting that she should still be the only American operatic artist who really made it as a film star (neither Grace Moore nor Lawrence Tibbett lasted anything like so long), and it is even more interesting that her success should have been made in silent films. I suppose only two of them were really good enough for her—*Carmen* and *Joan the Woman*. (I think her Joan of Arc was always quite as dear to her as any of her operatic characterizations.) This film was Cecil B. de Mille's first great "spectacular," and I still live in hope that someday some publisher of eight-millimeter films will dig it out and make it available again. De Mille continued to direct Miss Farrar as long as she remained with Lasky, and though her vehicles varied in quality, they were certainly much better than anything that came her way after she—most unfortunately, I fear—transferred to Goldwyn. *The Hell Cat, Shadows, Flame of the Desert, The World and Its Woman*—such vehicles afforded scope for none of her gifts, and even at the time they spoiled her image and lowered her reputation. I remember one of my high-school teachers would not go to see *Joan the Woman* because, she said, "I cannot imagine Geraldine Farrar in a spiritual role." This lady had not followed Miss Farrar's lyric career very closely. Of course many opera-goers thought of her first as Carmen, and, later, as Zaza, her last smash-hit at the Metropolitan; her triumph was front-page news from coast to coast the morning after, and it was as Zaza that she sang her last performance at the Metropolitan to such frenzied acclaim as the house never witnessed before nor ever saw again. Yet Elisabeth in *Tannhäuser*[3] and the Goose Girl in *Die Königskinder* were closer to her, enlisted deeper resources of her personality, and were generally rated by connoisseurs as finer achievements than Carmen or Zaza or Thaïs or, for that matter, Cio-Cio-San, which was probably the role in which the public loved her best, and whose popularity was so great that it very likely curbed the scope of her repertoire. Even as late as the time she wrote *Such Sweet Compulsion* she was still thinking of Gatti-Casazza as "stupid and inconsistent" in not allowing her to return to Elisabeth and the Goose Girl during her last seasons. Carmen she played much more on the surface, and vivid and theatrically effective as the characterization was, it was also decorous, refined, operatic, compared to what others have offered at the Metropolitan and elsewhere, both before and since. "When I sing Carmen," she once said, "unless, by the end of the first act, every man in the audience feels like sending his card backstage, that performance is a failure." Of course. So is any Carmen. But when the gentlemen got backstage, if they ever reached it, they would have behaved like gentlemen or else lived to regret it.

I myself saw some of Miss Farrar's early films before I had ever heard her sing, but the voice came at last, at the Auditorium in Chicago, on Sunday afternoon, October 12, 1919. She was the first great singer I had ever heard in person, and the day marked

[3] This was the only Wagnerian role she ever sang, but she told me that she had also prepared Eva, Elsa, and Sieglinde.

112

the beginning of a new era in my life. "My Mother Bids Me Bind My Hair," "For Music," "Summer Fields," "New Love, New Life," "In the Meadow," "Eastern Romance," "In the Silent Night," "The Wounded Birch," "The Snowdrop"—these are some of the songs she sang, and much of the enchanted wonder of that afternoon lingers in the very titles. (I wonder how many people know that Miss Farrar never ceased to love fairy tales as long as she lived.) Thereafter I never missed an opportunity to hear or see her in any aspect that came my way.

She handled her large correspondence with a precision and promptness that would have done credit to a banker, but I think it must, especially in later years, have become a burden to her, and I often wondered whether we were really doing her a kindness by making so much as we did of her increasingly venerable birthdays, for she always felt she had to write to everybody who had sent her even a card, and this chore kept her chained to her desk for weeks every spring. I have said that she had her austerities—though she was warmhearted, she was never a sentimentalist—and I think she was a little wary about taking on new people; it was always easier for strangers to get a photograph from her than a letter. Once she had accepted you, on the other hand, her loyalty knew no wavering. Though I never asked her, I have always wondered whether she remembered that the first time I wrote her, to ask a question about one of her records, she answered me in her own distinguished handwriting but signed the letter "S. Blein, Secretary"! In 1925, however, while I was still at the University of Chicago, I wrote a boyish little essay about her and published it in a campus magazine.[4] When it reached her in Buffalo, on a concert tour, she *telegraphed* her "preliminary thanks" and followed this with a long letter. In 1929 I published my *Geraldine Farrar: An Authorized Record of Her Career*, in a limited edition of 350 copies which she signed. Besides an essay, this contained a complete list of her operatic roles, with dates and casts of her first appearance in each, a chronology of all her

[4] *The Circle*, Vol. III, No. 4 (February, 1925).

operatic appearances in New York, a list of her records and films, some concert programs, and a selected bibliography.[5] During the preparation of this book I was continually bombarding her with requests for odds and ends of information, and all my letters were answered immediately. Only once did she fail me. She was on tour, and she only had time to write and say that she was too busy to tell me what I wanted to know now; if I would be patient she would send the information as soon as possible. It came the next day. In June, 1957, reissues of some of her records occasioned an article of mine about her in *High Fidelity*, which I think she liked, though, like me, she was disgusted by the title the editors insisted upon using: "Geraldine the Great."

During the early years of our correspondence most of her letters concentrated upon musical and theatrical affairs; later, as her own career receded, she was more inclined to discuss more general concerns, for the way in which the world—and our America—were wagging pleased her no more than it did me. One of the most interesting letters she ever sent me was written after the abandonment of her plans to appear in a Broadway production of the Lehár operetta *Frasquita* late in 1927, partly because of illness and partly because she was dissatisfied with the way the production was being handled. But the message I prize most of all was the one she sent me in 1935 after my mother's death. I did not know when I sent her the news that she had buried her father at almost the same time, but her own grief did not prevent her from composing what was by all means the most comforting letter I received. "We must be worthy of our parents—and of ourselves," she wrote. And she ended: "Put your trust in Time—he has gentle ways."

I never met Miss Farrar's mother, who died early in 1923. She

[5] My list of roles, with relevant data, was reprinted in an appendix to *Such Sweet Compulsion* (Greystone Press, 1938); the film data reappeared in the number of *The Record Collector* (Vol. XIII, Nos. 9–10) devoted to Geraldine Farrar. This serial, published and edited by James F. E. Dennis, Ipswich, Suffolk, England, contains the fullest available list of her recordings, both published and unpublished.

114

had been almost her daughter's other self, and when she went away she took about half Geraldine's interest in singing with her. I did meet her father, whom she greatly resembled physically, when I went to Ridgefield, Connecticut, in 1928, to talk about the plans for *Geraldine Farrar: An Authorized Record of Her Career,* and I have always remembered one amusing thing he said. Having heard her name pronounced both Făr'-ēr and Fȧ-rär', I asked her which pronunciation she employed. Before she had a chance to reply, her father cut in. "Well, now, I'll tell you," he said. "If you go up to Boston, where people still know how to speak English, you will hear Făr'-ēr. But if you go down to New York, where they talk this polyglot lingo, why there, of course, you'll hear Fȧ-rär'." Dictionaries often give the first pronunciation for the famous Victorian cleric, Canon Farrar, who was a relative, and the second for Geraldine. She herself seemed rather indifferent about the matter: her operatic colleagues, most of whom were not Americans, always tended to accent her name on the last syllable, and she had grown tired of correcting them. One day, when she was feeling more than usually frivolous, an interviewer asked her about her name, and she replied, "Well, when I introduce my mother to anybody, I generally call her Mrs. Făr'-ēr, but when I pronounce my own name I make it rime with 'hurrah.'" This time she caught a much bigger fish than she had intended, for this happened to meet the eye of the distinguished scholar George Philip Krapp, and it caused him to give both pronunciations of the name in a biographical dictionary he compiled, tagging the second (Fȧ-räh') as the name of an American prima donna, thus pronounced by her own fiat. Mark Twain said that humor was out of place in a dictionary, but sometimes the absence of a sense of humor produces still more unfortunate results.

When Geraldine Farrar was acting as commentator for the Saturday afternoon radio broadcasts of the Metropolitan Opera during the 1934–35 season, it fell to her to speak of Marcella Sembrich, who had just died. What she said was that Sembrich had "just joined the glorious company of the immortals." Now

115

that she herself has gone away from this world, these words come back to me as peculiarly appropriate to her. She was brought up in New England Unitarianism, and though during her later years she went to church only on special occasions, her religion was no less sincere and no less comforting for being very informal. She never attended a séance, but when *Such Sweet Compulsion* was published, many persons were surprised, and some were dismayed, to find that she firmly believed herself to be in contact with her mother's spirit. Indeed, she elected to write part of the book from her mother's point of view, not her own, and this was the part, she told me, that gave her most satisfaction.

Unless they share her kind of "sensitiveness," those she has left behind her will now have to rely for what they still have of her upon their memories and upon her many fine records. Henry Edward Krehbiel remarked of her Goose Girl that "memories of the picture she presented walking through the massive town-gates followed and surrounded by her white flock will die only with the generation that witnessed it." The same thing might be said of many other pictures she created, and the recorded moments are happily subject to no such limitation of memory. One's choices here must, of course, be largely a personal matter. For myself I suppose that if I could take only two of Miss Farrar's recordings to the proverbial desert island, I should choose the two selections she recorded from *Die Königskinder*—the heartbreaking poetry and pathos of the Goose Girl's death aria, "Weisst noch das grosse Nest?" and the charmingly childlike "Lieber Spielmann," which she never sang at the Metropolitan, since in the opera it belongs to another character.[6] If you wish to experience her dramatic intensity at its best, I would refer you to the "Vissi d'arte" from *Tosca* and the *Zaza* aria, "Mamma usciva di casa." The young voice heard in Micaëla's air from *Carmen* is of

[6] Fortunately these selections are now available again, after many years, in the Farrar record issued by Rococo Records. All admirers of Miss Farrar owe a great debt to William H. Seltsam, who brought out many hitherto unpublished recordings through his International Record Collectors Club of Bridgeport, Connecticut.

116

quite unearthly purity; so are almost all her duets with Edmond Clément, but especially the selections from *Mefistofele* and *Romeo et Juliette.* All the Mozart pieces are exquisitely sung also, Lilli Lehmann's training being clearly reflected in the "Allelujah" from the "Motette Exsultate"; the Gounod "Serenade" is charming; so, in their different ways, are "Ben Bolt" and "At Parting." It is a pity she was not allowed to record more Lieder, and in German; in her recording heyday there was much less market for these in America than there is today. But there is no use going on, for there are beauties to be found everywhere. I don't suppose "The Holy City" is a musical masterpiece, but there are turns of phrase in Miss Farrar's recording of it that I should hate to relinquish. Nor could I wish to have missed what seems to be one of her rarest and least popular records, Chadwick's "Love's Like a Summer Rose."

Miss Farrar's earlier autobiography, *Geraldine Farrar: The Story of an American Singer,* which Houghton Mifflin Company published in 1916, after it had been serialized in *The Ladies' Home Journal,* is only a sketch, and compared to *Such Sweet Compulsion,* it is superficial—she herself once referred to it as "that trite blurb of mine"—but it has good things in it nevertheless, and here is one of them:

> I have been asked, in summing up these experiences of my artistic career, so far, if it has all been worth while? From my point of view, yes. That is, what you believe to be the most complete fulfillment of yourself and the gratification of your ambitions is always worth while. Fortunately for me the adventurous and inquiring turn of my mind does not allow my ambitions to become narrowed or stationary, and that may possibly account for the unusual phases in my musical career.
>
> It is, however, distinctly *not* worth while, to my mind, unless Fortune smiles upon you in abundance, for art is not the medium stratum of life, but its flowered inspiration and emotional poetry: it demands and obtains its sacrifices and sorrows which modify and chasten its glory, and your own soul best knows the toll you pay.

117

As Far As Yesterday

Here is the sound common sense which all who knew Miss Farrar would expect from her. "If I can live," she once said, "so that those who come in contact with me find encouragement and enrichment, that is all I ask of life. Far more important to me than being a great artist will be, when the final curtain is drawn, to have succeeded in being a great human being." She understood the Emerson who did not wish to be a writer but preferred to be "a man writing." She was not a singing machine, and she disliked, after her retirement, being thought of as "a defunct canary." She was a great singer because she was a great woman. To have known her in either aspect is to have found one's life permanently enriched, and to have had both privileges is to have been fortunate indeed.

118

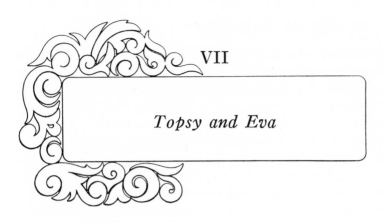

VII

Topsy and Eva

FOR SOME REASON OR OTHER, my tastes have always tended to be rather more "highbrow" in music than in some other areas where I might be supposed to be better informed. Consequently I have never cared much for that form of entertainment which, for want of a better term, is called "musical comedy." As a child I was taken to such shows of the period as *The Time, The Place, and the Girl*; *The Girl Question*; and *A Knight for a Day*, which starred the then-popular Mabel Hite. Later I saw the Dolly Sisters in *Oh, Look!* after which one of my parlor tricks was a pretty good imitation of Harry Fox singing "I'm Always Chasing Rainbows." When the old-fashioned musical comedy began to transform itself into whatever takes its place now, I got in on the ground floor by seeing *Blossom Time* and *The Student Prince*, but I did not very industriously pursue my explorations. The dominant tendencies in modern serious drama do not greatly charm me, and I have sometimes suspected that if the true spirit of the theater lingers anywhere in our world, it is in the musicals that it must be looked for (George Jean Nathan once pointed out that when people stopped building theaters that looked like theaters and began to build theaters that looked like undertaking

119

parlors instead, what was presented on the stage also began·to alter itself to correspond), but I am now inclined to leave the documentation of this impression to the investigations of others.

Of course I was taken to see Montgomery and Stone in *The Wizard of Oz*, and I fancy this was my first musical.[1] Naturally I was charmed, though I recall being vaguely troubled by the show's departures from the book I knew by heart. (If I had been a child when the M-G-M film was made, in which the whole Oz adventure became a dream of Dorothy's in delirium, I am sure I should have stalked out of the theater in indignation.) But I think more magic clings for me, though only with the vaguest pegs to hang it on, to two other musicals of the early 1900's which seem largely to have disappeared from theatrical history.

The first was an extravaganza called *The Top of the World*, whose scene was laid at the North Pole and in which I believe Santa Claus was one of the characters. That is nearly all I remember about it except a general atmosphere of white glitter and one buxom lady in white tights whom I did not think at all pretty, yet the very vagueness contributes to the atmosphere of wonder which lingers with me to remind me of an occasion when I escaped from the world of actuality into a better world of the mind. As a matter of fact, the transition was gracefully prepared for. *The Top of the World* was presented at the lovely Studebaker Theater, which is on Michigan Avenue, always for me the most enchanted part of Chicago, and before the show began my mother and I stopped off to see a relative by marriage who kept a floral shop in Van Buren Street, between Michigan and Wabash, where the atmosphere seemed almost as romantic to me as on the stage itself, and where the kind lady gave me a flower so that I might carry the flavor of her establishment away with me.

My other early memory is even vaguer, for I cannot even remember the name of the show. All I know is that I saw it at the

[1] In David Ewen's account of this work in his *Complete Book of the American Musical Theater* (Holt, 1958), the book on which it is based is described as taken from L. Frank Baum's "novel"; Dorothy's last name is transformed from Gale to Dale; and the Tin Woodman becomes "Tim Woodman"!

120

Great Northern, that it had a Chinese or Japanese setting, and that in the last act a good part of the stage was occupied by an enormous grinning Billiken. Now Billiken was a benevolent-looking Oriental idol, a kind of good-luck symbol, of whom miniature reproductions soon flooded the novelty shops of America, so that he became as omnipresent as whatever people fastened to the radiator caps of motor cars at a later period, and if, as I assume, he originated in this show (I cannot recall ever having seen him before, and he endured for years afterwards), then it must have exercised considerable influence, yet I have never been able to identify it. I once asked the late Charles Collins, of the Chicago *Tribune*, whom I had reason to believe well-nigh omniscient in such matters, about it, but he did not know any more than I did. There are fairy tales in which children go to a land where they find all the toys they have ever lost; perhaps there is also a land where we can refurbish our lost memories. Or perhaps not, for if I could see this show again, I might not enjoy it nearly as much as I did then unless I could also be the boy who saw it, and that, I fear, I can never be.

Once, however, during my adult years, I was enthralled by a musical comedy, and this was *Topsy and Eva*, with the Duncan Sisters. The book was by Catherine Chisholm Cushing, and the music was credited to the girls themselves, who had previously done "kid" acts in a number of big musicals, including Fred Stone's *Tip Top*. *Topsy and Eva*, which put Rosetta into the blackface she never got off again, opened in 1923 in Los Angeles, but its greatest success was in Chicago, where it played for over a year at the Selwyn Theater. I do not know how many times I saw it, but I was present on the last night, when, in imitation of the "Tom-shows" of days gone by, all the characters were doubled.

I expected the Duncan Sisters to go on to other big musicals (my pet project for them was an *Alice in Wonderland* with Vivian as Alice and Rosetta as the White Rabbit), but this did not happen. Though the success of *Topsy and Eva* in New York did not match its acclaim in Chicago, they found themselves "stuck" with the name characters much as Joe Jefferson was "stuck" with Rip Van Winkle or Rose Melville with Sis Hopkins, and they went on playing them in vaudeville and, later, night-club engagements across the world until Rosetta was killed in an automobile accident late in 1959.

I had met Vivian once, very briefly, in Chicago, but I became better acquainted with the sisters when they came to Seattle, where I was then living, in 1928, to play the Pantages circuit. Or perhaps I should say I became better acquainted with Vivian, for although Rosetta was never other than charming to me, she had the habit of disappearing into her dressing room between the grueling four-a-day schedule they were playing and leaving her sister to entertain their visitors. It was obvious that Rosetta was a temperamental young lady whose spirits alternated between the heights and the depths, but this is no wonder, for her energy on the stage (and I suspect off it, when she was really interested) was tremendous, and no girl's physique could have entered the strain, which must have been even more psychic than physical, without cooling-off periods in between.

Vivian, on the other hand, was a gorgeous peaches-and-cream kind of girl, right off the candy box, and with a disposition to match. She was pretty enough so that not even her heavy stage make-up (it was about the heaviest I have ever seen on anybody, and it would have been quite out of the question to take it off between shows) could make her other than very well worth looking at. One night we dined together at a neighboring cafeteria (she still in make-up), and I cannot honestly say that we did not attract attention. I often suspected that she was considerably bored with us all, but she never ceased to be the gracious hostess, and the atmosphere backstage was as decorous as in church.

Structurally *Topsy and Eva* was an old-fashioned musical comedy, in which no excuse was too flimsy to stop the story for a song-and-dance number. For all that, the story-line was im-

122

portant. "Tom-shows" had been a part of the American theatrical picture since the 1850's, and their fascination was in the American blood. The Duncan Sisters gathered the last great Uncle Tom harvest because they had the wit to see that theatrical taste had not changed so much as "smart" people supposed, and that all that was needed to give Topsy and Eva a new lease on life was to apply a modern veneer.

None of the countless Little Evas of the past can possibly have been prettier than Vivian Duncan, and none can have undertaken the character more determined to project the last essence of its sweetness. What made her acceptable in a day when most of them would have been rejected out of hand was that whenever her role was in danger of turning uncomfortably saccharine, she would turn about and "kid" it. Either she would wickedly sham fainting in order to get something she wanted, or offer plain aid and encouragement to the enemy of all things sentimental, present on the scene in the person of Miss Topsy, or else she would break out with spirit, doing funny, jazzy things with her voice. Thus she was at once romantic and realist, a fairy child and a hard-headed little girl of earth.

Topsy was a rather more complicated matter, for Topsy was an outrageous person even in Mrs. Stowe's novel, and she certainly did not grow more demure in Rosetta Duncan's tender hands. As Eva inherited the stage tradition of the angel child, so the mantle of the long inexhaustible blackface comedian fell on Topsy's shoulders, and her remark that Al Jolson was her "mammy" was no idle jest. Now blackface comedians are traditionally men. To give the role instead to a young and attractive girl and then have her beat her predecessors at their own game, marshaling six or seven times as much exuberance as any of them were ever able to command—all this may not seem like a very long step to take. But it is the kind of step that makes history in the theater.

Outrageousness was by no means all Topsy had however, nor could it alone have accounted for her reception. She added

123

charm to incongruity, and the combination proved irresistible. Whether or not one liked all the things she said and did—she ad libbed freely, and, like all such players, she was not always the same—it was impossible not to like her. The tiny, half-naked little figure of the first act, so inadequately enclosed in somber rags, so essentially helpless for all her impudence, made an immediate appeal, and the effect thus gained was never forfeited.

Many spectators, of course, were under the impression that she was the dominant figure. In a way this was true, but it was only half true. The Duncan stage partnership was not a rivalry; both sisters were necessary to the effect that was created, and neither could have done without the other. Vivian had no such prolonged "scene" as fell to her sister with "Topsy's Prayer," or, later, in vaudeville, with the remarkable "Curbstone Blues," and she always *did* much less, but what she *was*, was tremendously important. Even very great actors sometimes do their best work when they seem to be doing nothing, for it is cruelly difficult to do nothing on the stage, and it is even more difficult to make nothing into something. Certainly Rosetta's dynamism gained much from having Vivian's lovely restfulness as a background. Repose is as necessary in life as action, and as necessary in art as in life, and two Topsies would have destroyed each other and the audience with them. When Vivian was called upon to take the center of the stage she never had any difficulty in doing so, and when she stretched out her arms in the calcium glare and cried, "O Topsy, don't go!" she awakened more emotion than it was altogether reasonable to expect the situation to generate. Often, however, she seemed to be merely observing what Rosetta was doing, with sympathy, yet with a certain detachment too, much as she viewed her visitors backstage.

The Duncan Sisters suggested a fresh wholesomeness which was not the quality most frequently encountered in the musical-comedy stars of their time, but they also had a good deal of tart commentary on hypocrisy and pretension, much of which was no less effective for being implicit rather than explicit. One does

124

not often associate this with attractive girls, and at one time I thought Rosetta might develop along the lines later laid down by Elaine May. Their mockery of our musical aspirations in "Vocalizing" was delightful; so too was their burlesque of our sentimentality in "In Sweet Onion Time." I have never heard anybody sing the Negro spiritual "Heav'n, Heav'n" better than they did, and they brought art worthy of much better music to such numbers as "Baby Feet Go Pitter Patter Cross My Floor."[2] I am not sure whether they could have sung *Hänsel und Gretel* or not, but I should have liked to see them try. Their career was a record of splendid generosity; they always gave freely of their means and of themselves, and I am sure many theatergoers must remember them, as I do, with great affection.

2 Nearly all these numbers and others were recorded on Victor records.

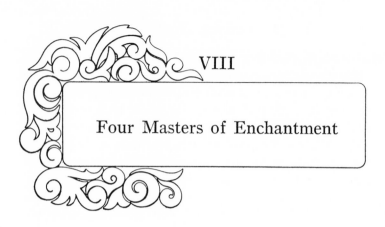

VIII

Four Masters of Enchantment

Howard Pyle (1853–1911)   N. C. Wyeth (1882–1945)
Maxfield Parrish (1870–1966)   Arthur Rackham (1867–1939)

WHEN HOWARD PYLE DIED I was only eleven years old and had
never heard of him; as the saying is, I did not even know he was
sick. I had not had the good fortune to which every child is en-
titled of being brought up on his *Robin Hood,* and my discovery
of *Harper's Magazine* came a few years later, by which time I had
to look him up through the back numbers. I did better with
Arthur Rackham, whom I first encountered the day I bought a
copy of *St. Nicholas* with one of his Mother Goose pictures as a
frontispiece and carried it home through Douglas Park, gazing
upon it from time to time enraptured. Later I became the "only
begetter" of one of Rackham's books, for it was I who, in 1931,
suggested to George Macy that he have the Limited Editions
Club bring out an edition of *The Chimes* by Charles Dickens and
get Rackham to illustrate it. Both the publisher and the artist
agreed, and I contributed a long introduction, which was later
reprinted in *Dickens and the Scandalmongers.*
   Being done as it is entirely in black and white, *The Chimes* is

126

is hardly a typical Rackham book, but I have always loved it, entirely apart from my own association with it, and I do not relish it least in the informal little sketches scattered through it here and there, almost as if the artist had thrown them off in moments of abstraction. Rackham and I corresponded about it, and after he had read *The Man Charles Dickens*, he wrote me an interesting letter in which he discussed Dickens' "cockney" qualities, a subject on which he considered himself an authority, since he was fond of referring to himself as a "transpontine cockney," or one born south of the Thames.

The contact thus established between Rackham and Macy led to the artist's later being assigned *A Midsummer Night's Dream* in the monumental Limited Editions Club Shakespeare. He had already illustrated this play twice, once for the Heinemann–Doubleday, Page edition of 1908, and once privately in a set of pictures now in the New York Public Library, but surely none of his other work was ever quite so beautifully reproduced as that in the L.E.C. *Dream*.[1] Then, at the very end of his life, the artist did *The Wind in the Willows* for Macy,[2] and it is hard to believe that these gay, intensely imaginative pictures were completed with great difficulty, in the strain of mortal illness and under the very shadow of death. Rackham might indeed never have found the strength to finish them except that their creation realized for him at last the achievement of a long frustrated ambition. He had been Kenneth Grahame's first choice as illustrator when *The Wind in the Willows* was first published, but he had been obliged to decline because of the pressure of other work. This he had regretted ever since, and when Macy at last quite unexpectedly suggested that he do the book for the Limited Editions Club, he was so pleased that he insisted upon putting it ahead of *The*

[1] Published in 1937. None of the artists considered in this chapter got the opportunity to design their own books; consequently the illustrations are seldom an integral part of the volume in which they appear. In many of Rackham's books, the pictures are mounted on stiff green or brown paper.

[2] Published by the Limited Editions Club in 1940. There were later, popular-priced editions by the Heritage Press and, in England, by Methuen.

127

Crock of Gold, which he had also undertaken, and which, as it turned out, he did not live to begin.

N. C. Wyeth and Parrish, too, were still active during my grown-up life, and I was one of the reputed 200,000 Americans who bought Parrish's "Daybreak" with delight when it appeared in the art stores in the early twenties. I once tried to get a book out of Wyeth too, for it seemed to me that Mrs. Behn's *Oroonoko* (in which I felt a vested interest both because I had written about the author[3] and because I had a cat who had been named for her hero) was a predestined subject for him. He replied that though he had never read the book, he knew enough about it to recognize its congeniality to his type of treatment, and that he would be delighted to do it if I could find a publisher who was interested, but this time I failed.

Both Wyeth and Parrish, as everybody knows, were among the most gifted of Pyle's many pupils, and have carried on the Pyle tradition in American art which Wyeth later furthered phenomenally by founding a kind of family dynasty of painters which now includes not only his famous son Andrew[4] but two daughters—Henriette (Mrs. Peter) Hurd and Carolyn (Mrs. John) McCoy—and which now seems to be descending to a third generation with Ann McCoy Weymouth and James, son of Andrew. Both John McCoy and Peter Hurd studied informally with N.C., and another son, Nathaniel Wyeth, who is an engineer, married Pyle's niece, Caroline Pyle, herself a painter. Henry C. Pitz finds no comparable painting group in America since the days of Charles Wilson Peale. Rackham, of course, being an Eng-

[3] "In Praise of Mrs. Behn," *The Colophon*, Pt. XVIII (1934).

[4] Andrew Wyeth illustrated one book in collaboration with his father: *The Red Keep, A Story of Burgundy in the Year 1165*, by Allen French (Houghton Mifflin, 1938). N.C. did the color frontispiece, and the many black-and-white line drawings are by Andrew. In his own view, however, Andrew was "just a clever water-colorist—lots of swish and swash" when his father died. Now he was "really on the spot" and felt impelled to prove that what that "wonderful, remarkable person" had started in him "was not in vain." Newell Convers Wyeth and one of his grandsons were killed near their home at Chadds Ford, Pennsylvania, on the morning of October 19, 1945, when their station wagon stalled at a grade crossing in the path of a freight train.

128

Four Masters of Enchantment

lishman, had no connection with the Pyle-Wyeth-Parrish group, though he did have a certain affinity of spirit with them in some aspects, more particularly with Parrish.[5]

All four of these artists led good lives, and no child who loved their pictures will ever be shocked by anything which he learns about their personalities. Parrish, who never taught, moved in a narrower orbit than either Pyle or Wyeth, but his New Hampshire neighbors loved him and rejoiced to find him always his same reliable self. He alone, among the subjects of this chapter, was a handsome man, sparely built and with a finely-chiseled face, though with no suggestion of sharpness. Both Pyle and Wyeth were big—"a large, ruddy well-built man," writes W. J. Aylward of Pyle, "with a head firmly set on broad shoulders, six feet and over, clad in gray tweeds with a bicycle cap perched on

[5] The careers of both Pyle and Rackham have been, if not exhaustively, at least very charmingly commemorated in two well-illustrated volumes by Charles D. Abbott—*Howard Pyle: A Chronicle* (Harpers, 1925)—and by Derek Hudson—*Arthur Rackham: His Life and Work* (Heinemann; Scribners, 1960). There are also extensive bibliographies for both: Willard S. Morse and Gertrude Brincklé, *Howard Pyle: A Record of His Illustrations and Writings* (Wilmington Society of the Fine Arts, 1921); Sarah Briggs Latimore and Grace Clark Haskell, *Arthur Rackham: A Bibliography* (Los Angeles, Suttonhouse, 1936). The other two careers still await adequate recording. The best thing on Wyeth is Henry C. Pitz, "N. C. Wyeth," *American Heritage*, Vol. XVI, No. 6 (October, 1965), 36–55, 82–84; see, also, the same author's "The Brandywine Tradition," *American Artist* (December, 1966), and two articles by Wyeth himself—"For Better Illustration" *Scribner's Magazine*, Vol. LXVI (1919), 638–42, and his introduction to Abbott.

Parrish, who lived in Cornish, N.H., shunned publicity, did his best to discourage both interviewers and photographers, and rejoiced when the snows blocked access to his house in winter, though he was too kindly ever to be rude to those who penetrated his defenses. He illustrated far fewer books than any of the other three and was much more given to magazine covers, calendars, and advertisements; this fugitive work now stands badly in need of collection. So far as I know, neither Pyle nor Wyeth ever did any advertisements, and Rackham did only a few, some of which are reproduced in Latimore-Haskell. Both, however, did much magazine work, of which a good deal, but by no means all, of Pyle's was collected in *Howard Pyle's Book of Pirates*, edited by Merle Johnson, and *Howard Pyle's Book of the American Spirit*, edited by Francis J. Dowd (Harpers, 1921 and 1923). Among the most useful articles about Parrish are Homer Saint Gaudens, "Maxfield Parrish," *Critic*, Vol. XLVI (1905), 512–21; Christian Brinton, "A Master of Make-Believe," *Century*, Vol. LXXXIV (1912), 340–52; M. K. Wisehart, "Maxfield Parrish Tells Why the First Forty Years Are the Hardest," *American Magazine*, Vol. CIX (May, 1930).

graying thin hair. Through silver-rimmed glasses, he fairly beamed good-humored kindliness." He clung to the dignity and formality which was prized in his time, and there seems to have been an aura about him; one gathers that, kind as he was to his pupils, he held himself somewhat apart, and the great inspirational power which he radiated was not wholly unconnected with this detachment, as he himself may well have been aware. Wyeth was more rugged and exuberant and more gifted with the common touch. Human contacts were easy for him, and he had the great gentleness that can be so touching in large, very forceful men.

Pyle, I am sure, was the greatest of the group, and there is no disrespect toward the others involved in saying this, for Wyeth would have gone to the stake for the same opinion (what Parrish believed, on this and on other matters, he kept largely to himself). For one thing, Pyle was writer as well as artist; in the beginning he was not even sure which interest predominated. The choice he finally made was, I am sure, the right one, but the wonder tales he published in *Pepper and Salt* and *The Wonder-Clock*[6] are as fine in kind as anything we have in America, and *The Merry Adventures of Robin Hood*[7] is certainly one of the unquestionable children's classics, nor do the four King Arthur books stand far behind it.[8] It is interesting by the way to note that all these books comprise old-world lore; there was nothing in Pyle which moved in the direction of the tendency later manifested by L. Frank Baum, Carl Sandburg, and others to find fairy-tale material in contemporary American life.[9]

[6] Harpers, 1886 and 1888, respectively. To these one might well add the delightful stories he used to publish in *Harper's Magazine* (sometimes in the Christmas number, gorgeously illustrated by himself). See "The Mysterious Chest," Vol. CXVIII (1908), 1–18; "The Salem Wolf," Vol. CXX (1909), 1–12; "The Dead Finger," Vol. CXXIII (1911), 489–502; and "The Painted Pitcher," Vol. CXXIII (1911), 829–39.

[7] Scribners, 1883.

[8] *The Story of King Arthur and His Knights*; *The Story of the Champions of the Round Table*; *The Story of Sir Launcelot and His Companions*; *The Story of the Grail and the Passing of Arthur* (Scribners, 1903, 1905, 1907, 1910).

[9] Parrish illustrated Baum's *Mother Goose in Prose* (Way and Williams, 1897),

Four Masters of Enchantment

When Wyeth wrote, in his memorial tribute to Pyle, that "an artist must be greater than his works," he showed himself a true disciple of his master. "There is nothing in the world," wrote Howard Pyle, "that will inspire the purpose of youth like the combined strength of spirituality and practical assistance." Though he refused to go to college and had little formal instruction in art, Pyle was not so foolish as to suppose that any spiritual force can make itself felt in art without sound technique, but technique for its own sake did not interest him, and if you had told him that the subject of a picture was of no importance and that composition was all, he would have replied that he had no interest in an art divorced from life. For him, the imagination was the creative element in painting, and all the rest only "a dead husk" unless "the divine life of creative impulse" was enclosed within it. "For after all, a man is not an artist by virtue of clever technique or brilliant methods; he is fundamentally an artist in the degree that he is able to sense and appreciate the significance of life that surrounds him, and to express that significance to the minds of others." He knew his value as an artist and as a teacher, and though he charged no tuition in his summer classes at Chadds Ford, he chose his pupils very carefully, not proposing to waste himself either upon those who had no gift or on those who, having it, were not willing both to work hard and to live right.

Like Parrish, Pyle came of Quaker forebears (he was related to Bayard Taylor), but his mother turned Swedenborgian, and he followed her into this faith. How seriously he took it can be understood by those who read his correspondence with Howells, as given in Abbott, and the 1890 letter to H. M. Alden, which was printed in an eight-page pamphlet called *Sabbath Thoughts*, of which I have a copy and which must be very rare, since it is not listed in the Morse-Brincklé bibliography. As a painter, he was, nevertheless, basically a realist in method, and

but this antedates *The Wizard of Oz*, and Baum himself was still using old-world materials.

he did not care much for allegory. "I doubt whether I could paint 'Massachusetts Crowned with Plenty,' or 'Massachusetts Standing a Bulwark for Freedom against Tyranny,' " he wrote when the question of his doing some murals for the State House was under consideration, and he added, "I do not know whether I could paint a decorative subject in tones of blue and silver or blue and gray, but I am very sure I should not venture to make the attempt." Yet he did touch allegory in such pictures as the series on "The Travels of the Soul," which he both wrote and illustrated as the Christmas feature of the *Century* for 1902,[10] and the delicate mysticism which informs his picture of Joan of Arc enraptured before her saints in Domremy meadows[11] makes it one of the most beautiful things he ever did. His long fairy tale, *The Garden Behind the Moon*,[12] seems very George MacDonald–like, but it may have derived only from Swedenborg. In 1903 he published through Harpers a novel written nine years earlier, *Rejected of Men*, which caused one clergyman to describe him as "the Richard Strauss of historical portraiture and reproduction!" *Rejected of Men* puts the Christ story in a modern setting. The tale is told from the point of view of the Pharisees, and the hero meets death in the electric chair.[13]

The tentative, troubled young people of today may well be alienated by what they might consider a certain smugness in the young Pyle confidently setting out to build his career, and I doubt that many of them could altogether sympathize with the letter to Howells in which he announces that he and his wife

[10] Vol. XV, 167–74.

[11] An illustration for Mark Twain's essay, "Saint Joan of Arc," in the 1904 Christmas number of *Harper's Magazine*, Vol. CX, 1–12. Pyle's pictures were reprinted when the essay was later republished by Harpers in book form.

[12] Scribners, 1895.

[13] For the mystical note in Pyle, see further two short stories: "In Tenebras," *Harper's Magazine*, Vol. LXXXVIII (1894), 392ff., reprinted in *Shapes That Haunt the Dusk* (Harpers, 1901), and "To the Soil of the Earth," *Cosmopolitan*, Vol. XIII (1892), 217ff. Other pictures which suggest allegory are the frontispiece to Edwin Markham, *The Man with the Hoe and Other Poems* (Doubleday & McClure Co., 1900), and the picture called "The Closed Door" in Houghton Mifflin's special 1893, two-volume edition of *The Autocrat of the Breakfast-Table*.

Four Masters of Enchantment

"hope shortly to have that greatest of all blessings befall us—to give another life to this dear, beautiful old world," but objectors should remember that he was not condemned to live in their age of scientific "progress" and global meddling. Pyle was certainly an optimist, but he was no cheerful idiot. "Even in my infancy, the fear of death and annihilation hung over me like a cloud, and that cloud was not dissipated, but became rather more dark and dense as I advanced into youth and adolescence." The death of a son was a terrible sorrow, and when he went to Italy at the end of his life to embark upon a new career as a mural painter, he was compelled by illness finally to face the fact that this was not to be.

But religion was his sure solace always.

> I always feel within myself that after all we are only here to learn in this life that which we shall carry forward in the life to come. In that life the flower of perfection will not spring from the things in which we have succeeded, but from the things in which we have failed. Were this life all that we had to live, such disappointments would be terrible indeed, but as it is not the only life we have to live they are only the seed implanted for the rich fulfillment.

Whether he was right or wrong in the specific articles of his creed, he never accepted anything on authority—not even Swedenborg's authority—but reasoned it out and tested it in his own life and learned that he could live by it and could not live without it. In 1894 he wrote Howells, "I have found that whatever remains of turgid doubts yet lingered in my mind are now clean gone, never, I believe, to return, and only the truth is left as light as day."

As a boy Pyle pored over *Punch* and loved the pictures of Leech, Doyle, and Tenniel. He chose the illustrator's life—always despised by the aesthetic snobs—as deliberately as, at a later date, Gerald Moore chose to be an accompanist for singers rather than a concert pianist. "My mother and I . . . liked the pictures in the books the best of all. . . . Even to this very day I still like the pictures you find in books better than wall pictures." But he was not disposed to undervalue the illustrator's function, even in comparison to that of the author, for he believed that the two rounded the circle "instead of advancing in parallel lines upon which it is almost impossible to keep them perfectly abreast," and he wished as illustrator, to be able to exercise his imagination freely and to fill out the text instead of narrowly confining himself to it.

The worlds which Pyle inhabited as graphic artist were many, the most important among them being American history, especially the Colonial Period (with fascinated side-glances toward what John Fiske described as "the golden age of piracy"), medievalism, and faerie. About the last-named he never had any doubts and was prepared to go to the literary barricades at any time to defend it against assailants who proposed to make the minds of children as dull as their own. But for some reason he seems to have been happier when he was satisfying his romantic impulses with pirates than with knights and ladies; possibly this was because piracy was much more closely tied to the colonialism he knew so well. Under one of his pirate pictures, he wrote:

> It is not because of his life of adventure and daring that I admire this one of my favorite heroes; nor is it because of blowing winds nor blue ocean nor palmy islands which he knew so well; nor is it because of gold he spent nor treasure he hid. He was a man who knew his own mind and what he wanted.

Taken as a whole, his medieval pictures were probably the most spectacular he ever did, but though I cannot perceive that he ever did them less carefully than he did other things, yet he seems to have felt a certain shoddiness in them, or at least in the medieval tales that *Harper's* sent him for illustration (perhaps he merely felt a certain danger of being swallowed up by "a fake mediaeval type," as he called it), and he finally rebelled against doing more of them.[14]

[14] Of course these objections did not apply to the medieval black-and-white pictures which he made for *Robin Hood* and the King Arthur books; these were deeply rooted in his own interests. His own swashbuckling story for boys, *Men of*

Four Masters of Enchantment

The gorgeous color processes which became practicable for American magazines around the turn of the century brought a quality of vivid drama to Pyle's work which it had inevitably lacked before, but the more spectacular pictures are not always the best. Wyeth, for example, placed the King Arthur black-and-white pictures at the top of his bent, and some would put the *Robin Hood* and the wonder tales even higher. Both in color and in black and white, Pyle strove hard to avoid repeating himself. *Robin Hood* relies more on outline and less on shading than the King Arthur pictures, and the use of the scroll as a semi-framing device in *Pepper and Salt* gives a somewhat different effect from that achieved in the more Pre-Raphaelitish *Wonder Clock*. In the little volume which contains three of Holmes's poems, *Dorothy Q, Together with a Ballad of the Boston Tea Party & Grandmother's Story of Bunker Hill Battle*,[15] the "Dorothy Q" drawings are considerably more sketchy than those for the other two poems, and to my way of thinking, some of his very best drawing was done for another Holmes book, *The One-Hoss Shay, with its Companion Poems*,[16] which first appeared in 1891 and was republished, and transformed by the addition of color in 1905, to which I would add that the humor of "The One-Hoss Shay" itself is no more successfully realized than the rich terror of "The Broomstick Train." If there is humor in some of these latter pictures also, there is certainly none in the witch picture captioned "Dark, dim, Dante-like solitudes," which, ever since I first saw it, has flashed before my mind every time I have seen a dark wood.

Pyle's color plates are not all of a piece either. The illustrations for Erik Blögh's story, "The Pilgrimage of Truth," which was the *Harper's* Christmas feature in 1900,[17] use a method similar to

Iron (Harper, 1891), came closer to the kind of literature he criticized, but *Otto of the Silver Hand* (Scribners, 1888) did not gloss over the dark side of medieval life.

[15] Houghton Mifflin, 1892.
[16] Houghton Mifflin.
[17] Vol. CII, 1–17.

that later employed by C. B. Falls which I have not encountered elsewhere in Pyle, and the Captain Kidd pictures[18] are different again. He was always sensitive enough to adapt his style to his subject-matter. The Oriental "Sword of Ahab" pictures[19] suggest Dean Cornwell; the picture of Estrecel, with its subdued color, facing the first page of Grace Rhys's story, "The Charming of Estrecel,"[20] recalls seventeenth-century portraiture, while the vivid red "Lola"[21] is quite as Spanish as it needs to be. And in the somber pictures he did for W. D. Howells' brooding poems, *Stops of Various Quills*,[22] which seems to me one of Pyle's great achievements, his own optimism has not at all prevented him from catching and projecting and reinforcing the somber spirit of the poems.[23]

But I think there can be no doubt that Pyle's greatest contribution was made in the field of American history. These pictures are unmistakably the product of the same mind which produced

[18] John D. Champlin, Jr., "The True Captain Kidd," *Harper's Magazine*, Vol. CVI (1902), 27–36. The pictures are reprinted in *Howard Pyle's Book of Pirates*.

[19] A story by James Edmund Dunning, *Harper's Magazine*, Vol. CIX (1904), 327–37.

[20] *Harper's Magazine*, Vol. CIX (1904), 327–37. In the portrait of "Holy Mr. Herbert," sitting under a tree, in Marjorie Bowen's story of that title, *Harper's Magazine*, Vol. CXX (1910), 839–46, the quiet tone of the picture is again admirably adapted to the character of the subject.

[21] In Percival Gibbon's story of the same title, *Harper's Magazine*, Vol. CXVIII (1909), 248–56.

[22] Harpers, 1895.

[23] Pyle's moons are always enchanting: see the third color plate illustrating Olivia Howard Dunbar, "Pierre Vidal, Troubadour," *Harper's Magazine*, Vol. CVIII (1903), 10; the illustration for Mrs. Henry Dudeney, "A Sense of Scarlet," *Harper's Magazine*, Vol. CXIV (1907), 399–404; and the second of the two plates for Pyle's own story, "The Salem Wolf," *Harper's Magazine*, Vol. CXX (1909), 1–12. In photogravure we have the picture of "The Mountain Home" in *The Autocrat of the Breakfast-Table*; in black and white, see the picture of p. 30 of the *Dorothy Q* book, and in *Howard Pyle's Book of the American Spirit*, "Along the Canal in Old Manhattan," p. 51; "A Game of Bowls," p. 67; and "A Pennsylvania Cave-Dwelling, XVIII Century," p. 97. With the frontispiece to "The Salem Wolf" it is interesting to compare the fox in Wyeth's end papers for Henry David Thoreau, *Men of Concord* (Houghton Mifflin, 1936). Wyeth's moon in the picture facing p. 32 in the Bulfinch-extracted *Legends of Charlemagne* (David McKay, n.d.) does not seem to me very successful as a moon, though it is an impressive composition.

the medieval pictures, and they have the same sort of charm, but this time there can be no question that they are based upon wide and intimate knowledge.[24] Pyle illustrated many historical pieces for *Harper's*, including the writings of both Woodrow Wilson and Henry Cabot Lodge, and he did not hesitate to correct even Wilson when he thought him wrong. "I can say with all sincerity," wrote the future President, "that the more you test my details the more I shall like it. I am not in the least sensitive on that point," thus expressing an attitude which, most unfortunately for all of us, he failed to carry over into his later political controversies. Whatever else they may have disagreed about, Wilson and Lodge agreed about the merit of Pyle's pictures, and he was greatly admired by Theodore Roosevelt (whom he himself warmly admired) also. Mark Twain thought extremely well of him. The great William Morris praised his *Robin Hood*, and in *Otto of the Silver Hand*, Joseph Pennell found it hard to say where Dürer left off and Pyle began.

N. C. Wyeth was born in Needham, Massachusetts, and grew up on the banks of the Charles. Like Pyle, he was blessed with a mother, in his case of Swiss extraction, who understood him and encouraged him and furthered his ambitions. His first commissions, received while he was still one of Pyle's pupils, were for covers for *Success* and *The Saturday Evening Post*.

Wyeth could do charming sketches in black and white,[25] but primarily he was a colorist. He painted rapidly, often finishing a picture in two or three days, and instead of being read to while he worked, as Pyle was, he apparently preferred to listen to the phonograph. He tended to paint on a larger scale than Pyle, his colors were likely to be brighter,[26] and his exuberant energy (he

[24] In spite of his phenomenal industry, Pyle managed to get through many volumes, partly through having himself read to while he worked, his choice of books ranging all the way from Swedenborg to Darwin.

[25] It is interesting today to take a look at Kate Douglas Wiggin's *Susanna and Sue* (Houghton Mifflin, 1909), in which Wyeth plays second fiddle to Alice Barber Stevens; the color plates are hers, and only the little black-and-white drawings at the beginning of each division were entrusted to him.

[26] Cf., for example, the Pyles in the Teachers Room at the Boston Public

137

excelled in scenes depicting violent action)[27] fairly spilled over the edges of the canvas. I should say that his picture of the children playing on the beach and gazing up at the giant they see in the clouds[28] is more romantic than anything Pyle ever did, very successfully combining the world of sense with that which lies within the mind. In some of the books he did comparatively late in his career—especially in *Men of Concord* and in Kenneth Roberts' *Trending into Maine*[29]—Wyeth found a less romantic type of subject matter than generally fell to him in the children's classics to which he devoted so much of his career, but it can hardly be without significance that the most realistic of all these books —the Kenneth Roberts—should contain a picture of a sea serpent which is about the most extravagant thing he ever did.[30] I cer-

---

Library with Wyeth's *Men of Concord* pictures, of which one—Bronson Alcott in the Old Granary Burying Ground—is in the Boston Athenaeum and several more are in the Concord Public Library.

[27] The picture facing p. 66 in Cooper's *The Last of the Mohicans* (Scribners, 1919) is a fine example of Wyeth's use of action, here present not only in the dynamic figures but in the waterfall behind them. *The White Company*, by Conan Doyle (McKay, n.d.), is full of action pictures, and there is a particularly gorgeous one facing p. 162 of Sidney Lanier's *The Boy's King Arthur* (Scribners, 1917), but where material is so abundant, it seems unnecessary to particularize.

[28] See *American Heritage*, Vol. XVI, No. 6 (October, 1965), 36. Somewhat similar to this in general conception is the sinister picture on the title page of *Treasure Island* (Scribners, 1911), where the pirates see a hanged man in the clouds. Parrish's picture of Atlas, in *A Wonder Book and Tanglewood Tales*, is as imaginative as Wyeth's giant, but the absence of the children deprives the picture of comparable contrast. Parrish does achieve triumphant contrast, however, in his illustration for Eugene Field's "Seein' Things" in *Poems of Childhood* (Scribners, 1904), and the wonderful picture facing p. 134 of Kenneth Grahame's *Dream Days* (John Lane, n.d.) captures every boy's dream of fighting pirates.

[29] Little, Brown, 1938.

[30] Wyeth did dragon pictures on the cover of his *Legends of Charlemagne* and, most exuberantly, on the end papers of Edna Johnson and Carrie E. Scott, *Anthology of Children's Literature* (Houghton Mifflin, 1940); see, also, the Winged Horse, facing p. 78 of the *Charlemagne*. If one compares Wyeth's dragons with Parrish's picture of the Reluctant Dragon in *Dream Days*, one perceives at once that Parrish has extracted all the ferocity from his bumbling, shambling, endearing beast, and replaced it with humor. This is, of course, exactly what Kenneth Grahame's story called for, but this does not alter the fact that only this kind of dragon could have been congenial to this artist. Compared to either Pyle or Parrish, Wyeth's pictures in general have little humor, though there is a delightful example of it in the picture of Thoreau and the Three Reformers in

tainly would not say, however, that all Wyeth's best pictures involve action, or, for that matter, high color. His death of Robin Hood[31] has little of either, yet it seems to me very touching. So, too, is the picture of Chad's vigil by Melissa's bedside in *The Little Shepherd of Kingdom Come*,[32] and the snow pictures in *The Black Arrow*,[33] though in quiet tones, are very beautiful. In *The Little Shepherd*, again, the charmingly graceful picture of Melissa against the background of her house shows Wyeth's ability to focus upon a single still figure when he chooses to do so.

In *Rip Van Winkle*[34] the colors are unusually rich even for Wyeth, and these pictures are notable too for their treatment of light, always one of the great delights of Wyeth's work. In the frontispiece the village in the sun-bathed valley nestles under the lowering mountains and the storm-clouds in the background. As Rip leaves his house, sunshine soaks its dilapidated front and the scolding woman in the doorway, highlighting the unlovely qualities of both, while he and his children stand shaded in the foreground. Sun sifts through the heavy trees in the picture before the inn, and again at the close, where Rip, returned, is out fishing in the woods with the children, but when he goes to the mountains only the peaks are illuminated. Henrik Hudson's men bowl in dark blue shadows, but there is light in the heavy clouds behind them. And when Rip returns to his ruined home, he stands shadowed in the open doorway with the blazing light behind him, casting his shadow forward upon the floor.

Light sifts through the trees again as John Alden brings Priscilla home after their marriage in *The Courtship of Miles Standish*,[35] and it soaks the rocky hills near Plymouth, when, earlier in

Men of Concord. He also used many fewer grotesques than Parrish, and when they appear, as in the illustration for "Hark, hark, the dogs do bark," in *Anthology of Children's Literature*, they lack the Parrish wit and sense of fun.

[31] In Paul Creswick, *Robin Hood* (McKay, 1917). Cf. Pyle's treatment of the same scene in his Robin Hood book.

[32] By John Fox, Jr. (Scribners, 1931).

[33] By Robert Louis Stevenson (Scribners, 1916).

[34] McKay, 1921.

[35] Houghton Mifflin, 1920.

the poem, he goes on his strange errand to her, with a glimpse of the sea in the background. Wyeth's trees, though less imaginative than Rackham's, are almost as characteristic, and there is a lovely interplay of tree and shade and sunshine in the plate facing page 156 of *Robin Hood*. In the picture of Mary and Joseph on their journey in Henry van Dyke's *Even Unto Bethlehem*,[36] the sunshine breaks through the clouds in visible beams. In the frontispiece Wyeth did for Mary Johnston's novel, *The Witch*,[37] the house before which the two characters are standing is treated much like Rip Van Winkle's house, except that in this case the shadow cast by the overhanging thatched roof adds an effective contrast, but in the two Civil War novels he illustrated for Mary Johnston—*The Long Roll* and *Cease Firing*[38]—Wyeth kept the color level down, making war as unromantic as the author made it. There is light in the clouds behind Stonewall Jackson in the frontispiece to *The Long Roll*, but the man and his horse are themselves both unlighted and swathed in mist. Mist and mud, not warm blood, are used in the battle scenes too, and the suggestion of cold in the picture called "The Vedette" almost causes one to shiver.

When Wyeth's edition of George Herbert Palmer's translation of *The Odyssey of Homer* was published by Houghton Mifflin in 1929, in one of the handsomest books ever made for him, he seemed to be deserting realism for a less representational style; the same tendencies appear more mildly in the *Anthology of Children's Literature* and in some of Wyeth's magazine work of the period, but the shift, if there was a shift, was not developed and did not long continue.[39] Incidentally, the picture of Emmaeus the swineherd, a somewhat elongated, terribly mournful

---

[36] Scribners, 1928.

[37] Houghton Mifflin, 1915.

[38] Houghton Mifflin, 1911 and 1912.

[39] Dudley Lunt, "N. C. Wyeth, 1882–1945," *Horn Book*, Vol. XXII (1946), 333–38, says that Wyeth began painting in egg tempera on gesso panels during his last years. His easel pictures seem to have been more restrained than his book illustration, bringing him much closer to his son Andrew.

figure, standing with his great dogs against a background of stockade and Greek isles, has always seemed to me one of Wyeth's fine achievements.

The work of Maxfield Parrish was less varied than that of either Pyle or Wyeth, but in a sense he was even more a creator of wonder. Parrish has an affinity with such painters as Boutet de Monvel and Puvis de Chavannes. In sharp contrast to Wyeth, the master of action, he either could not do action at all or did not care to do so; at any rate, he rarely attempted it.[40] The world of his pictures is, for the most part, a static world, and it is this, I think, which accounts for the impression of monotony which those who do not admire him complain of. Like Wyeth, he visited the American West,[41] but when he tried to paint it, he turned it into a country of his own mind, and the pictures he did for Ray Stannard Baker's "The Great Southwest"[42] are noteworthy for the absence of all characteristic "Western" notes. Parrish's trademarks include sun-kissed castles perched precariously in the mountains and bathed in a golden glow in the background of his pictures while the figures in the foreground are soaked in "Maxfield Parrish blue," pillars and vases with light and shadow playing over them, bold checks in clothing or properties, and enchanting little glimpses of other scenes peeping out here and there from the background of the main composition. In the famous mural of "The Pied Piper" at the Sheraton-Palace Hotel in San Francisco, there are actually three such glimpses—one the inevitable castle, one a peaceful river valley, and one which looks very much like a Western desert. The most elaborate and beautiful book illustrated by Maxfield Parrish is *The Knave of*

[40] It must be admitted, however, that in Parrish's picture of the Fisherman and the Genie, in *The Arabian Nights: Their Best-Known Tales*, edited by Kate Douglas Wiggin and Norah A. Smith (Scribners, 1909), a strong sense of impending development is presented.

[41] He also visited Italy and did an elaborate series of colored illustrations for Edith Wharton's *Italian Villas and Their Gardens* (Century Company, 1904). This early work may well have influenced his frequent use of architecture in his later paintings.

[42] *Century Magazine*, Vol. LXIV (1902), 5–15, 213–25, 361–73, 535–45.

As Far As Yesterday

Hearts, by Louise Saunders;[43] here the end papers are a variation of, and I think an improvement upon, the basic design he had already used in "Daybreak," and just before the play begins, the red-clad Manager draws back a green curtain just far enough to give you a tiny glimpse of the Arcadian landscape behind it.

Just after he had illustrated Kenneth Grahame's *The Golden Age*[44] and *Dream Days,* Parrish received this tribute from the distinguished art critic, Hubert von Herkomer:

> He has combined the photographic vision with the pre-Raphaelite feeling. He is poetic without being maudlin, and has the saving clause of humor. He can give suggestiveness without loss of unflinching detail. He has a strong sense of romance. He has a great sense of characterization without a touch of ugliness. . . . He has been able to infuse into the most uncompromising realism the decorative element—an extraordinary feat in itself.

This is much better than the remark once made by Parrish's father, Stephen Parrish, himself a painter, that his son was "more of an artisan than an artist," but Stephen's remark is not without point. The combination of highly romantic subject matter with intensely realistic methods was Maxfield Parrish's secret. Even in fairyland he never suggested anything (as Rackham, for example, often did); instead everything was portrayed, and in the minutest detail. Parrish, who was still driving his own car at ninety, had the American obsession with machinery, and many of the properties he painted in his pictures were first produced in the fully-equipped machine shop where he was as much at home as in his studio. Walt Disney is said to have invited Arthur Rackham to come to Hollywood to work on *Snow White and the Seven Dwarfs.*[45] Parrish would have made a greater "art director" for films than any they have ever had, particularly if he could

43 Scribners, 1925.
44 John Lane, 1900.
45 John Russell Taylor, *The Art Nouveau Book in Britain* (The M.I.T. Press, 1967), 149.

142

have worked with Maurice Tourneur, with whom he could easily have achieved a meeting of minds, and who had himself been an assistant to Puvis de Chavannes and in this capacity had worked on the murals in the Boston Public Library. But I am sure he would rather have committed suicide than live in Hollywood.

There can, I think, have been few more self-sufficient men in this world than Parrish. In his youth he knew poverty and illness and hard physical work. In his heyday he was not puffed up by his great prosperity (he is believed to have earned a fortune by his calendar pictures alone, and John Jacob Astor was said to have paid him $50,000 for the "King Cole" mural in the Knickerbocker Hotel), but when in his old age he was neglected and often sneered at by those who imagined painting to consist of squiggles or black squares, it seems to have affected him not at all. He always knew exactly what he wished to do, and he did it; what others made of it was their business and not his. It may be that those who insist that he stamped himself upon the country around Cornish, New Hampshire, so that even the trees and the clouds look like those he painted are over-romantic, but there can be no doubt that the house he himself designed and built there will seem quite familiar to anybody who knows his pictures. I do not mean by this that it looks like a castle or that there is anything eccentric about it; it is simply quite the right kind of house for a man like Maxfield Parrish to live in. Parrish had the brain of a dreamer and the hands of a builder; unlike most dreamers, he never contented himself, therefore, with insubstantial dreams. As a child in the nursery he made his own toys, with every figure carefully designed and fully developed, and the subject matter he employed here was pretty much the same he was to use all his life. When he was a student at Haverford he decorated his chemistry notebook with gnomes and pixies which his instructor cherished for years and made his college room into a fairy wonderland that his friends rejoiced to visit. If ever a man created art for the love of it, it was he, and pictures ran out of him as music seems to have run through Schubert, so that he could hardly send off a letter without decorating the envelope so that it was cherished as a keepsake by its recipient.

There were raised eyebrows when Parrish was reputed to use an air-brush or to have mixed his paints with varnish to secure a certain effect. I do not know whether these things are true or not, but Quakers are a pragmatic people, and if Parrish could thus have secured an effect he aimed at, I am sure that he would not have been at all distressed because he had won it by unorthodox means. His startling color effects he secured by using only three or four basic colors, and painting one over another. I do not mean by any of this that Parrish was ever smug or cynical or self-satisfied about his work. As a matter of fact, it rarely satisfied him; sometimes he destroyed it. When he was sixty he said he thought he had painted one or two pictures which showed "promise." I may add that I have rarely seen a reproduction of a Parrish painting which did justice to the beauty of the original. When the little art gallery in Concord, Massachusetts, put on an exhibition of his work in the autumn of 1966, the picture called "Lanterns"[46] lighted up the whole end of the room in which it was hung. Yet his colors were not always brilliant, nor did he always startle. "The Fountain of Pirene" in *A Wonder Book and Tanglewood Tales* is a very dark picture, and the illustrations for "L'Allegro" and "Il Penseroso"[47] are certainly very subdued. In the picture of the Young King of the Black Isles in *The Arabian Nights*, which is a masterly composition, the color, though skilfully employed, is distinctly muted.

It has been observed that Parrish's classical scenes are more Gothic than Greek; if this was intended as a criticism of the *Wonder Book* pictures, it falls to the ground, for the same thing is true of Hawthorne's stories, and illustrations should harmonize with text. It is certainly true, however, that whether his scene be classical, Oriental, or medieval, Parrish never concerned himself

[46] Reproduced facing p. 38 in Palgrave's *Golden Treasury* (Duffield, 1911).
[47] *Century Magazine*, Vol. LXIII (1901), 163–69.

Four Masters of Enchantment

with the kind of accuracy that his master Pyle insisted upon. Whether this ever troubled Pyle I have no idea, but his views being what they were, he might well have made the same criticism of Parrish that he leveled against James Branch Cabell's stories ("they are neither exactly true to history nor exactly fanciful, and . . . I feel that they are not true to mediaeval life, and that they lack a really permanent value"). To the true romancer such criticisms are irrelevant, for the land of faerie is not bounded by time. In "The Merchant's Tale" Chaucer not only brought Pluto and Proserpine into old Januarie's medieval garden but permitted them to quote "this Jewe, this Salomon"!

Neither Pyle nor either of his pupils made much use of the nude. Pyle frankly did not care for it, and about the only examples of it I can recall in his work are the picture of the little naked children used as a frontispiece in his own *Twilight Land*[48] and some of the decorations in Markham's *Man with the Hoe*. Wyeth used it freely in his pictures for the *Odyssey*, where the nude Calypso is a lovely figure, but hardly anywhere else.[49] Though he did not care for life studies in art school, Parrish used more nudes than the others; in fact, his first "strike," his magazine cover for the "Midsummer Number" of the *Century* in 1897, is a nude.[50] But the strange, almost unparalleled distinction of Parrish's nudes is that one can hardly ever tell whether the figure portrayed is male or female! (In one case, that of the picture of "The Dinkey-Bird" in Field's *Poems of Childhood*, this even

[48] Harpers, 1894.

[49] One exception, oddly enough, is the frontispiece to S. Parkes Cadman, *The Parables of Jesus* (McKay, 1931), where the Christ Child is as exposed as even a Renaissance painter could have painted him. This picture does not seem to me one of Wyeth's triumphs, not at all for this reason but because of the uncharacteristically "pretty," almost coy, expression on the child's face. The general composition, with the sunburst halo effect in the background, is effective, however, and the Joseph-figure is pleasing.

[50] Parrish was awarded second, not first, prize in the competition which the magazine had conducted, only because he had characteristically disregarded the ground rules, and, following his daemon, had submitted a picture which required five printings where three had been specified. The judges were Elihu Vedder, F. Hopkinson Smith, and Henry B. Henderson.

occasioned controversy.) Now I know that chastity is an excellent quality in nudes, but it can be carried too far, and in at least one instance in Parrish it suggests an unpleasant ambiguity which the artist cannot possibly have intended.[51] There is nothing in kind in any of my American artists quite so charming as the naked Pandora, Epimetheus, and their companions in Rackham's pictures for "The Paradise of Children" in Hawthorne's *Wonder Book*,[52] and there are more mature female figures in Rackham which, while always handled with restraint and good taste, are not lacking in physical appeal. Parrish, on the other hand, has only one picture of Pandora, as a considerably older girl than the one Rackham chose to portray, and despite the text to the contrary, she is well covered.

Having introduced Arthur Rackham in the first paragraph, I have kept him waiting in the wings quite an unreasonably long time without inviting him to take the center of the stage. As I have already said, he had no connection with the other artists considered in this chapter except that, like them, he lived, as artist, in a world of the imagination and that he meant far too much to me to be left out. Like Parrish, he was an artist predestined, smuggling paper and pencil to bed with him as a child and drawing surreptitiously until the light failed. He was a fellow-student with Charles Ricketts at the Lambeth School of Art but spent five years as a clerk in an insurance office, which must inevitably remind one of how the greatest imaginative writer among Rackham's contemporaries, Walter de la Mare, put in a much longer stretch as a statistician for Standard Oil. Rackham's early photographs, with the high stiff collars and the small, steel-rimmed spectacles, look very much like those of a clerk; later, when his face became weather-beaten and deeply lined, he reminded many people of some of the quaint figures he liked to draw. Since he often used himself as a model, perhaps this is

[51] I may add that it would be difficult to make me believe that the legs of the standing figure on p. 27 of *The Knave of Hearts* could ever join his trunk, under his clothes, at the proper places.

[52] Hodder & Stoughton; George H. Doran, 1922.

not surprising; he was much less objective than Parrish. He was very fond of doing self-portraits[53] and caricatures of himself also, and there are a good many of these scattered through his books, clear down to the very last, *The Wind in the Willows,* where he is the clerk in the ticket-office window of the frontispiece.

Rackham studied Cruikshank, Caldecott, Doyle, Arthur Boyd Houghton, and Aubrey Beardsley, and was touched by foreign influences from both Germany and Japan. Art Nouveau may be seen in the waves in *Undine*[54] and elsewhere, and the picture facing page 73 in *Grimm's Fairy Tales*[55] shows this influence very clearly. At the beginning of his career he did "Sketches from the Life" and other topical pictures for *Pall Mall Budget* and other papers; he even illustrated an American travel book, *To the Other Side,*[56] the pictures being done from photographs. In *The Ingoldsby Legends,*[57] his style is still in process of development; I suppose these pictures might be called Rackham-in-embryo, though I find them very charming. He came much closer to the Rackham we know next year with the Lambs' *Tales from Shakespeare,*[58] but his real fame dates from the Grimm, first published in 1900 and subsequently altered and enlarged. The first pictures he did for Grimm are dark and a little crabbed and crowded compared to Rackham's fully-developed style, which appears more clearly in the supplementary Grimm collection, *Little Brother and Little Sister and Other Tales,*[59] and, of course, much later, in the Hans Christian Andersen *Fairy Tales,*[60] which con-

---

[53] See especially the frontispiece to Derek Hudson's *Arthur Rackham.*

[54] By Baron Friedrich Heinrich Karl de la Motte-Fouqué, in the W. L. Courtney translation (Heinemann; Doubleday, Page, 1909).

[55] In my copy, which carries the Heinemann imprint and no date. The book was first published by Freemantle in 1900 and reprinted and enlarged in 1907 and 1909. The 1909 edition was by Constable. Latimore-Haskell does not give the name of the American publisher of 1909.

[56] By Thomas Rhodes (George Philip & Son, 1893). Some illustrations from this book are reprinted by Latimore-Haskell.

[57] Dent, 1898; enlarged edition, 1907.

[58] Dent, 1899; Dent, Dutton, 1909.

[59] Constable; Dodd, Mead, 1917.

[60] Harrap; McKay, 1932.

tain some of the loveliest pictures he ever made, and which, one would suppose, he must have greatly enjoyed doing.

Rackham was more water-colorist than painter, and the coloring in his pictures is, generally speaking, much paler and more delicate than in the Americans I have been considering, though there is often a very effective bright color spot (in several instances, red berries) by way of contrast. He generally supplemented his color plates with numerous black-and-white illustrations in the text, and he also used silhouettes freely; these are his principal reliance only in *Cinderella*[61] and *The Sleeping Beauty*,[62] but he often employed them in a subordinate capacity in other books, occasionally even combining them with line drawing in a single picture.[63] Derek Hudson thinks his backgrounds became more impressionistic in later years and his colors cleaner and brighter. Certainly he could employ an impressionistic technique very effectively when he chose, as in the surpassingly lovely drop-curtain for *Hänsel und Gretel* which Hudson reproduces facing page 140 of his biography of Rackham. And he could do the lovely English landscape too, occasionally by itself, more often as a background, as in "Adrift" in *Arthur Rackham's Book of Pictures*,[64] with the pretty, terrified little girl in the boat drifting into the reeds in the foreground and the English town under heavy, threatening clouds on the opposite bank. He is always effective in his use of water, and the great winds blow through his pictures as freely as they blow through Meredith's poetry and prose. For all its delicacy, Rackham's is a much more active world than that of Parrish.

In a sense, I suppose we may say that the most ambitious thing Rackham ever did was the illustrations he made for *The Ring of the Nibelung*,[65] but while I certainly would not say that these pic-

---

[61] Retold by C. S. Evans (Heinemann; Lippincott, 1919).

[62] Retold by C. S. Evans (Heinemann; Lippincott, 1920).

[63] See Charles Dickens, *A Christmas Carol* (Heinemann; Lippincott, 1915), 84–85.

[64] Heinemann; Century Co., 1913.

148

tures are not successful, they do not represent the part of his work that I value most. To my way of thinking, he was at his superb best in such books as *Rip Van Winkle*, with its pendant, *The Legend of Sleepy Hollow*, which, though less elaborate, is equally good;[66] in *Peter Pan in Kensington Gardens*,[67] (though I do not care for the figure of Peter himself); and in any of the pictures he made for *A Midsummer Night's Dream*.[68] The delicacy and charm of the fairies here is incomparable, and the same may be said of the fairies in *The Tempest*[69] and, indeed, wherever he had occasion to draw them. It would be hard to choose Rackham's finest single fairy picture, but certainly high claims could be made for the last picture in the Limited Editions Club *Dream*, where Puck, having taken his curtain call, withdraws discreetly behind the folds, while fairies spill out at every conceivable point of opening, as if the stage and the whole world were crammed with them. But, then, the "curtain lecture" picture in *Rip Van Winkle* is almost equally good, and how could we have lived without No. 5—"By the Way"—in the *Book of Pictures*, where a princess pauses by the roadside to examine the fairies emerging from the ground with their pointed hats like red toadstools, and a plowed field stretches out to the horizon, with a tall gaunt tree in the foreground and a flight of birds darkening the sky?

Rackham's twisted, gnarled trees, often wearing human expressions and sometimes commenting upon the actions of the human characters, are almost equally delightful, and I could

[65] Latimore-Haskell lists only *The Rhinegold & The Valkyrie* (Heinemann; Doubleday, Page, 1910) and *Siegfried & The Twilight of the Gods* (Heinemann; Doubleday, Page, 1911). In my edition the whole tetralogy is bound between a single pair of covers as *The Ring of the Niblung* (Doubleday, Page, n.d.). The translations from the German of Richard Wagner are by Margaret Armour.

[66] *Rip Van Winkle*, by Washington Irving (Heinemann; Doubleday, Page, 1905). *The Legend of Sleepy Hollow*, by Washington Irving (Harrap; McKay, 1928).

[67] By J. M. Barrie (Hodder & Stoughton; Scribners, 1906).

[68] The commercially published edition was issued by Heinemann and by Doubleday, Page in 1908.

[69] Heinemann; Doubleday, Page, 1926.

walk out of my house now and within a quarter of an hour come to a tree which I never pass without thinking of Rackham and which I would give a good deal to be able to transplant to my own front yard. What could be more delightful than the picture of "Major André's tree" in *The Legend of Sleepy Hollow?* Rackham tree, Rackham fairies, Rackham witch, and Rackham witch's cat—they are all there, and this is almost more than we have a right to expect in a single picture in this world.

Rackham's old men and women are frequently delightful. He found himself quite at home with the phantoms in Dickens' *Christmas Carol* too, and his picture of the "Old Scratch" referred to parenthetically in this tale could hardly be bettered, but on the whole I have never been able to care very much for his supernatural grotesques. We are told that he did not enjoy doing his pictures for Poe's *Tales of Mystery and Imagination*,[70] very late in his career, and I would guess that he was much less *en rapport* with *Peer Gynt*[71] also than he was with such milder recreations as *The Vicar of Wakefield* and *The Compleat Angler*,[72] which belong to the same general period. But surely he made the Poe pictures more horrible, and more like a series of cartoons, than would have been necessary, and I should say that he had a tendency to do this with his grotesques in general; for this reason I have never been able to admire his *Comus*[73] as much as some do. Nor do I admire his dragons and his sea serpent (in the *Book of Pictures* and elsewhere), for the simple reason that they all seem to me to have more reptilian horror than wonder about them. His Santa Claus is interesting, though hardly the standard conception, either in the *Book of Pictures* or in *The Night Before Christmas*,[74] which was the title Rackham's publishers gave to Clement C. Moore's *A Visit from St. Nicholas*.

[70] Harrap; Lippincott, 1935.
[71] Harrap; Lippincott, 1936.
[72] *The Vicar of Wakefield*, by Oliver Goldsmith (Harrap; McKay, 1929). *The Compleat Angler*, by Izaak Walton (Harrap; McKay, 1931).
[73] By John Milton (Heinemann; Doubleday, Page, 1921).
[74] Harrap; Lippincott, 1931.

150

Four Masters of Enchantment

If this seems a chilly note on which to end my discussion of Arthur Rackham and this chapter, I certainly do not mean it as such. I hope I am not so foolish as to regard any one of the painters I have discussed as the equal of Michelangelo or Leonardo or Rembrandt, and if I were, I am sure nobody could possibly be more disgusted with me than the artists themselves. Nevertheless, their art has enriched my life, and I am thankful to have lived in a time when it was available. If you should offer me my choice between the originals of one of my favorite pictures by each of these artists, I might find it quite impossible to make up my mind, but if you should ask me to choose between any one of these and any example of the work of a number of far more illustrious painters whom I (or you) might name, I am confident that I should have no difficulty at all and that my choice would shock you.

IX

How It Feels
To Be a Writer

The Wizard of Oz had yet a deeper significance for me than I have indicated in my discussion of it. Not only did it bring me unbounded delight; it also showed me what I wished to do with my life. From the time I encountered it, at the age of six, I knew that I must become a writer. And as soon as I was able to hold a pencil, or use a typewriter, I began to write—for my family when they were interested, for the public as soon as it could be persuaded, and for myself when no other reader was available.

The family, I am sure, regarded all this as the amiable and comparatively harmless weakness of a bright boy. I certainly do not blame them for not considering the possibility of my earning a living through writing. I did not consider that myself, nor should I advise anybody else to do it, even today. If I had waited to begin to earn a living until the time came when I was able to support myself by my typewriter alone, I should have starved to death long before it came. What does surprise me is that it should not have been clear to everybody from the outset that, being what I was, no other profession than that of either a teacher or a clergyman was worth considering for me. But until I made this unmistakably clear by taking my own road—at which point I received the most generous co-operation from everybody concerned—I am sure all around me thought in the stereotyped terms of a business, sometimes even a technological, career, all of which must have been dust and ashes for me. Marilyn Monroe used to say that when she told people her sign was Gemini—"that's intellect"—they always laughed. When I told people I was going to be a writer, they did not exactly laugh, but they gave the impression of thinking that I had said something rather sweet or quaint or precious. The first exception was my fourth-grade teacher, Miss Mary F. Dwyer, who had the imagination to meet me on my own ground, which is always the most important thing an adult can do for a child. "Eddie," she said, "I want you to promise me that when you publish your first book, you will send me a copy." I promised faithfully and solemnly, and the promise was kept. She lived just about long enough to receive the volume.

Mathematics had always been to me what it was for Henry James—a "dreadful blight"—and when I encountered Geraldine Farrar's statement that if the Lord had intended her to learn the multiplication table, He would never have given her ten fingers to count on, I nodded in enthusiastic agreement. Yet when I graduated from grade school, I was enrolled, upon phenomenally stupid advices, in the technical course at the high school, whereupon I proceeded to learn how it feels to find yourself at the foot of your class instead of at the head.

In woodworking the first task assigned to me was to make a joint out of two little blocks of wood. Each side had to be planed smooth, after which the wood must be hollowed out so that the two pieces would fit together. The method of procedure was that as soon as you got one surface smooth and flat, you took it up to the teacher for an O.K., after which you went on to the next surface. I managed to get a few O.K.'s, but I could never get O.K.'s on all sides of my block. Before very long I became aware that my wood was now so reduced that even should I succeed in making it smooth and straight, it could never be utilized for the purpose designed, whereupon I gravely presented it to the instructor

153

with the announcement "It's gettin' kinda thin." He was a dour, unimaginative man who was already somewhat familiar to me because he lived in a house owned by one of my aunts, but I owe him a great debt. After he and I had agonized together for a number of weeks, he opened the prison door for me, by telling me there was no use going on: I must change my enrollment from the technical to the general course. This meant making up six or seven weeks of German, but this was unalloyed delight from the beginning. Mr. Abbott may have been motivated by no more humane impulse than his imperative need of getting rid of me, but I certainly would not blame him for that.

Oddly enough, I was finding algebra much easier than arithmetic, partly, I am sure, because I had an excellent teacher; neither did I have any trouble with the first half of plane geometry. But I had graduated from grade school the first of February, and when I was halfway through my second year of high school, we moved from Chicago to Oak Park. Oak Park High School had no midyear class, and this necessitated my taking the second half of my sophomore English, German, and geometry in summer school. Since Harrison had no summer session, this meant going to Crane, where I found the atmosphere very uncongenial. I sailed through the English and the German with my customary ease, but with the geometry my old enemy mathematics announced that the truce between us was over. The teacher was a very genial and highly competent, but extremely exhibitionistic, man, who had the habit of writing a proposition on the blackboard and passing over everything I did not understand with "obviously" or its equivalent. What was obvious to him was not at all obvious to me, and I soon did what I have always done under such circumstances; I stopped working altogether. Plane geometry thus became the only course I ever "flunked," which placed me under the necessity of repeating the whole year of it at Oak Park. Here, again, I had an excellent teacher and encountered no trouble. When I told her I hated mathematics and all the sciences, she was amazed. I must be mistaken about my-

154

self, she said, for I had a scientific mind. Later, at the University of Chicago, I was comforted when I heard Professor James Root Hulbert say that anybody who was worth anything at all was sure to flunk in something.

When I was younger in my academic life, I more or less adhered to the ideal of a "well-rounded education," but I have now become so doubtful about it that I am about ready to return to President Eliot's free elective system. If I may judge by my own experience, nobody ever learned anything in a course that he did not wish to take. Though I did well in algebra, not only has algebra been of no use to me whatever, but I remember absolutely nothing about it (I am not exaggerating) except that there were x's in it, while as for geometry, I recall only that "the square of the hypotenuse of a right triangle is equal to the sum of the squares of the other two sides," and I should not now have the faintest idea of how to go about proving that, while my indifference to it is absolute.

To be sure, the attitude I reveal here was not entirely absent even from my English classes. With two exceptions hereinafter to be noted (and even these were more apparent than real), I do not think any composition teacher I ever had either in high school or in college was of the slightest use to me. In high school I reveled in the "literature" portions of my "English" courses and yawned through the "composition" portions, yet away from school I was always scribbling. The explanation, I think, is simple. I have never been able to write anything on an assigned subject; that is why I could never have been a journalist. The choice of subject, the writing impulse must come from within; I cannot create to order.

The German language and the perspective of the ancient world, as it opened up before me in my history course, furnished the principal stimulation I received from my high-school work in Chicago, for the English courses there did not take me very far beyond the point where my excellent eighth-grade teacher, Miss Alice L. Burns, had left me. Oak Park was a different world,

155

but, interestingly enough, the primary stimulus here was in the direction of speaking rather than writing.

Not that this was entirely new to me. I loved "speaking pieces" even as a child and have dim memories of myself perched on a table spouting something which ended with "Mistah Woostah pwesents a vewy stately appeawance." In third grade we memorized a poem each month, beginning with "September" and "October," by Helen Hunt Jackson.

> The goldenrod is yellow;
> The corn is turning brown;
> The trees in apple orchards
> With fruit are bending down.

Why is it that I could still say that in my sleep but have forgotten all the rest?

My first real public speaking came about, however, through the Epworth League, first in Chicago and then in Oak Park. When I was fifteen I created a sensation by offering in the Epworth League at the Douglas Park Methodist Church so fervent a plea for the expansion of the church into the community (which sadly needed it) that something really had to be done about it. Unfortunately nobody had enough imagination to think of anything better than holding a week of special evangelistic services with home talent, which accomplished just about what might have been expected. It was quite natural, therefore, that, during the fall term of my senior year, I should have enrolled in a newly-established public-speaking course at Oak Park High, taught by Miss Margaret H. Dixon, who had become a good friend of mine as my English teacher the previous year. What was wholly unexpected was that, like Byron, I should, as a result of this course, wake up one morning to find myself famous, though over a much narrower area than he commanded.

Oak Park High School has always claimed to be very proud of the Class of 1917, but this is principally because Ernest Hemingway was a member of it. During our senior year Hemingway's

How It Feels To Be a Writer

weekly column in *The Trapeze*, Morris Musselman's extraordinarily finished performance in the class play, Clyde Fitch's *Beau Brummel*, and my "orations" all attracted much attention. Ernest's *Trapeze* column was modeled on the work of Ring Lardner and B.L.T. in the Chicago *Tribune*, and such copies of the paper as have survived now command fantastic prices, as do the monthly issues of the literary magazine, *The Tabula*, containing his early stories, and the classbook number of the same publication, which included the class prophecy in which I have always claimed he made me one of the first Hemingway characters. Taking his clue from my utter indifference to all sports and games, he made me a famous baseball player, and I can still remember the mischievous glance he cast at me, out of the corner of his eye, when he was reading it at our Class Day exercises.

The beginning of all this, so far as I was concerned, came when it was decided that Miss Dixon's public-speaking class should furnish the program for the pre-Thanksgiving assembly, and a number of us were asked to prepare talks. Mine was on the subject "America's Thanksgiving," and though I became aware that some of my classmates were strongly impressed by it during our rehearsals, it did not seem to me notably different from what I had been turning out for the Epworth League. When it came to the assembly, however, I might just as well have been the only person on the program, and I was completely unprepared for the storm of applause that greeted me and the acclaim I thereafter found myself enjoying among pupils, teachers, and townspeople alike.

Of course I was enrolled in all the speaking contests within hailing distance. I placed first at Lake Forest and third at Northwestern, though none of the Oak Park contestants did very well at Illinois. (I also won a scholarship at the University of Chicago in a competitive examination which had nothing to do with public-speaking.)

At Oak Park High School it was the custom for the faculty to choose the commencement speakers and allow the senior class to elect the valedictorian from among them. Since I was under the impression that the valedictorianship went automatically to the student with the highest grade-point average, and since I knew this was Edward Willcox, the thought that I might be valedictorian had never occurred to me. I had only my last two years at Oak Park, and many of my classmates did not know me at all well personally; I was amazed, therefore, when I almost literally swept the board. My triumph on Commencement night, June 14, 1917, was more than one of the most spectacular things that ever happened to me, it was one of the most spectacular things I ever witnessed, but I value it now not for the inflation it gave my ego but because it enabled me to understand how a great singer or actor feels on the night of an extraordinary triumph. Quite frankly, however, I am sure that much of the emotion came not from me but from the mood of the hour, for this was just about two months after the United States had followed the Pied Piper into World War I, and my subject was "Tomorrow." I soon changed my mind about the great crusade to make the world safe for democracy, and I have never been taken in by another since. Consequently the memory of my great night is not quite unalloyed satisfaction to me, nor can I even feel that I won my triumph quite legitimately.

After my graduation from high school, I was foolish enough for a time to think that I might become a professional "lecturer" (which, to be sure, was not quite so unreasonable in 1917 as it would be today), and for the time being I suppose my ultimate goal of writing shone more dimly through the mists than at any other time. It is amusing to remember that there was a rich man in River Forest, a Chicago banker, who, greatly impressed by my Commencement oration, wanted to do something for me. In the year of our Lord 1917, he could think of nothing more valuable than to send me to a phrenologist, who had his offices, as late as that, in McVicker's Theater building in the Loop, and who examined the bumps on my head and assured me with a perfectly

158

straight face that I had a skull much like that of Abraham Lincoln!

I had no desire to be Abraham Lincoln, but predestined writer though I was, I suppose there never was a time when I should not have been glad to be a great actor or singer. The latter possibility was ruled out by the popular prejudice in favor of singers who possess a voice, for my first and last great triumph in this field occurred when I sang "Love's Old Sweet Song," also acting as master of ceremonies, at the exercises which followed my "graduation" from second grade.

I have, however, had some success as a reader, and with proper training, I might have made an actor, but I had sense enough to know that I should hate the traveling and other hard conditions to which an actor is subjected, and I knew, too, that though I should have loved to give my life to Shakespeare, there was nothing much for me in the modern plays that were coming more and more into vogue. If I had known then what I afterwards learned, that Sothern and Marlowe never turned down any young man or woman who wished to read for them, I might well have gone to them on one of their visits to Chicago, but I think I knew, even then, that any creation of which I might be capable must be wrought in solitude, as the writer creates, and that to function creatively under rehearsal conditions, as an actor must, or to interpret as the director, rather than the inner monitor, might desire would be quite out of the question for me. Among all the wrong or foolish decisions I have made in my life, this surely was a wise one, and so was one other. When I became Oak Park's "boy orator" all the best advices were in favor of my studying law. I never gave this even a moment's consideration—those who urged it might just as well have addressed me in a foreign language—for the simple reason that the law and the matters with which the law mainly deals did not interest me at all, could indeed hardly be said to exist. I might, to be sure, have been a successful and spectacular advocate on special occasions, but I should certainly have performed very indifferently when my

159

emotions were not involved, and the strain of those "scenes" by which I might have shone would surely, had they come often enough, have killed me long before this.

Though I have always written to please myself first of all, I have never been bashful about wooing the printing press, and I began sending my things out very early. For a long time, of course, they all came back, but in the long run nothing that was publishable failed of publication, though, except for book reviews, I have always been more successful with book publishers than with magazine editors. Here, again, I am sure my irrefragable independence has been the root cause. Magazine editors have "policies" and "interests." So have I, and I have never considered dropping mine to take up those of somebody else.

When I was a child, one of the Sunday features in the Chicago *Tribune* was "The Bird Lover's League," conducted by one "Aunty Bee," the purpose of which was to teach children to love and protect wildlife. There was a pretty button, with some lovely ribbons on it, and there was a department in the paper to which children might contribute. I have no idea what I wrote about or when all this took place, but I do know that I "made" "Aunty Bee's" column a few times, and these must have been positively my first appearances in print. It is interesting that all this should have been in the newspaper for which I was later to review so many hundred books, but it still seems strange to me that we did not save the clippings.

Thereafter, of course, the movies swallowed me up, and my writing was drawn into the theatrical orbit. Late in 1911, *The Motion Picture Story Magazine*, as it was called in those days (it is now *Motion Picture*), invited its readers to write letters answering such questions as "Which of our writers is your favorite, and why?" "What kind of story do you like best?" and "Do you prefer to read the story or to see the film first?" I won the fifth prize, the only child to be thus honored. It was a year's subscription to the magazine, which was worth all of $1.50, but it was a great event nevertheless, and I remember as if it were yesterday,

160

going downstairs to the front door to get the letter, which was on special Christmas paper—one of the first typed letters I ever received—on the late afternoon delivery (yes, dear young reader who believes in progress and who imagines that communications are faster now than they were when I was a boy, we had *three* mail deliveries a day in 1911), tearing it open in eager expectation, and then rushing up the stairs like a banshee, yelling the wonderful news to my mother. They did not print the winning letters in the magazine, though they did announce the names of the winners, and some of my other lucubrations did appear later in their pages in the form of letters to the editor.

Then, in the summer of 1918, Kitty Kelly, who was the film critic of the Chicago *Herald-Examiner*, got the bright idea of inviting readers to submit "lay" criticisms of current films for her Sunday department. I did not need to be asked twice, and Miss Kelly liked what I wrote well enough so that I became almost a "regular" as long as her column lasted. At this time, Julian Johnson, editor of *Photoplay Magazine*, was probably the best film critic in America. I was one of his most eager readers, and he taught me a good deal about both films and a certain type of writing. In addition to his monthly reviews of individual films, Johnson produced annually an allover review of the year's films, and I shamelessly set out to imitate him. What is more I got two of my annual reviews published in a comparatively short-lived motion-picture magazine called *Photo-Play Journal*, one in December, 1918, and the other in November, 1919, and there would have been more if the editor, a man named Delbert Essex Davenport, had not thereafter relinquished control and left the enterprise in the hands of someone who knew not Joseph. The only other piece of mine which Davenport published was a rather pretentious essay called "The Photoplay and American Life," in November, 1918, but when he took off he had other manuscripts in hand, waiting to appear. I even interviewed a then rising and very beautiful young actress named Constance Binney for him when she was playing in Chicago, with Henry Hull, in Rachel Crothers' play, *39 East.* Thus Miss Binney has the distinction, for whatever it may be worth, of being the only human being who was ever interviewed by me!

By this time I had of course got it through my head that I was not going to write the kind of books L. Frank Baum wrote—this was what I expected at the outset for the excellent reason that this was the only kind of book I knew—but it took me a comparatively long time to find anything else to put in the empty place. My interest in *The Atlantic Monthly* during my high-school days, which led to the essays of Agnes Repplier and Samuel McChord Crothers, taught me that there was such a thing as non-fiction writing, and of course I tried to write essays too, but this did not seem to be quite the thing either. Then, when I was in my early twenties, I decided to try my hand at book reviews. I do not know where the idea came from—I have written elsewhere that it was suggested to me by Dr. Crothers, after he had read one of my essays, but on looking back to his letter, I find that this is wrong; what he actually suggested was short articles, which might fit more easily into an editor's plans. When I began book-reviewing, I was so ignorant that I knew neither that reviews were assigned by the editor nor that publishers furnished review copies; I drew books out of the public library and wrote reviews and submitted them! Unbelievable as it seems, it not only worked, but I began at the top, and the first reviews of mine that ever appeared in print were in *The Saturday Review* (a piece on Agnes Repplier's *Under Dispute* in one of the very first issues), *The Atlantic Monthly, The Yale Review,* and *The Virginia Quarterly Review.* In the early numbers of the last of these, which began at just the right time for me—1925—I find that I filled more pages than any other writer. Its editor, the late Dr. James Southall Wilson, must have been a long-suffering man; certainly he was very kind to me, and he gave my morale a considerable boost.

By this time, however, two other important things had happened: I had finished my work at the University of Chicago, and

162

How It Feels To Be a Writer

I had encountered Gamaliel Bradford. The composition courses "English 4 and 5," taught by David Allan Robertson, later president of Goucher College, and the novelist Robert Herrick respectively, were the exceptions above referred to, among the writing courses in which I was enrolled. And this was their secret: neither man ever told me what to write, for they both knew that if you need to be told, then writing is not for you. They asked me what I *wished* to write about, and when I had written it, they read it and praised what was good in it and tried to correct what was bad. All this was immensely important to me; I had at last encountered two persons in whose judgment I had sufficient confidence so that I could believe in myself because they believed in me. At the same time, I was also in contact with Edith Rickert, the greatest teacher I have ever had, and though I generally think of her first in connection with the understanding of scholarship in general which she imparted to me, her encouragement was important to me as a writer also.

Gamaliel Bradford (1863–1932) too came to me first through the *Atlantic*.[1] Under the influence of Sainte-Beuve, Bradford had developed a type of biographical writing which he called "psychography." It differed from regular biography primarily in two respects: it was organized topically, not chronologically, and it concentrated not upon the outward events of a man's life but upon an analysis of his character and personality. I knew at once that this was what I had been waiting for, and I produced my first psychographs in Robert Herrick's "English 5"—one dealing with Richard Mansfield and the other with Marie Bashkirtseff.[2]

[1] My most detailed consideration in print of the writings of Gamaliel Bradford is in my article, "Gamaliel Bradford, Psychographer," in *The Twenties: Poetry and Prose, 20 Critical Essays* (see Appendix for details); cf. also "Psychography and Such," *Boston University Graduate Journal*, Vol. XII (1964), 100–12. The emphasis here, however, is more on my own career than on Bradford's.

[2] "Richard Mansfield, Portrait of an Actor" appeared, in a revised form, in *Sewanee Review*, Vol. XXXVIII (1930), 150–60; "Marie Bashkirtseff in Retrospect," in *South Atlantic Quarterly*, Vol. XLIII (1944), 63–75. This was not the Mansfield paper afterwards published in *Merely Players* (1966).

As Far As Yesterday

Bradford might very reasonably have been offended by my "Richard Mansfield" when I sent it to him, for I had imitated him almost as slavishly as, in another field, I had imitated Julian Johnson. His greathearted generosity made this impossible for him; instead he welcomed me in the warmest possible manner and even told me that I would probably carry psychography farther than he had been able to take it. This was the beginning of a friendship which was cultivated through hundreds of letters and two extended visits of mine to Bradford and his wife at Wellesley Hills, Massachusetts, and which was broken off only by his death. Whatever an established writer can do for a newcomer, Bradford did for me.

My actual book-publishing began timidly and locally and unpsychographically, however, while I was teaching at the University of Washington in Seattle. My colleague and friend, the late Glenn Hughes, brought out two pieces of mine in his "University of Washington Chapbook Series," and my first title between hard covers, *Values in Literature*, was published by the University Book Store for use in my own classes. The year 1929 was an *annus mirabilis* for me: I published four titles—two locally, two through regular publishers, besides a great deal of matter which appeared serially; I never brought out four books again within a single year until 1966. And one of my 1929 books was my first major work, *The Man Charles Dickens*, which, through Bradford's good offices, was accepted by Houghton Mifflin Company.[3]

This study began through doctoral-dissertation agonies and exigencies. After I had decided that, for convenience' sake, I would take my doctor's degree at the University of Washington, where I was teaching, instead of going back to the University of Chicago for it, as I had originally planned, my adviser, D. D. Griffith, and I decided that I would do something on Dickens, but for some time I had no definite subject in mind. One night,

[3] For full bibliographical information about all my books, see the Appendix to this volume.

164

feeling none too happy about my uncertainty, I went for a walk, and while I was standing looking at some magazines in a store window, the solution of my problem came to me. Of course. How could anything else have possibly been considered? For me there could be only one subject. I would do a psychograph of Charles Dickens. It was published both here and in England and enjoyed a remarkable press. If it did not make me rich, it did bring me a great deal of satisfaction.

The Man Charles Dickens was followed, after an interval of two years, by *Jenny Lind*, which I suppose stemmed ultimately from my maternal grandfather's enthusiasm for that singer, which had become a legend in the family. This was a much shorter, somewhat lighter book than the Dickens, but Houghton Mifflin made a beautiful, lavishly-illustrated volume out of it, and I thought it a rather more graceful piece of portraiture than its predecessor. Both Bradford and Geraldine Farrar reviewed it in the Boston *Herald*. And then I struck a snag.

I had not yet produced a book composed of varied portraits on a common theme, which was the typical Bradford pattern. So I wrote something which I called "Eve in Modern Dress," containing studies of Marie Bashkirtseff, Isadora Duncan, Mary Garden, Julia Marlowe, Jane Addams, Katherine Mansfield, Willa Cather, and Mary Johnston. But by this time the depression was very bad, and Ferris Greenslet entertained well-founded doubts concerning the selling power of such a book. If I would wait a year, he said, Houghton Mifflin would probably publish it, but not now. I said, "Give me a contract calling for publication a year from now, and I will wait. Otherwise I will submit it elsewhere." He would not agree to this. Bradford, from his deathbed, sent me word that he thought I had done just right.

Unfortunately nobody else was willing to take a chance on "Eve in Modern Dress" in 1932 either,[4] though several publishers

---

[4] The studies of Julia Marlowe, Isadora Duncan, and Mary Garden finally appeared, much revised, in *Seven Daughters of the Theater* (the Julia Marlowe had previously appeared in *Modern Drama*, Vol. I [1959], 244–55) and that of

165

praised it warmly, and it has been long since dismembered. So I put it away and turned to Mark Twain, whose centenary was due in 1935. All was not smooth sailing here either; in fact, I was more discouraged at this point than at any other time in my life. After I had had two rejections, I defied fate, swearing that if I could not place this book, I would write nothing else. Fortunately Miss Bernice Baumgarten came to my rescue and placed the book with the Yale University Press. Bernard De Voto "boomed" *Mark Twain, the Man and His Work* on the front page of *The New York Times Book Review,* and Carl Van Doren was equally enthusiastic in the *Herald-Tribune.* It turned out, of course, to be one of my most successful books, and it was just in time to pay the expenses of my wife's first confinement! It also, though I did not know it yet, marked the end of the first stage in my writing career and was the last psychograph I was to do for twenty years.

One day, not long after I had finished the Mark Twain, Thomas J. Wilson, later director of the Harvard University Press, but then in charge of the college department at Henry Holt, walked into my office and asked, "How would you like to write a history of the novel for us?" I replied, "You must be psychic," for it so happened that I had been turning over that very idea in my mind, but had, as I thought, rejected it as too grandiose. I exhumed it at Tom Wilson's bidding and received a contract calling for a history of the English and American novel in two years. I at once told Mr. Wilson that could not be done but signed the contract upon receiving his assurance that time-extensions would be granted as needed and that I would have no trouble with the firm, which promise was faithfully kept. For the English portion I read hundreds of novels and heaven only knows how much

---

Jane Addams in *Chicago*. The Mary Johnston was published in *Sewanee Review,* Vol. XLIV (1936), 188–206, and condensed in *Cavalcade of the American Novel*. Earlier studies of Willa Cather and of Katherine Mansfield had appeared, respectively, in *Sewanee Review,* Vol. XXXVII (1929), 221–39, and in *English Journal,* Vol. XVII (1928), 272–84; some of the Cather, as designed for "Eve in Modern Dress," was taken up into *Cavalcade of the American Novel*. The Marie Bashkirtseff has appeared only serially; see Note #2, above.

166

biography and criticism. By this time I had split the project in two, and it was only the *Cavalcade of the English Novel* which appeared in 1943. Both it and its American companion, which followed in 1952, have been in continual demand in both college and trade editions ever since.

Cavalcade of the English Novel might have appeared a little sooner if Harcourt, Brace had not meanwhile seduced me into editing the Victorian section of *The College Survey of English Literature*, which appeared, in two volumes, in 1942. And this was important not only for its own sake but, as will shortly appear, because it gave me an idea.

Eight years had passed between the Mark Twain book and the English *Cavalcade*. I did not expect the American novelists to be less demanding, and I was not happy over the prospect of another eight-year gap between publications. Now it happened that at the mid-forties in America the popularity of anthologies was at an all-time high. Practically every possible and impossible subject was being anthologized, and many of these books were doing very well. There was an anthology of deathbed utterances, and I even remember an anthology of stories about snakes! Having been made anthology-conscious by *The College Survey*, I began to wonder whether I might not throw off a few trade anthologies while I was working on the American *Cavalcade*, thus keeping my name in the publishers' announcements and enticing a few coins into my pocket. By 1950 I had published eleven such books, but by that time the cream was pretty well skimmed off. I only placed two more during the rest of the fifties, and so far I have had only one in the sixties.

My success was due to two circumstances. First, *The Fireside Book of Christmas Stories* (1945) was a Book-of-the-Month Club "premium," and, second, it was my good fortune to be represented at this time by an extremely able, sympathetic, and energetic agent named Frances Pindyck, who was, for me, one of the by-products of my friendship with Walter de la Mare. She was de la Mare's American agent, and I first met her name when she wrote me in connection with some project she had in hand relating to him. I found her so completely congenial that I soon asked her if she would not take me on, and I never had a better piece of good fortune than when she said yes. After she gave up the agency business, she turned me over to Diarmuid Russell, who has taken good care of me ever since.

Bobbs-Merrill brought out all four of my "Fireside" anthologies, hoping, of course, that each one would sell as well as the first, but unfortunately this never happened. Bobbs-Merrill did not absorb me, however, for my success attracted other publishers to me, none of whom, I fear, found in me quite what they had been looking for.

The most disastrous failure, and the one that caused me the most grief, not so much on my own account as because of the loss to its publisher, Mrs. Eileen J. Garrett, who was always such a generous and faithful friend, was that of *The Story of Jesus in the World's Literature* (1946). This was the longest and most elaborate of my anthologies; it was expensively produced; it had pictures by Fritz Kredel; it was heavily advertised; the Religious Book Club took it; it had rave reviews. Not only its publishers but the whole book trade expected a smashing success. The first printing order was for 25,000 copies, but when everybody said, "You'll be out of stock for Christmas," this was raised to 40,000. I still shudder to think how many of them went to the remainder houses at twenty-five cents a copy.

Nobody ever found out why, though various diagnoses were attempted. The author of the most ambitious of these came up with the idea that the book was too good and contained so much that the reader felt overwhelmed. But the basic trouble was that most readers did not get close enough to be overwhelmed. My own guess is that the volume was under a heavy handicap from the start by being printed, because of its great length, on very large-size, double-column pages of the sort the American reader associates with textbooks rather than with holiday reading.

This was not, however, the only queer anomaly of my career

168

as an anthologist. For *The Fireside Book of Christmas Stories* itself came very close to being destroyed before it managed to get itself born.

What happened here was that the prospectus was originally prepared not for Bobbs-Merrill but for a very distinguished publisher whom I shall not name here. But by the time it was ready, the editor who had commissioned its preparation had been drafted in the current global crusade in behalf of democracy, Christianity, and civilization, and his successor, whose name would be familiar to everybody in the book business if I chose to set it down here, turned the book down on the ground that it contained too many familiar, oft-anthologized stories, which just did not happen to be true. This gentleman, thus, began a not wholly undistinguished career as an editor by losing a Book-of-the-Month Club selection for his employer.

In 1952, *Cavalcade of the American Novel* finally appeared, and I had at last finished with a project that had been hanging over my head for many years. I knew too that I was practically through with anthologizing, and that if I were ever to get back to psychography, in which I had never lost my interest, it was high time that I went about it. Certainly, I wanted no more eight-year projects. Since I was now living in the Boston area, where manuscript material was much more readily accessible to me than it had been in the West, I decided to turn my attention to New England writers. After one more college book for Holt—*A Preface to Literature* (1954)—I went back to first principles with Henry Wadsworth Longfellow. I am glad to remember that I was the last scholar to work with Longfellow's manuscripts in his own house before they were removed on loan to the Houghton Library at Harvard. The results of my study were *Longfellow: A Full-Length Portrait* (1955), the only modern book which was both based upon original source material and which also covered the whole life (it was later rewritten and republished as *Henry Wadsworth Longfellow: Portrait of an American Humanist*), and *Mrs. Longfellow* (1956), a volume of

169

selections from the letters and journals of Longfellow's second wife, the beautiful, admirable, and at last unfortunate Fanny Appleton.

I discovered that Mrs. Longfellow's letters and journals were a virtually untapped treasure comparatively early in my Longfellow researches, and therefore when John L. B. Williams heard that I was working on Longfellow and wrote from Longmans, Green & Co. to express his interest, I replied that I wished to contract for the two books together. This I did with some qualms of conscience, for while I had no doubts concerning the value of Mrs. Longfellow's manuscripts, I was not sure about their sales potential. Longmans took both books, and Mrs. Longfellow rewarded them. As if to show once more that you can never tell about a woman, she far outsold her husband, picked up a small book club selection, and even sold newspaper serial rights in Boston!

John Williams was the only editor who ever published me through three different houses. In 1929, when he was with Appleton, he accepted *A Guide to Bernard Shaw*, which was my first book to appear through a regular publisher; he was with Bobbs-Merrill when they brought out my "Fireside" anthologies; and now he was with Longmans. It might reasonably be assumed from this that we were very close and always saw eye to eye, but this was far from being the case. One day, when we were walking down the street in New York, together with another member of the Longmans firm, Theodore Roosevelt's name came up somehow, and I remarked, "He would make a good subject for a psychograph." "Yes," replied John, enthusiastically, "he would!" I had long felt that I ought sometime to make up my mind about Roosevelt, who had been one of my childhood heroes but whom I had never studied closely as an adult. Having celebrated Mark Twain's centenary in 1935, I therefore decided that I would take on his in 1958, though I was somewhat hesitant about doing a political figure. I wanted to call the book "T.R.: A Centenary Portrait," but Williams christened it *The Seven Worlds of Theo-*

dore Roosevelt. I did not like this at first because it seemed too much of a "steal" from *The Lowells in Their Seven Worlds,* by Ferris Greenslet, though I finally accepted it and came to think well of it. But the basic trouble between John Williams and me was, that though we were never other than friendly, he would never let me work on anything unless he happened to be interested in it. He wanted the Longfellow because *he* liked Longfellow and thought it was time for a new book about him, and he wanted the Roosevelt for much the same reasons. But though he loved the theater himself, he would not let me touch a theatrical subject, because he had got it firmly fixed in his head (heaven only knows how or why) that theater books never sell. After *The Seven Worlds of Theodore Roosevelt* we could not agree upon another subject, and so when Sheldon Meyer came along from the Oxford University Press, which was doing well with the anthology of Chaucer criticism I had done for their "Galaxy" series, and asked me whether I was free, I said I was, and we embarked upon the series of studies of American writers which began in 1961 with *Nathaniel Hawthorne, Man and Writer,* and whose end is not yet. Then John felt somewhat aggrieved toward both Oxford and me, but I could not see that he had any cause to be.

Since 1961 my books have nearly all been published by either Oxford or the University of Oklahoma Press. The beginnings of my very happy relations with Oklahoma were very casual. I was asked to write an introduction to *The Art, Humor, and Humanity of Mark Twain,* edited by Minnie M. Brashear and Robert M. Rodney, and this led to my telling the director of the press, Savoie Lottinville, that I would like to rewrite *Mark Twain: The Man and His Work* and bring it up to date. He said he would like to publish it, and we have been together ever since. Every now and then somebody asks me why, living in Boston, I publish in Oklahoma. They would not ask that if they knew either Mr. Lottinville or his successor, Edward A. Shaw, but the East is still very provincial in some respects. In addition to my books on

171

literary subjects, I have done the *Chicago* volume in Oklahoma's "Centers of Civilization Series," and I also gave them a long-pondered book on *The Movies in the Age of Innocence* (1962), which brought me more mail than anything else I have ever written, and which has, I believe, made some contribution to the revival of interest in silent films which is now under way in this country.

My principal business, however, for both Oxford and Oklahoma, has been, and will, I think, continue to be, psychography. I am no longer an imitator of Bradford; I learned my trade from him, but I now practice it in my own way. Bradford was a magazinist, and his magazine audience was always wider than his book audience; I leave the magazines alone. I never brought out a composite book until 1964, when Oklahoma published *Seven Daughters of the Theater*, which was followed in 1966 by a companion volume of studies of eight actors called *Merely Players*. As a writer, I do not consider myself as talented as Bradford was; if I were to try to sum up the differences between our respective uses of the psychographic method in a word, I should say that I am more of a research man than he was and that he was more of an essayist than I am.

Of course I have also been associated with a considerable number of abortive projects whose history need not be detailed here, for I have always had far more ideas than I had time to work out. It used to be said of Roswell Smith that he came down to his office at the Century Company every morning with three new ideas, and that it took the staff until noon to convince him that two of them were not good and the rest of the day to carry out the third. This is very much the way it has been with my writing, though now that I am in the fortunate position of having a publisher available for any reasonable project that I might conceive, I think I have a tendency to spawn somewhat less wildly than I once did. I am also sure, however, that no matter how long I may live, I shall not have time to get everything I wish to say down on paper.

172

How It Feels To Be a Writer

My most startling recent departure was the publication of a novel about Mary Queen of Scots, *Nine Before Fotheringhay*, which I brought out in London, through Geoffrey Bles, in 1966, under the pseudonym "Julian Forrest." The basic idea of this book was to tell Mary's story from the point of view of nine different persons from a vantage-point fixed just before her execution. The concluding narrative, which is her own, is not intended to clear up everything, the whole truth being rather intended to emerge in the reader's mind as the distillation of all that he has heard. I wrote this work about a decade ago, but American publishers shied from it because, although they found much good to say of it, they thought that it was not "really" a novel. Just what the difference may be between a book that is merely a novel and a book which is "really" a novel was never spelled out to me.

Finally, my friend Norah Lofts, that gifted novelist, read it, admired it much more than it deserves, decided that it would appeal more to English than to American publishers, and sent it to Miss Juliet O'Hea at the Curtis Brown agency, after which its publication by Bles shortly followed. I took a pseudonym not because I wished to conceal my identity but because I thought it well to mark off this book and any other possible successors in kind from the rest of my very different output.

Like other writers I have had many wry and ironical encounters in the course of my writing career. Librarians have been uniformly kind and co-operative. Apparently there is something about the profession which makes it impossible for a person to be anything else; perhaps all our so-called statesmen and diplomats ought to be trained as librarians first. Other scholars have ranged all the way from the most selfless, overwhelming generosity (as with such persons as John B. Pickard, Roland H. Woodwell, and Thomas Ollive Mabbott) to a shocked fear that somebody else might possibly invade their preserves (as with— well, if you have ever done any work in American literature, you will probably be able to fill in the blank yourself).

When my *Jenny Lind* was in preparation, Houghton Mifflin

Company, distinguished publishers though they are, wanted me to call it "Jenny Lind: Portrait of a Nightingale," to which I replied in effect, "Over my dead body." But I remembered Lily Langtry, who, I had been told, wished to call her autobiography "Lily Leaves," and would have done so if George H. Doran had not held out for *The Days I Knew*. If Lily and I could only have switched publishers, we might both have been happy.

The "Fireside" label on my Bobbs-Merrill anthologies was borrowed, with their kind permission, from Simon and Schuster, who had used it some time before on *The Fireside Book of Dog Stories*. When that work appeared I wrote them to ask whether they would be interested in my doing a companion volume on cats. Had they said yes, I might have begun my career as an anthologist earlier, and under their auspices, but they said no, on the amazing ground that there were not enough people interested in cats to make such a book profitable, surely one of the most quaint decisions in the history of publishing. I wonder what they think of the plethora of cat books that have appeared since.

One of my anthologies was copy-edited by an idiot who found the style of the various distinguished authors represented in it below her own high standards, whereupon she set to work to rewrite them, thus, of course, voiding all our permissions, and forcing her employers to reset everything her stupidity had altered.

Once the director of a celebrated university press made tentative arrangements with me for a biography of James Russell Lowell but was blocked by a member of his learned advisory board who wished to know why a book about Lowell should be considered. I told him not to try to explain. You teach the ignorant, but when there is no mind there to work with, you are defeated before you start.

My Abraham Lincoln anthology was once "reviewed" by a writer who not only had not read it but had not even examined it sufficiently to discover that it was an anthology. He wrote that it was a good biography but that he himself was so devoted to

How It Feels To Be a Writer

Carl Sandburg's biography that he just did not see why another was needed.

As I originally wrote *A Guide to Bernard Shaw*, it contained a good many quotations from Shaw's own work. When I wrote him for permission to use these, he did not bother to reply. (From what I have since learned, I think I have good reason to suspect that his secretary did not bother to bring the matter to his attention.) I rewrote the book, omitting all quoted matter, but I have always been sorry I did not send him a copy inscribed "To Bernard Shaw, in the sincere conviction that this is a better book now than it would have been if he had permitted me to include quotations from his writings." This might well have stung him into sending me one of the famous post cards that would have been interesting reading at the time and might have been negotiable now.

When I wrote my two *Cavalcades* I sent out each chapter for criticism to persons whom I regarded as authorities on the various authors, periods, or types. I sent the chapter on the Gothic novel to Montague Summers, who was equally famous for his learning and his eccentricities. Summers was kindness itself; he could not well have been kinder. He sent me all sorts of data which I could not possibly have used in a general book, and he went on sending me Christmas cards and other greetings for years. But about the only criticism he had was that in one passage I had quoted from Marjorie Bowen. Marjorie Bowen was a good novelist, and he had no objection to what she had said, but he insisted that her reputation as a scholar was not good and that it would give anybody a start to see her quoted in a scholarly book. So would I please take out the quotation from Marjorie Bowen? (It was never Summers' custom to use one word where a dozen would do.)

Meanwhile I had sent my chapter on Jane Austen to the foremost authority in the world, R. W. Chapman, at Oxford. Like Summers, he did not find much wrong with my general discussion. But at one point I had quoted Montague Summers, and he

175

said he wished I would take that out, as Summers' reputation as a scholar was not good.

A few of the writers treated in chapter-length studies in my *Cavalcades* were still alive when I wrote, and in these instances I sent my chapters to the writers themselves. It was in this connection that, quite without intending it, I caught a very big fish.

My chapter on H. G. Wells, which is anything but unsympathetic on the whole, begins with a kind of summary of his shortcomings and eccentricities. Though Mr. Wells was on record as being completely indifferent to criticism, and committed to the thesis that criticism was quite worthless, this apparently got under his skin sufficiently so that he went to the trouble of rewriting my whole first section, refuting every one of the objections alleged, and sometimes even causing me to quote myself as "a clever critic" and proceed to my own confounding. This was sent to me in typescript, with corrections in Mr. Wells's own hand, but with a covering letter from his secretary.

When I received it, I decided to have some fun. If Mr. Wells would not write me except through his secretary, I would not communicate with him except through mine, and never mind that I didn't have one. I went downstairs to the office of the Graduate School, where a girl whom I knew worked, and said, "You are hereby appointed my secretary, and you are going to write a letter for me to Mr. Wells." What she told him was that Mr. Wagenknecht was greatly interested in the material Mr. Wells had sent him, though somewhat puzzled as to how it might be most effectively used. On the whole, he thought it might be best to leave the text unaltered and to print Mr. Wells's version of it in a footnote. Now what did Mr. Wells think of that?

I knew that he would not permit me to do anything of the kind, and of course I would not have done it even if he had been willing. But quick as the airmail can travel came another letter, this time from a different secretary, saying, No, no, no, no, Mr. Wagenknecht must not do that. The material had been sent only for Mr. Wagenknecht's own use, and Mr. Wells wished to avoid any appearance of either criticism or co-operation.

I revised my chapter on Wells, using any of his suggestions that I found in order (I think there are still about two sentences in my opening paragraphs which *he* wrote, including the one about "Peterpantheism"). Finally the time came to gather permissions covering the use of quoted matter. When I wrote to Macmillan, who had published many, though not all, of the Wells books from which I had quoted, they replied that they had no jurisdiction, Mr. Wells having reserved all reprint rights to himself. At this point I thought I was in for it, for I could not believe that he would permit me to quote anything. He was more generous than that, and I apologize to his shade. My letter was very promptly acknowledged, and I was told that I might quote anything I liked but that I must make no acknowledgement. Clear to the end, he was faithful to his principle of avoiding all appearance of criticism or co-operation.

When the story was relayed to Walter de la Mare, he remarked in substance that authorship makes asses of us all.

This chapter has not been written because I am so foolish as to believe that anybody will be interested in the experiences related because they happened to me. But there are a great many people in America who are interested in writing, though, to be sure, many of them are more interested in talking about it than in doing it (those who can write, write, and those who can't write go to writers' conferences), and it may be that some will be glad to have this candid account of how one man, without exceptional talent, built a writing career, such as it is. As Oliver Wendell Holmes once remarked in a similar connection, I leave inferences and morals to the reader; there is no extra charge.

This leaves, then, but one final question: "And what is the good of it all?" in reply to which I can only say that if it has to be asked, then no answer is possible. Of course I am never satisfied with anything I write, and of course I see flaws in everything that I have written. Nevertheless it is my honest conviction that

As Far As Yesterday

I have achieved a fuller and more satisfying expression of myself in writing than I have achieved anywhere else, or than I could possibly have achieved in anything else that I might have done. Here I have done what I was sent into the world to do, and here I have fulfilled my destiny so far as it was within my power to do so.

At the end of the Preface to his correspondence with Ellen Terry, Bernard Shaw answered those who might complain that "it was all on paper" by reminding them "that only on paper has humanity yet achieved glory, beauty, truth, knowledge, virtue, and abiding love." I cannot read this without a pang; I think there is deep sadness in it; but there is acceptance of the human lot too; and though it is not (thank God!) the whole truth, I fear there is some truth in it for all those who were born to write, and whose only comfort must be that their reproach is also, in some measure, their compensation. Dr. Johnson said that only a fool would write a book except for money, but when he made that statement, he was himself a fool, not only unwontedly but amazingly too. I should say that *only* a fool writes a book for money; if it is money that you want most of all, there are always much more effective ways of getting it. Nobody ought ever to write anything, and nobody ought to try to do anything in any art, unless he wants to do just that beyond anything else in the world. And nothing that is done on any other basis is good for anything. William Vaughn Moody knew whereof he spake when he wrote:

> *Heart, we have chosen the better part!*
> *Save sacred love and sacred art*
> *Nothing is good for long.*

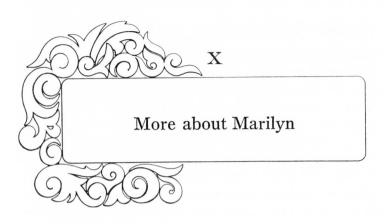

X

More about Marilyn

MARILYN MONROE died in the night of August 4–5, 1962. Though she had been a legend during her lifetime, her legend was the creation of studio press agents, and any resemblance it bore to any person, living or dead, was, as the saying is, purely coincidental. Since her death a more truthful legend has begun to develop, and it appears now that she may well be remembered for generations as exemplifying how an innocent, sensitive person, incapable of malice and free of guile, can be victimized and finally destroyed by a conscienceless and commercially motivated society.

Because I wrote about her in *Seven Daughters of the Theater*, I have perhaps been more in touch with the development of this legend than many persons. I will give just three examples out of many to illustrate the spell she still exercises.

Shortly after the publication of the *Daughters*, I was asked to give a lecture on the movies before a club of very elderly, very dignified Boston ladies. As Will Rogers might have put it, I suspected that, so far as Marilyn was concerned, the trouble with my audience would be not that they were ignorant concerning her but that they knew too many things about her that weren't

179

so, and I tried to clear up misunderstanding by devoting about one-quarter of my lecture to her. Afterwards I received a letter from one of the oldest and most genteel of the group. I am very glad you said what you did about Marilyn Monroe, she wrote in effect. I saw her only a few times, but what I felt for her was close to a personal affection. I soon learned that most of my friends did not agree with me about her; so I did not talk about her very much. But I went right on feeling the same way.

This is the first instance. The second relates to a distinguished midwestern writer who walked into my living room one day, picked up a copy of the *Daughters* from the table where it was lying, looked at her picture on the jacket, and remarked quietly, "Even yet, I can hardly bear to think that she is dead."

But my most interesting experience came in the unlikeliest of places and connections, one day when my wife and I were in the midst of a conference with a banker on Boston's State Street. He got to talking about the various (perfectly legitimate) devices which various film stars used to reduce their income-tax indebtedness, and he spoke of one particular star who, he said, was so greedy that she had to collect every penny the minute it was due, even when she could save money by spreading her collections over a longer period. "Don't forget," I remarked, "that Marilyn once walked out on a salary conference with 'I don't care about the money; I just want to be wonderful.'" "Ah, yes," he replied, "but the trouble is there was only one of her." And from here he went on into what I can only describe as a rhapsody on the subject of Marilyn Monroe, ending with the declaration that she had to die because the contrast between what she was and what the rest of us were like was so overwhelming that we simply could not endure having her about. Which, I submit, is not exactly the kind of talk one expects to hear from a banker, in Boston of all places, and in the midst of a business conference.

I was both late and early in encountering Marilyn Monroe. My first contact was made while she was still modeling, or at least while her modeling pictures were still in active circulation.

180

More about Marilyn

What I saw was a picture of her, in very brief shorts, standing beside a bicycle, but she was not advertising the bicycle but some kind of bell that could be attached to a bicycle. "This pretty little girl," said the legend, "shall have music wherever she goes." She was a pretty little girl indeed; I had never seen a prettier one, nor one that was sweeter looking, and though I did not save the picture, and did not identify it with her in my mind for many years, I never forgot it. Later, in a magazine which I have never been able to find again, I encountered a two-page spread of the photographs André de Dienes took of her at Jones Beach in the summer of 1952. But I heard very little about her during the early years of her screen career, when she was playing supporting roles, and it was not until after *Life* had begun to run publicity about her that I ever saw her on the screen. *Don't Forget to Knock* was the first picture I encountered, and having been misled by the buxom picture by Philippe Halsman which *Life* ran on its cover for April 7, 1952, and which I have never liked, I went expecting to see a young Mae West. I could hardly believe my eyes when I encountered this small, delicate-looking, obviously hypersensitive girl.

In this chapter, which is essentially a series of addenda to what I wrote about Marilyn in *Seven Daughters of the Theater*, I shall confine myself largely to commenting on what has been written about her since my book appeared. But first I must refer to two items which were in existence before I wrote but which I had not then seen. I had heard about Sidney Skolsky's *Marilyn*,[1] but I did not know that it had been published in movie-magazine format. This kind of publication is almost as ephemeral as the daily paper, and the libraries I consulted could find no trace of it. Of the other more ambitious attempt, *Marilyn Monroe*, by George Carpozi, Jr.,[2] which is in pulp paperback format, I had never even heard.

Pictorially the Skolsky item is excellent, but considering how

[1] Dell Publishing Co., 1954.
[2] Belmont Books, 1961.

well the author knew the star, the text is not very revealing, and at this date no informed student of Marilyn Monroe is going to learn much from it that he does not already know. The Carpozi is much longer (222 closely-printed pages). Stylistically it belongs wholly to the pulp paperback world, but it has autobiographical value for the very large number of Marilyn's own words which are quoted in it.

In 1966 came Edwin P. Hoyt's *Marilyn: The Tragic Venus*,[3] the most ambitious study of its subject since Maurice Zolotow's biography of 1960. Unfortunately this turned out to be something of a hatchet job. Mr. Hoyt evidently conducted his "research" on the principle of believing everything anybody told him to Marilyn's discredit, even when it conflicted directly with what had been recorded by others or by the actress herself. It is obvious that he relied heavily upon Nunnally Johnson, whom he refers to again and again, and who "boomed" his book in advance of publication. Johnson despised Marilyn until shortly before the end of her life, when he did a kind of right-about-face concerning her, without, apparently, ever achieving a consistent all-over view.

This, however, would not trouble Mr. Hoyt, who is capable of asserting on pages vii and 76 that Marilyn was the mistress of the aged Joseph M. Schenck (on page 76 Schenck even wished to marry her) and also of affirming on page 48 that "the facts indicate that Marilyn was telling the truth" when she denied any such connection. On page 68 "Marilyn was not used. Marilyn was not pushed. Marilyn was the user and the pusher." But on page 208, "She had been used by many, she had been a laughing stock of Hollywood," and on page 266, "She was used by many."[4] On page 67 "Marilyn was not a rich man's whore; she was a courtesan of the old school," and on page 101 "she had the morals

[3] Duell, Sloan and Pearce.
[4] When Twentieth Century Fox took Marilyn off suspension, following her marriage to Joe DiMaggio, Mr. Hoyt tells us that this "was really a generous gesture considering the fact that she had done nothing for them except earn more money than any other star on the payroll in 1953."

of an animal," being, in fact, exactly like the girl she played in
Niagara (which would mean that she was a potential murderess
also), but on page 215, she "was not a tramp," and on page 269
"she was a *natural,* an innocent soul who lived for thirty-six years
in a corrupt and corrupting world." Of course it may be that there
are fine distinctions here which my coarse mind cannot grasp,
for Mr. Hoyt's difficulties with logic and with Marilyn are nothing compared to his difficulties with the English language. He is
devoted to utterly meaningless distinctions, and his ability to
write sentences which mean absolutely nothing is unsurpassed
by that of any other writer I know.

Even the pictures in *Marilyn: The Tragic Venus* have obviously been chosen to show Marilyn in her least attractive poses.
All, that is, except the picture on the jacket, which is lovely
(attractive photographs on jackets sell books). But about the
only good thing in the book itself is that Mr. Hoyt points out that
the evidence to support the view that Marilyn committed suicide is quite inconclusive. Though even the official verdict (rejected by everybody who knew her well) did not venture beyond
"probable suicide," nine persons out of every ten have always
taken it for granted that she took her own life.[5] It is very characteristic of Hoyt's method that he should tell us that Zsa Zsa
Gabor, then the wife of George Sanders, was jealous of her husband's interest in Marilyn Monroe when they played together in
All About Eve but neglect to mention that this did not prevent
Sanders, when he wrote his autobiography,[6] from going out of
his way to describe Marilyn as the most decent woman in Hollywood, in sharp contrast to some others in much better odor, on
whom he pulled no punches. Mr. Hoyt never saw a Monroe film

[5] Thus *Life,* hitherto always very friendly to Marilyn, spoiled its record when
it observed the second anniversary of her death by publishing a pseudo-profound,
characteristically lofty, and utterly worthless article by Clare Boothe Luce, "What
Really Killed Marilyn" (August 7, 1964), and decorating the cover with a
photograph captioned "Marilyn Monroe eight years before her suicide." (When
it is the boss's wife who chooses to have a brainstorm, it must be difficult for an
editor.)

[6] *Memoirs of a Professional Cad* (Putnam, 1960).

during her lifetime but became interested in her only because of the mystery of her death. For him, once more, then, she was a "case," a "thing," which was what she hated being most of all, and good biographies are written not about "cases" but about persons. All in all, the most interesting, and by all means the most naïve, statement in his book is this reference to his investigations: "Among those who were close to her—even many with whom Marilyn had broken—there was a protectiveness that I have never encountered in dealing with any other personality, living or dead."

Don't try to find out why, Mr. Hoyt. You will die without knowing.[7]

Marilyn: The Tragic Venus was followed in 1967 by a novel written in much the same spirit: Alvah Bessie's *The Symbol*.[8] Mr. Bessie, of course, denies that the girl in his novel is Marilyn (which is to say that he makes the conventional and legally advisable disclaimer of having taken any of his characters from life), much as Arthur Miller denied that the girl in *After the Fall* was Marilyn. And I completely agree: in both cases the girl certainly is *not* Marilyn! But both writers included enough that *suggests* Marilyn so that nobody could read the novel or see the play without her image in mind, and since neither writer is an idiot, both must have intended and desired just that. *The Symbol* is indeed from first to last a *roman à clef*, suggesting not only Marilyn but almost everybody who ever crossed her path (thus

---

[7] In 1966 came also an English book, *Who Killed Marilyn Monroe? or Cage to Catch Our Dreams*, by Charles Hamblett, published by Leslie Frewin, but this volume contains so little about Marilyn that its title can only be described as a "steal." Mostly it consists of an account of the author's adventures in Hollywood, including his interviews with a great many persons, among them a promiscuous high-school girl whose connection with the matter in hand is not obvious. There is a chapter on the making of *The Misfits*, obviously not derived from firsthand knowledge (the source is not indicated), but the only thing in the book that has any particular value so far as Marilyn is concerned, is contained in a few very well-chosen and extremely profane remarks by the director Henry Hathaway, who holds forth with simple justice on pp. 145–47 on how she was mistreated and her talent wasted by the film moguls.

[8] Random House.

184

the Joe DiMaggio role is taken by a football, not baseball, star, and the Arthur Miller role not by a playwright but a painter). This is not exactly subtle, but the *roman à clef* is seldom that, nor does it often achieve literary value. Certainly *The Symbol* does not, but the oddest thing about it is that the author's attitude toward the girl he calls Wanda Oliver is not really unsympathetic or entirely lacking in understanding, which suggests that he might have produced a much better book if he could have persuaded himself to relinquish his ambition of giving a pig's-eye view of Marilyn's life and thus produce a Hollywood variation of *Fanny Hill*.

I cannot attempt a comprehensive coverage of the material that has appeared about Marilyn in the magazines. There is too much of it, and a good deal of it has appeared in Europe. *Paris Match* and *Marie-Claire* have been very mindful of anniversaries; a serial about her has appeared in the German *Stern* and a longer one in the Italian *Gente*.[9] In this country, perhaps the most valuable single article was Ralph Hatteresley's "Marilyn Monroe: The Image and Her Photographers," in *Popular Photography*, January, 1966, which was based on interviews with Richard Avedon, Philippe Halsman, Bert Stern, Elliot Erwitt, Doug Kirkland, and John Bryson. It has been remarked before

[9] The articles in *Stern* ran from August 7 through August 28, those in *Gente* (by Domenico Compana) from August 31 through October 19, 1966. Of *Paris Match* see especially the issues for August 17, 1963 and December 31, 1966, and of *Marie-Claire* the issue for anuary 18, 1965. In this country, see *Life* (November 14, 1966–"Behind the Myth the Face of Norma Jean," by Richard Meryman) and two items in the movie magazines: Gene Ringgold, "Marilyn Monroe: Her Legend Triumphs Her Tragedy," *Screen Legends* (August, 1965), which, despite its silly and incoherent title, is a comprehensive career article, with many illustrations, and Adele Whitely Fletcher's deeply-felt " . . . So That the Memory of Marilyn Will Linger On," *Photoplay* (September, 1965): "There never was anyone who tried harder to be a right person." I am not discussing such items as Frank A. Caprell's *The Strange Death of Marilyn Monroe* (The Herald of Freedom, 1964), in which an attempt was made, for only too obvious reasons, to hold a well-known political figure responsible for Marilyn's death, and Carlo Curti's *Skrouras, King of Fox Studios* (Holloway House Publishing Co., 1967), which attributes the filth it gathers to an unnamed person now dead. It seems a pity that these writers did not get together beforehand; they might at least have avoided cancelling each other out.

185

that people who met Marilyn off screen did not find her particularly provocative, and her photographers seem to have thought her less beautiful physically than she was generally rated, but they did value her, and prize their association with her, for other reasons. Richard Avedon, for one, made it clear at the outset that if the interviewer had come to him in search of gossip, the interview was over before it had begun, thus manifesting an integrity one can only wish were more widespread, but he was glad to talk about the impression Marilyn had made upon him and did so freely. Avedon found Marilyn "very easy to work with," "very original," "completely creative," "very considerate to every assistant," "never provoking in any way," and "infinitely more patient, more demanding of herself, more careful than I would have been." Bert Stern, too, called her "truly creative," "a marvelous, marvelous person, and a wonderful model." Elliot Erwitt, though admitting that he thought her "a bit of a nut," called her "absolutely charming, sweet, pleasant, kind, immediate, considerate," and John Bryson found her "a very warm, sensitive, shy creature"; he thought it "a fascinating experience to watch her at close range over a long period and to learn that many of the legends about her were untrue." He added, "I'm proud to have been her friend, and to have photographed her. She was a good girl." And Avedon added, "I often think of her."

When I wrote about Marilyn in *Seven Daughters of the Theater*, I had read all the material about her which had appeared in the standard magazines, but since I had not read any movie fan magazines for many years, and since this material is not indexed, I had seen very little of what had appeared here. The general view is that this stuff is not worth reading, and I certainly have no intention of going to bat for it. Nevertheless, the fan magazines do record, first and last, a good deal of data about screen personalities, and the biographer cannot ignore all of it without risk of missing something. Thanks to the industry of Mr. Ray J. Butler, of San Francisco, and Mr. Malcolm Willits, of

More about Marilyn

the Collectors Book Shop in Hollywood, I have now seen a good deal of it.

I should say that the thing which interested me most was that almost from the beginning of her career, there were people who knew what was being done to Marilyn, and I pause to salute John Curtis, who, in December, 1952, had an article in *Movie Fan* called "You've Gotta Stop Kickin' This Girl Around." And then, of course, there was also another type of article. Turn, for example, to the November, 1956, issue of a periodical called *Screen*. The cover carried the nakedest picture of Marilyn that the art editor could find, with this lettering: "Confessions of Hollywood's Sexiest Queen. Marilyn's Uncensored Story. Gossip! Gossip! Gossip!" The following quotations are typical of the dreadful things she said in the shocking interview inside: "I don't hurt anyone intentionally. Why should anyone want to hurt me or my career?" And again: "Life is funny, isn't it? The things that people take for granted are denied to a few of us. So we appreciate them—and want them—more than anything else."[10]

From the point of view of understanding and evaluation, I should say that the three best items about Marilyn have come out of England. The first is Dame Edith Sitwell's tribute, in her

[10] For biographical data, I should say that the following are the most important of the articles in popular magazines that I have seen (I list them on the chance that they may be useful to others who may wish to write about Marilyn Monroe): Richard Cottrell, "I Was Marilyn Monroe's Doctor," *Ladies Home Companion* (January, 1965); Natalie Kelley Grasco, "I Was There When Marilyn Posed," *Movie Stars Parade* (July, 1953); Jim Henaghan, "My Love Affair with Marilyn," *Motion Picture* (July, 1955); Tom Kelley, "Why Marilyn Monroe Posed for My Nude Calendar," *Filmland* (February, 1954); Natasha Lytess, "The Private Life of Marilyn Monroe," *Screen World* (November, December, 1953); Dorothy Manning, "The Woman and the Legend," *Photoplay* (October, 1956); Marilyn Monroe, "This is My Past," *Motion Picture* (December, 1952); N. Polsky, "And the Lord Taketh Away," *Modern Screen* (November, 1957) (an account of how Marilyn's neighbors at Amagansett reacted when she lost a baby); Sidney Skolsky, "I Love Marilyn," *Modern Screen* (October, 1953); Emmeline Snively, "The Secrets of Marilyn's Life as a Model," *Modern Screen* (July, 1954); Bill Tusher, "Marilyn Owes Me Everything," *Movie Mirror* (May, 1957) (an interview with Natasha Lytess); Susan Wender, "Marilyn Enters a Jewish Family," *Modern Screen* (November, 1956).

187

posthumous autobiography, *Taken Care Of*.[11] Dame Edith used few words, but she made every one count. "In private life," she tells us, Marilyn "was not in the least what her calumniators would have wished her to be. She was very quiet, had great natural dignity (I cannot imagine anyone who knew her trying to take a liberty with her), and was extremely intelligent. She was also exceedingly sensitive."

Dame Edith was amazed by the "will-power she must have needed in order to remain the human being she was, after the cruelty with which . . . she was treated. . . . It arose partly, I think, from the envy of people who are devoid of beauty, and partly from the heartless stupidity of those who have never known a great and terrifying poverty. There are people, also, who cannot believe that beauty and gaiety are a part of goodness."

The second is from David Robinson, "MM: The Last Pictures," in the British magazine *Town* for November, 1962.[12] Wrote Mr. Robinson in part:

> Part of her triumph as well as her tragedy was that the time was out of joint for Marilyn. She was so extraordinary and exciting because she was an anachronism. No one nowadays has deprived and unhappy childhoods, but Marilyn had. . . . The illegitimate birth, the orphanage and cruel or careless foster-homes, the terrifying precocious encounter with sex, are like some Victorian saga. Victorian, too, was the great central drive for self-improvement. Marilyn was Samuel Smiles' favourite girl. . . .
>
> She was at her best as an intuitive artist; and an intuitive artist is in danger of losing his spontaneity through self-improvement. It did not affect Marilyn, simply because it was so completely in character. It was no accident that so many of the girls she portrayed—the Milwaukee chorus girl who falls in love with the Prince, the singer in *Some Like It Hot* with a weakness for gentlemen in pebble-glasses, and the heroine of *Let's Make Love* with her knitting and night classes—were all like her, Cinderellas trying to escape from the

[11] Atheneum, 1965.
[12] Actually this too predates the publication of *Seven Daughters of the Theater*, but I did not see it until long afterwards.

188

kitchen. . . . She was as sexy as Jean Harlow, and as innocent and vulnerable as Lillian Gish: and it is not by chance that one compares her with standards of sexuality and of innocence from an era earlier than her own. Both the potency of her sexual challenge and the poignancy of the childlike quality that accompanied it belonged to more heroic days of cinema. . . .

Her honesty, her frankness, her directness, too, were heroic; and found a peculiar response in days when these virtues are largely forgotten.

Finally, we have Alexander Walker's fine tribute in *The Celluloid Sacrifice*, a study of the mystique of the feminine film star.[13] Though subtitled "Aspects of Sex in the Movies," the scope of the book is considerably broader than that, and the first star to be considered at length is Mary Pickford. ("Feminine Personality in the Movies" might have come closer to it.) Not only is Mr. Walker well aware of the applicability to Marilyn Monroe of Clara Bow's statement toward the end of her career: "Being a sex symbol is a heavy load to carry, especially when one is very tired, hurt and bewildered." He also shows how, as her career progressed, Marilyn progressively "liberated herself from the flesh and stood out against the trend of the times," finally making her appeal "virtually immaterial, in the sense of impalpable and intangible." Among all the harsh things that have been said against Arthur Miller for writing *After the Fall*, nothing cuts much deeper than Mr. Walker's observation that it is *The Misfits* rather than the later work which now looks "like his attempt to exorcise her spirit." He continues: "The moral appears to be that in the films it is far less harassing to live with a 'body' than to settle for marriage to a 'soul.' In life, too, the same perhaps applies."

I fancy we shall not do much better than that. I do not think it necessary to judge Marilyn, to wrap her up neatly in a bundle, or to "close" the subject. As she so often insisted, she was not a "thing." She was a human being, and human beings have—or

13 The American edition was published by Hawthorn Books in 1967.

are—souls, and of the soul there is no end. Of course she was scarred, psychically if not morally, by the cruel conditioning of her life. Not only was her childhood a horror; she never had the environment that her kind of personality needed. And on this point I can only repeat what I have written elsewhere, that Marilyn played the best game of anybody I know, with the worst hand.

The strangest of all the paradoxes of her strange career is that one of the most adored women in the world should also have been one of the most abused women in the world. What was it that made those who did not love her wish to hurt her and ridicule her? Granted that she sometimes made herself vulnerable, who ever tried to help her to be anything else? I do not know the answers to these questions, but it may be that my banker-friend's explanation is the right one. Unfortunately the old saying that we are made so that we must needs love the highest when we see it is true only for the best of us. Some of us are so constituted that we must needs hate the highest when we see it and wish to stamp on it and destroy it. And some peculiarly vulnerable people seem to have been brought into the world only to inspire sadism in those who are not worthy to undo the latchets of their shoes.

For all this, there is always still some soul of goodness in things evil, as Shakespeare perceived, and I never cease to be thankful and amazed and surprised that, in spite of all the mud that was flung at Marilyn, there were so many people everywhere (some of them highly sophisticated, intelligent people and some of them very unlearned, simple souls) who instinctively trusted her and sensed the truth about her and clung to it stubbornly even when they could not substantiate the faith that was in them.

Many years ago there was a film star against whom a false accusation was senselessly brought and who contemplated a libel suit. What, asked her attorney, do you expect to gain? Obviously, she replied impatiently, she expected vindication. But why, the lawyer went on, do you think you can get it that way? The people

190

who care for you are not going to believe this nonsense, and they are the only people that you need to concern yourself about. Yes, there are others who will believe it, because they want to believe it. But they would go on believing it if you were to win twenty lawsuits. And that should not trouble you at all.

Sir Herbert Tree once remarked that every man has the God he deserves. But mysticism is not only a matter of knowing God. It is only those with some quality of awareness who ever have the faintest inkling of the nature of even another human being. Hence Sir Herbert's statement has a wider applicability than he perhaps intended. It applies to God but it applies to people also. It even applies to books and music and pictures and lilacs and kittens and sunsets. It applies to Marilyn Monroe.

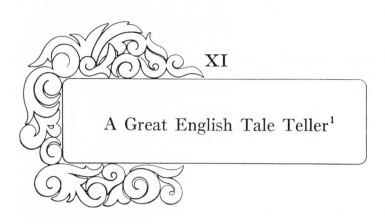

XI

A Great English Tale Teller[1]

WHY DO ENGLISHWOMEN as a class write better historical novels than anybody else? I do not know, but the fact seems to me undeniable. Of course a sense of history is all around you in England, but it is no closer to women, surely, than to men. I must not write here of the writers of today, but it is good to know that the gift has not died out. Among those who are still happily producing, I should find it hardest to get along without Norah Lofts, though H. F. M. Prescott's novel about the Pilgrimage of Grace, *The Man on a Donkey*, is surely one of the greatest of all historical novels. I must not overburden this page with names, but both Prudence Andrew and Alison MacLeod are well worth mentioning among writers of recent emergence. My subject here is, however, the lady generally known as Marjorie Bowen, which was the name she signed to most of her 150 or so books. To the census-taker she was Gabrielle Margaret Vere Campbell Long, and she died in London, two days before Christmas, in the year 1952.

[1] This chapter is reprinted in substance from my article, "Bowen, Preedy, Shearing & Co.: A Note in Memory and a Check List," *Boston University Studies in English*, Vol. III (1957), 181–89. Copyright, 1958, by the Trustees of Boston University.

192

A Great English Tale Teller

I suppose that when so prolific a writer passes at the age of sixty-seven, one does not ordinarily make much of a point of the unwritten books which one has lost. Yet it was impossible for at least one of her readers to avoid this sense of loss in thinking of Marjorie Bowen, for to me her novels, like her personal letters, were a source of exhaustless and unfailing delight, and she poured them out with such unceasing, apparently effortless, prodigality that one almost seemed in the presence of some great natural force that must continue to flow forever. I think it was Tennyson who once remarked of Miss Braddon that he was now confining his novel-reading entirely to her, finding her more uplifting than Mrs. Henry Wood. My enjoyment of Mrs. Long's books made it easy for me to understand what he meant, and I have often said that I could never go to a desert island for the simple reason that her works were too bulky to take along.

I have never ceased to marvel at how little appreciated she has been. How can anyone who has written so much manage to escape the notice of so many people? In this country most readers seem to know only the crime stories which she published late in her career under the name of Joseph Shearing, and when I search for the few Marjorie Bowen books which my own collection still lacks, I am unfailingly presented *The Hotel* or *The Death of the Heart*, by the excellent Elizabeth Bowen, since surely *this* must be the writer I am looking for! Hugh Walpole called Marjorie Bowen the greatest historical novelist England had produced in a generation; she was praised enthusiastically by Walter de la Mare, Compton Mackenzie, William Roughead, and other good judges. Graham Greene has generously acknowledged his debt to her, and she collected as a matter of course reviews for which any writer in his senses would give his eyeteeth. At the very beginning of her career she got off to an excellent start in America under the warm sponsorship of no less a writer than Mark Twain, to whom, in gratitude, she dedicated her third novel, *The Master of Stair*. Of critical evaluation of her work as a whole there has, however, so far been much less than she deserves. The contemporary novel must indeed be rich in talent if we can afford to overlook such a writer as this. Only where, one wonders, is it keeping itself?

I have spoken of Mrs. Long as a storyteller, and I do not write disparagingly; neither do I offer the phrase as a comprehensive or all-inclusive designation of her work. She did not neglect characterization; the backgrounds in her historical novels are rich, accurate, and based on wide and scholarly knowledge; she knew too that a work of fiction is the expression of an author's and a civilization's sense of values. Few writers since Wilkie Collins have come within hailing distance of her as a creator of "atmosphere" in fiction, and this is often of a weird or sinister variety, for she was, among many other things, one of our best writers of stories of the supernatural. In one special technical device I know no writer who has ever surpassed her: she knew how to embody the whole spirit of a story in an object or a symbol, which would thereupon proceed to brood over her terrain like a malevolent, implacable god. But she always remembered something which a great many of her contemporaries forgot—that prose fiction is a branch of *narrative* art. From the beginning of her career to the end she was never ashamed to enthrall the reader's imagination or to supply him with "a tale that holdeth children from play or old men from the chimney corner."

That, no doubt, is one reason why she is neglected. She was an abnormally sensitive woman who did not enjoy the times in which her lot was cast, though being also an abnormally strong one, she voluntarily took upon herself not only her own share of their burden but, like her Victorian predecessor, Mrs. Oliphant, often assumed the burdens of others also. As a writer, however, she had no desire to chronicle either the horrors or the infidelities of our days; instead, she preferred to use her tireless imagination to create a world that was more to her liking. There are no "trends" to be studied in her novels. Fiction to her was not sugar-coated sociology; it was an art. If you would read her, you must read her as an artist; the significance of her pages rests within themselves and not in any references they may contain to that which lies outside.

Her range as a writer was very wide. She experimented endlessly, writing, for example, every conceivable kind of historical novel that can be written. She was Marjorie Bowen; she was George R. Preedy; she was Joseph Shearing. And both Preedy and Shearing won their spurs unaided before anybody knew that either was to be identified with the other or with Marjorie Bowen.

She once wrote a fiercely honest autobiography called *The Debate Continues*. There are sensational things in this book, but when I call it a fiercely honest autobiography, I do wish to imply that it was in the least like Isadora Duncan's autobiography, for such books are less honest than exhibitionistic. Isadora set a fashion for "true confessions" in modern autobiographical writing, but in reading the books which followed in her train we need to remember that hypocrites do not always try to make themselves seem better than they are; sometimes they take up currently-fashionable sins so that they may appear worse. You may be willing to confess sexual delinquencies which a Victorian could never have revealed, but are you willing to set down the humiliating account of the last time you made a fool of yourself? of how somebody slighted you in a painful way? In the Isadora Duncan sense, Mrs. Long had nothing to reveal. But, as Middleton Murry once expressed it in another connection, she made a holocaust of her whole life and came as close as a human being can come to painting an unprejudiced picture of herself; this she did neither for self-aggrandizement nor for self-denigration but simply to enlarge the world's knowledge of human nature. And her over-all description of herself in this volume is "a woman who earned her living by writing fiction—with occasional essays in that kind of history deplored by historians."

If you write to earn your living, you are not always at your best; Mrs. Long, accordingly, left it to the reader to do some of the sorting which more fastidious writers do for him. Her reputation has suffered on this account, much as Trollope's suffered long ago. Yet I must say that I did not always agree with her evaluations of her books; some of the "potboilers" that she disliked most seemed to me to have more of her essential quality in them than did some of the works with which she had taken more pains. Neither do I believe, as many do, that her work would have been better in quality if she had written less, for writers of her kind must create freely and easily or else they cannot create at all. It is astonishing that a human being who possessed such exhaustless patience in the business of living should have had so little patience as an artist. Mrs. Long was so good a woman that to know her even slightly was to think better of human nature. Her loyalties were absolute and unquestioning, her tolerant understanding vast and overwhelming. But her attitude toward art was very much like Sir Walter Scott's, and there is no denying that she was often unpardonably careless in matters of detail. It was the large design that interested her, the broad imaginative conception, the great sweep of the brush. She had no patience to search out the *mot juste*; indeed, she could hardly bear to read her proofs. I do not believe that such a book as Virginia Woolf's *To the Lighthouse* was at all beyond the range of her talents, but her temperament being what it was she could not possibly have written it. She professed indeed to think meanly of her work, but though I know she was completely honest about this, I was never able to believe that she interpreted her attitude quite correctly. She was much too earnest a woman to devote her life to something she did not seriously believe in, and had she not known the value of her work she could never have been so grateful for appreciation as she always was. The real difficulty, I believe, was that she had never been able to satisfy herself: there was always a gap between her glorious dream and the embodiment she had been able to achieve for it. Once her creative impulse had exhausted itself and the book was done, she had, therefore, very little interest in it.

There were other contradictions in Mrs. Long. She had a wildly romantic temperament but her principles and conduct might have been approved by the strictest classicist. Her spirit was deeply religious; her "views" were, in some aspects, "rationalistic." She was one of the kindest women who ever lived; yet much of her work bears a deceptively "hard" surface. In some of her books, she has hardly a sympathetic character, and even some of the historical personages of whom she has written—Lady Hamilton, for example, Mary Queen of Scots, and even, in a measure, John Wesley—have been most unsympathetically portrayed.

Here again, though I have not always agreed with her judgments in individual cases, I am confident that it would be a great mistake to attribute any of this to what we sometimes call "debunking" tendencies or to a desire to degrade human nature. On the contrary, Mrs. Long's vision of human nature was so high that when she wrote of a human being, it was impossible for her to do other than apply the highest possible standards to him and to report her findings without fear or favor if she believed that he fell short. To do less than this would have been to trifle with truth. As for her crime stories, though they often dealt with very sordid matters indeed, she never handled them in a sordid manner. It would be idle to pretend that her love of drama did not make this kind of literary material attractive to her, but her mysteries are not "whodunits"; neither did she ever exploit evil for evil's sake. Extreme situations bring out extreme tendencies in human nature, and it was here that her interest lay. And if she sometimes attacked, it must be remembered that she sometimes rehabilitated also. She rehabilitated Mrs. Maybrick, for example, in *Airing in a Closed Carriage*. At the very end of her career, one of her very few attempts to handle an American theme, *To Bed at Noon*, deals with the old subject of the Kentucky Tragedy. I am proud to think that I was "the only begetter" of this book, for it was I who suggested the subject to Mrs. Long, and she did me the honor to dedicate the novel to me. In writing it, however, she completely transformed the sordid character and motives of the actual participants in this notorious murder case and conceived her personages on a scale and plane of being much more congenial to her own idealistic mind.

This chapter is not a critical study of Mrs. Long's work (though such a study greatly needs to be made) but a frankly personal note. It is not necessary therefore that I should here discuss individual books by Mrs. Long. Her trilogy about William III—*I Will Maintain, God and the King,* and *Defender of the Faith*—has always been regarded as one of her most substantial achievements. Different aspects of the Renaissance are considered in the very dissimilar kind of trilogy which comprises *The Golden Roof, The Triumphant Beast,* and *Trumpets at Rome,* while *God and the Wedding Dress, Mr. Tyler's Saints,* and *The Circle in the Water* concern the religious life of seventeenth-century England. But if I go much beyond these, I merely list my personal preferences, and I lack the space to support such choices here.[2]

[2] Those who desire a bibliography are referred to the article cited at the beginning of my *BUSE* article or to the less complete list appended to my review-article, "The Amazing Mrs. Long," *New York Times Book Review* (May 2, 1943).

198

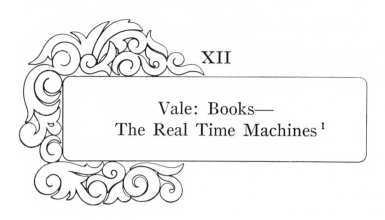

XII

Vale: Books— The Real Time Machines [1]

My text is from Emily Dickinson:

There is no frigate like a book
To take us lands away.

Only for my purpose, I would rather make it "ages away."

In 1905 H. G. Wells published a still live romance called *The Time Machine*, which greatly stimulated the imagination of the young J. W. Dunne and very likely influenced his later speculations (in *This Serial Universe* and elsewhere) about traveling in time. In Dunne's wake, the production of novels and plays concerned with time-traveling threatened, especially in England during the thirties and forties, to take on the dimensions of a small industry. *Berkeley Square*, by John Balderston and J. C. Squire (which derived from Henry James's unfinished novel, *The Sense of the Past*); *Lovers' Meeting*, by Lady Eleanor Smith; *A Traveler in Time*, by Alison Uttley; *The Man Who Went Back*,

[1] This chapter represents the substance of an address delivered by the author of this book at the dinner meeting of the Massachusetts Library Association, on June 10, 1966, at the Sheraton-Boston Hotel. It appears here much as it was published in the Association bulletin, *The Bay State Librarian*, Vol. LVI, No. 3 (July, 1966).

As Far As Yesterday

by Warwick Deeping; *The Middle Window*, by Elizabeth Goudge; *Uncle Stephen*, by Forrest Reid—these are only a few of the titles which come to mind. Americans took to the theme less enthusiastically, but we had at least one successful play—*The Star Wagon*, by Maxwell Anderson, and two fine novels by Robert Nathan—*Portrait of Jennie* and *But Gently Day*. Moreover, there were many other writers, like Virginia Woolf, who, though they did not go in for what might, in the widest sense, be called a subdivision of science fiction, still furnished evidence to support the thesis that the idea of time haunts the imagination of the modern writer, almost beyond all others.

If, as Dunne suggested, time is a fourth dimension of space, perhaps actual time-traveling may someday be possible. I do not know; neither does it concern me here. What I am interested in is the fact that for many generations now every human being who owned even a small shelf of books written before his own time might be said to be in sure possession of not one but a number of time machines, each ready to take off unerringly for its particular destination whenever he should choose to give the signal. It seems to me that this is a fact of tremendous human and moral significance. It also seems to me that at the present moment some of its implications are in grave danger of being overlooked.

When in this day and age we speak of books, I think we must be understood to be including also those two wonderful modern adjuncts to the printed page, films and recordings. In a sense, both resurrect the past more directly than books themselves. Caruso and McCormack, both long dead, reproduce at the command of anybody who owns their records countless songs and arias which they delivered before World War I. Chaplin and Mary Pickford are both in their seventies as they go about their business in the world, but on the screen they are still in their wonderful twenties, and Marilyn Monroe will never be any older or less lovely there than she was when she died. Yet neither films nor records can, after all, take us back very far in time, and though they may surpass the book in their ability to show "the

200

very age and body of the time his form and pressure," we may well doubt that they will ever rival literature in its power to take us inside the heart and mind of a day that has passed.

But why, it may be asked, is all this important? Why not be content with the time you inhabit?

Well, because, to begin with, the present is in a very real sense the only time that we can *not* possess. The present is only a bridge over which we step from the past into the future; moment by moment it slips away from us; in the very process of having it we transform it into what has been. Without memory and anticipation life would be a poor thing indeed. Very few human activities are significant only for their duration, and most of the things we do we should stop doing at once if we were sure there was to be no future. I suppose one of the most profound utterances of dramatic criticism is that of Christopher Sly, watching the players in *The Merry Wives of Windsor:* " 'Tis a most excellent piece of work, madam lady; would it were done." Even pleasant experiences would become intolerable if indefinitely prolonged, and one of the most mournful lines in Tosti's mournful "Good-Bye" proclaims that "all the tomorrows shall be as today." In her terrible story, "Where Their Fire Is Not Quenched," May Sinclair devised the most horrible punishment that any imagination has conceived: her sinners are simply condemned to go on committing the same sin forever!

But there is more to it than that, for, in another sense, we do inhabit the present and only the present. Matthew Arnold was fond of talking about seeing life *sub specie aeternitatis*. This is a large order, and I should be the last to deny that there are aspects in which nothing less will serve. (Incidentally, books can help here too.) But my present aim is less ambitious. The trouble with most of us is not merely that we do not see life *sub specie aeternitatis* but that we are imprisoned in the century, the decade, the year, the month, the week, and sometimes even the moment. If things happen to be going badly now, there is something in us which urges that they have always gone badly, and we are even inclined to waste determination worthy of a much better cause in repelling the comforters who would tell us that tomorrow or the day after the sun will shine again. I have no idea how many suicides could be prevented if the prospect could be reached at the psychological moment and persuaded not to relinquish the idea of suicide but merely to postpone its execution for a month. But I believe that the saving of life thus effected might be considerable.

In her trenchant essay, *Ethics in Modern Art*, Marjorie Bowen inquires why an ability to enjoy *Ulysses* should unfit a reader for enjoying *Clarissa Harlowe*. Exactly. When Kaiser Wilhelm II told Richard Strauss that he preferred *Der Freischütz* to Strauss's works, Strauss replied, "Your Majesty, I also prefer *Der Freischütz*." The trouble is that there are too many people in the world who, enjoying Joyce, do not wish to enjoy Richardson, or who, relishing *Salome*, feel themselves therefore under a moral obligation to sneer at Weber. You hear people talk patronizingly about "pre-Frank Lloyd Wright" architecture or "poets of the pre-Eliot variety," as if Wright had somehow done something to the architects who existed before him or Eliot had hopelessly smeared all earlier English poetry, and, not to mince words, I submit that this is damned idiocy. (As a matter of fact, Wright himself chose to live at the Plaza Hotel while he was working on the Guggenheim Museum.) I believe that people who take up the narrow-minded and rigorously contemporaneously-minded attitude that I have been trying to describe are unnecessarily depriving themselves of a great deal of legitimate enjoyment, but I am not primarily concerned about that. What really concerns me is that I fear they are developing thinking habits which will sooner or later prevent them from thinking straight about anything.

To put the matter as bluntly as possible, I do not see why such terms as "new," "original," and "different" should always be employed as terms of approbation, nor why "traditional" and "old-fashioned" should always be employed pejoratively. This does not at all mean that I have a grudge against the twentieth century or that I sigh for "the mediaeval grace of iron clothing." I do not believe that all new buildings are ugly nor that all old buildings are beautiful. I should be very cold to the idea that women ought to return to bustles and pompadours, nor should I care to don a Roman toga myself. Much of the past—perhaps most of the past—was iniquitous and is fit only for burning. But the point is that it never was fit for anything else and that the same thing is true of much, perhaps most, of the present. "Things are so," as E. H. Sothern once remarked, "because they are so, and not because you, I, or the cat believe them to be so." And things—and people—are beautiful or good or sound or true or what-have-you because these qualities are inherent in themselves and not because they happen to be in vogue in a particular period. Many of the houses that were erected in New England in the seventeenth and eighteenth centuries are still beautiful because they were erected by people who had a sound sense of design and who knew how to build, but New England—and America-at-large—is also covered by other houses and public buildings put up by people who lacked these qualifications. They are no uglier now than they were when they were built, and people of sound architectural sense knew it then quite as well as we know it now. If there are more who know it now, this simply means that in this particular area the standard of taste has risen, and this should cause us to rejoice. And when the time comes when all the up-to-date people find the concrete towers and glass boxes that are going up all around us today so intolerably ugly and "old-fashioned" that they will be impelled to pull them down, I should be glad to be remembered as one person, representative of many, who knew that they were quite as ugly before they became old-fashioned.

What I am saying is, of course, that it is the devotees of the latest thing who are themselves enslaved to all the vices of which they accuse the rest of us. They are the real provincials and the real conformists. Because they are too ignorant to know anything

203

about any age except the one in which they live, they accept all its atrocities at face value, and because they have no taste or judgment of their own, they admire the things—and only the things—that those who happen to have caught the ear of the age tell them it is safe to admire. Even I can remember when Verdi was definitely "out"; now he is as "in" as Bach and Wagner themselves. But Gounod and Massenet are still "out," though there are signs that here too the tide is turning. What mysterious changes will they be found to have suffered, I wonder, when they come "in" again?

G. K. Chesterton was never more penetrating than when he reminded us that our age is only an age and not the Day of Judgment. Every age was modern once, and every age except our own has, in its turn, been superseded. Medieval men, whose minds were quite as keen as our own, were as confident that the schoolmen had found the truth as we are that it has been possessed by the nuclear physicists. How can we, at this juncture, be quite sure who was right?

Most ages mark gains in some area or other; all register losses. (Even in medicine an advance in one area sometimes entails retrogression in another, and the "miracle drug" which cures a hitherto incurable disease may itself create a fresh pathological condition.) Why, then, is it so important that we should "vibrate" to the age we live in, or "tune in" to its wave-length? and why is it a sign of moral turpitude to be, in one aspect or another, antipathetic toward it? Of course I would not have one fail to make use of the advances that one's age has registered. But there is little danger of that. The great danger lies always in the other direction. For better or for worse, we are a part of our age. We share its outlook whether we will or not, and it exerts inevitable pressures upon us from multitudinous directions. At the same time we *know* that since no one age has ever possessed itself of all the virtues and advantages, the modern temper alone cannot possibly be completely adequate to serve all our needs, and since we cannot secure sufficient detachment from it to judge it dispassionately, we must know too that we cannot be *sure*, however the situation may appear to us, that we are not inhabiting a backwater. Ignoring Matthew Arnold's *sub specie aeternitatis* for the moment, would it not seem better to seek to vibrate to *humanity* rather than merely to the age we happen to live in?

My whole point is, of course, that this is just what books make it possible for us to do. The real Road to Yesterday is to be found in any book that you find readable, no matter how old it may be. And unlike the characters in the play, you will not experience any great difficulty in getting back, though it is true that the landscape may look better or worse to you because of your excursion. Literally, of course, all books belong to yesterday, for a book is the author's present only while he is writing it; it has become his past by the time he reads his proofs, to say nothing of the time it reaches the reader.

Is Virgil, then, better than Thomas Mann? I cannot answer that question. You will have to discover by experiment which is better for you. But this I know: that Virgil is *different* from Thomas Mann; that as Thomas Mann commands something that the world has gained since Virgil, so Virgil commands something that the world has lost. And I know, too, that as reading Thomas Mann is to commune with the best thinking of the twentieth century—and to share the minds of that thinker's readers throughout the world—so to read Virgil is to share in the minds of poets and scholars for the last two thousand years. And that, I believe, *is* an advantage.

But you do not need to confine yourself to the giants. Sometimes the minor writers make the best time machines, for in many ways they reflect their times more directly. Once Mrs. E. D. E. N. Southworth was at least as popular in America as Frances Parkinson Keyes is today. Whittier admired her greatly, and she herself never met a human being who had not read at least one of her books. Young readers of today have never heard of her. Possibly you prefer Mrs. Keyes to Mrs. Southworth. Possibly you prefer Mrs. Southworth to Mrs. Keyes. (Or possibly

205

you feel that you can get along very well without either of them.) But if you do prefer Mrs. Southworth—or, if you wish, for a few hours, to take a holiday in her time, escaping from your own—is there any reason why you should not take *The Hidden Hand* down from either your shelves or those of the public library and read it? It may be that you prefer James Russell Lowell's *Atlantic* or Bliss Perry's *Atlantic* to that of Edward Weeks or the *Atlantic* of 1966. It may be that you find more to interest you in the *Harper's Magazine* of, say, 1908, when Howard Pyle was at the height of his vogue, than you do in the *Harper's* of today. Well, so long as the paper and the ink last, it is there for you. And these are only crude illustrations chosen out of available thousands.

Current newspapers and magazines always do their best to prevent our escaping from our own time. "Timely" is the magic word here. Except for *American Heritage*, no magazine could be expected to print an article on the Millerites (who, in the middle of the nineteenth century, believed that the Second Coming of Christ was imminent, and went out to welcome Him). The Millerites were obviously crazy; why should anybody waste space on them? But the crazier a contemporary phenomenon is, the more sure it will be of commanding space. If a "theologian" proclaims that "God is dead," which is a contradiction in terms, he can find a hearing everywhere and will even be discussed as if what he had to say were worthy of serious consideration.

There are, of course, currents and countercurrents in every age. "Dominant" interests are often made to seem dominant by what almost amounts to a conspiracy among those who control public channels of information. But even the interests that are truly dominant are often opposed or ignored by millions of people. We are not all as contemporary-minded as the newspapers would have you believe.

To conserve the best of the past and to add to it—this, I suppose, is the ideal in any area of human endeavor, and attitudes are important because, in the last analysis, thought is creative.

206

Vale: Books as Time Machines

I do not know, and I do not suppose that in the present state of human knowledge anybody really does know, just where the real limits of creative thinking lie. In one of Mary Johnston's novels a wise man says: "What ye strongly expect and build for ye shall receive—having constructed it." It is true that we can be blown up by the Bomb even if we choose to ignore it; that people were not protected against yellow fever by their ignorance that infection was carried by mosquitoes; and that you can still smoke yourself into lung cancer or emphysema though you stubbornly refuse to admit the validity of medical findings. Up to an undefinable limit, however, thought is still creative, and having lived through the period between two world wars, I cannot but believe that we helped to think the second into being by expecting it, and, of course, by allowing the conditions to exist which produced it.

Either God exists or He does not exist. If He does not, your believing in Him will not create Him, though you will, no doubt, derive from your faith, some, though not all, of the advantages which you might derive from His existence. If He does, and you deny His existence, this will not blot Him out of being, and you will still have to live in a world that He created, but you will automatically cut yourself off from fellowship with Him; so far as what the mystics call "the practice of the presence of God" is concerned, He might just as well not exist. So it is too with the values of the past and with all human values. Othello's loss of faith in Desdemona did not change her, but it meant the end of their marriage nevertheless and of both their lives. Civilization means standing on the shoulders of our predecessors, not standing beside them as the animals do; that is why, building on the foundations which others have laid, we are able to make progress and not merely to repeat an endless pattern. It seems strange that those aggressive "moderns" who seem most committed to the idea of progress should have chosen to ignore this. In art as in life, it would appear that we have now come to a place where it is

207

important to remember—or, if necessary, to learn—that, as Samuel McChord Crothers once reminded us, there is a difference between being original and being aboriginal.

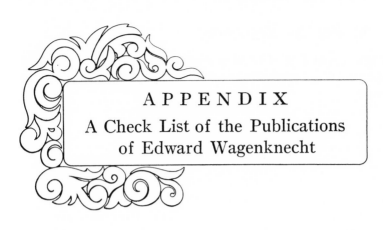

APPENDIX

A Check List of the Publications
of Edward Wagenknecht

(Up to and Including *As Far As Yesterday*, 1968)

A. Books and Pamphlets Written by E.W.

1. *As Far As Yesterday: Memories and Reflections.* Norman, University of Oklahoma Press, 1968. Pp. 224.
2. *Cavalcade of the American Novel, From the Birth of the Nation to the Middle of the Twentieth Century.* New York, Henry Holt and Company, 1952. Pp. 575. Frontispiece.
   Now published by Holt, Rinehart and Winston.
3. *Cavalcade of the English Novel, From Elizabeth to George VI.* New York, Henry Holt and Company, 1943. Pp. 646. Frontispiece.
   Cavalcade of the English Novel, 1954 Edition, with Supplementary Bibliography. New York, Henry Holt and Company, 1954. Pp. 686. Frontispiece.
   Now published by Holt, Rinehart and Winston.
4. *Chicago.* "The Centers of Civilization Series." Norman, University of Oklahoma Press, 1964. Pp. 181.
5. *Dickens and the Scandalmongers: Essays in Criticism.* Norman, University of Oklahoma Press, 1965. Pp. 162.

209

6. *Edgar Allan Poe: The Man Behind the Legend.* New York and London, Oxford University Press, 1963. Pp. 276. Frontispiece.

7. *Geraldine Farrar: An Authorized Record of Her Career.* Seattle, University of Washington Book Store, 1929. Pp. 91. Four illustrations.

    Limited edition of 350 copies, signed by Geraldine Farrar.

8. *A Guide to Bernard Shaw.* New York and London, D. Appleton and Company, 1929. Pp. 128.

9. *Harriet Beecher Stowe: The Known and the Unknown.* New York and London, Oxford University Press, 1965. Pp. 267. Frontispiece.

10. *Henry Wadsworth Longfellow: Portrait of an American Humanist.* New York and London, Oxford University Press, 1966. Pp. 252. Frontispiece.

    A revised version of Section A, #14.

11. *Jenny Lind.* Boston, Houghton Mifflin Company, 1931. Pp. 231. Sixteen illustrations.

    The substance of this book, in a revised version, is included in Section A, #24.

12. *John Greenleaf Whittier: A Portrait in Paradox.* New York and London, Oxford University Press, 1967. Pp. 264. Frontispiece.

13. *Lillian Gish: An Interpretation.* "University of Washington Chapbooks," No. 7. Seattle, University of Washington Book Store, 1927. Pp. 27. Frontispiece.

    Reprinted in substance in Section A, #18.

14. *Longfellow: A Full-Length Portrait.* London and Toronto, Longmans, Green & Co., 1955. Pp. 370. Frontispiece.

    See Section A, #10.

15. *The Man Charles Dickens: A Victorian Portrait.* With an Introduction by Gamaliel Bradford. Boston, Houghton Mifflin Company, 1929. London, Constable, 1930. Pp. 365. Four illustrations and two facsimiles.

    The Man Charles Dickens: A Victorian Portrait. New and

210

Revised Edition. Norman, University of Oklahoma Press, 1966. Pp. 269. Four illustrations.

16. *Mark Twain: The Man and His Work*. New Haven, Yale University Press; London, Oxford University Press, 1935. Pp. 301. Frontispiece.
Mark Twain: The Man and His Work. New and Revised Edition. Norman, University of Oklahoma Press, 1961. Pp. 272. Frontispiece.
Mark Twain: The Man and His Work. Third Edition, with a Commentary on Mark Twain Criticism and Scholarship since 1960. Norman, University of Oklahoma Press, 1967. Pp. 302. Frontispiece.

17. *Merely Players*. Norman, University of Oklahoma Press, 1966. Pp. 270. Twenty-six illustrations.
Psychographs of David Garrick, Edmund Keau, W. C. Macready, Edwin Forrest, Edwin Booth, Sir Henry Irving, Joseph Jefferson, and Richard Mansfield.

18. *The Movies in the Age of Innocence*. Norman, University of Oklahoma Press, 1962. Pp. 280. Ninety-one illustrations.

19. *Mrs. Longfellow: Selected Letters and Journals of Fanny Appleton Longfellow (1817–1861)*. New York and Toronto, Longmans, Green and Co., 1956. London, Peter Owen, Limited, 1959. Pp. 255. Twelve illustrations.

20. *Nathaniel Hawthorne: Man and Writer*. New York and London, Oxford University Press, 1961. Pp. 233. Frontispiece.

21. *Nine Before Fotheringhay: A Novel about Mary Queen of Scots*. London, Geoffrey Bles, 1966. Pp. 320. Frontispiece in color.
Published under the pseudonym "Julian Forrest."

22. *The Personality of Chaucer*. Norman, University of Oklahoma Press, 1968. Pp. 155.

23. *A Preface to Literature*. New York, Henry Holt and Company, 1954. Pp. 381.

24. *Seven Daughters of the Theater: Jenny Lind, Sarah Bernhardt, Ellen Terry, Julia Marlowe, Isadora Duncan, Mary*

Garden, Marilyn Monroe. Norman, University of Oklahoma Press, 1964. Pp. 234. Thirty illustrations.
See Section A, #11.

25. *The Seven Worlds of Theodore Roosevelt.* New York and Toronto, Longmans, Green & Co., 1958. Pp. 325. Frontispiece.

26. *Shakespeare: A Man of This World.* Chicago, privately printed, 1947. Pp. 11.
An address given before the Friends of Literature at Annual Shakespeare Birthday Dinner, May 10, 1947. Two hundred copies of the edition were enclosed in stiff paper covers and signed by the author.

27. *A Tribute to Clarine Seymour.* Privately printed, 1920. Pp. 15.
Clarine Seymour was a very promising young actress in D. W. Griffith's company who died early in her career. This tribute to her is an extract from an address given in Oak Park, Illinois. A friend of the Seymour family had it printed; I forget how many copies Mr. Seymour told me were made, but I am sure there were no more than ten. Some of these were elaborately bound in leather, others enclosed in paper copies. I have one of the latter variety, which is the only copy I have ever seen.

This item antedates by seven years my next earliest publication.

28. *The Unknown Longfellow.* Boston, Boston University Press, 1954. Pp. 32.
"University Lecture," April 8, 1954.

29. *Utopia Americana.* "University of Washington Chapbooks," No. 28. Seattle, University of Washington Book Store, 1929. Pp. 40. Frontispiece.
A critical study of the Oz books of L. Frank Baum, reprinted in part in Section A, #1.

30. *Values in Literature.* Seattle, University of Washington Book Store, 1928. Pp. 96.

    The first edition of this book, which was intended for college sophomores, was case-bound. There were revised editions, in paper covers, in 1935, 1937, and 1941. The 1935 edition added two appendices; the 1937 edition added a new chapter on "Realism and Romance."

31. *Washington Irving: Moderation Displayed.* New York and London, Oxford University Press, 1962. Pp. 223.

B. Books Containing Sections by E.W.

1. *The Story of Jewish Culture,* by Philip A. Langh, Herbert H. Gowen, Warren J. Hastings, and Edward Wagenknecht. Seattle, *The Jewish Transcript,* 1935. Pp. 73.

   E.W.'s contribution is "The Story of Jewish Literature: The Bible," pp. 20–37.

2. *The Twenties: Poetry and Prose: 20 Critical Essays.* Edited by Richard E. Langford and William E. Taylor. Deland, Florida, Everett Edwards Press, Inc., 1966. Pp. 101.

   E.W.'s contribution is "Gamaliel Bradford, Psychographer," pp. 53–58.

C. Anthologies Edited by E.W.

1. *Abraham Lincoln, His Life, Work, and Character. An Anthology of History and Biography, Fiction, Poetry, Drama, and Belles-Lettres.* New York: Creative Age Press; Toronto, McClelland and Stewart, 1946. Pp. 661. Ten illustrations by Sue Williams.

   Introduction by E.W., pp. xi–xvii.

2. *Chaucer: Modern Essays in Criticism.* "A Galaxy Book." New York, Oxford University Press, 1959. Pp. 413.

   Introduction by E.W., pp. v–vii.

3. *The Collected Tales of Walter de la Mare.* New York, Alfred A. Knopf, 1950. Pp. 467.

213

Twenty-four tales, chosen by E.W., with de la Mare's approval. E.W. contributed an introduction (pp. vii–xxi) and "A Partial Check-List" (pp. 465–67).

4. *The College Survey of English Literature.* Edited by B. J. Whiting, Fred B. Millett, Alexander M. Witherspoon, Odell Shepard, Arthur Palmer Hudson, Edward Wagenknecht, and Louis Untermeyer. New York, Harcourt, Brace and Company, Inc., 1942. Volume I, pp. 1,140. Volume II, pp. 1,172. Illustrated with a drawing and four pages of photographs at the beginning of each of the seven periods.

E.W. edited, introduced, and annotated "The Victorian Period," Volume II, pp. 375–938.

There was also a "Shorter Edition" in one volume (pp. 1,290), 1942. In 1951 this version was revised by Alexander M. Witherspoon.

5. *The Fireside Book of Christmas Stories.* Indianapolis, The Bobbs-Merrill Company, 1945. Pp. 660. Forty-four drawings by Wallace Morgan.

Introduction by E.W., pp. xi–xviii.

Now published by Grosset and Dunlap.

6. *The Fireside Book of Ghost Stories.* Indianapolis, The Bobbs-Merrill Company, 1946. Pp. 593. Decorations by Warren Chappell.

E.W. contributed a general introduction (pp. xi–xxiii) and short introductions to each of the ten sections, in addition to two stories: "The Ghost in the Chamber," by Edward Wagenknecht (pp. 339–47) and "Unto Salvation," by Julian Forrest (pp. 192–200).

Later published by Grosset and Dunlap.

7. *The Fireside Book of Romance.* Indianapolis, The Bobbs-Merrill Company, 1948. Pp. 589.

E.W. contributed a general introduction (pp. 7–15) and short introductions to each of the eight sections.

8. *A Fireside Book of Yuletide Tales.* Indianapolis, The Bobbs-

214

Merrill Company, 1948. Pp. 553. Four full-page illustrations in color and four in blue ink by Warren Chappell.

Introduction by E.W., pp. xi–xix.

Later published by Grosset and Dunlap.

9. *An Introduction to Dickens.* Chicago, Scott, Foresman and Company, 1952. Pp. 880.

E.W. contributed a Preface (pp. v–vii), plus introductions and annotations to all selections.

10. *Joan of Arc: An Anthology of History and Literature.* New York, Creative Age Press, 1948. Pp. 421.

E.W. contributed a general introduction (pp. 1–39), plus individual introductions to each of the six sections.

11. *Murder by Gaslight: Victorian Tales.* New York, Prentice-Hall, Inc., 1949. Pp. 437.

This volume contains Miss Braddon's novel, *Lady Audley's Secret*, and short pieces by Dickens, Wilkie Collins, Charles Reade, and Amelia B. Edwards. E.W. contributed an introduction (pp. 3–13). The subtitle was arbitrarily tacked on by the publishers without the editor's consent.

12. *Six Novels of the Supernatural.* "The Viking Portable Library." New York, The Viking Press, 1944. Pp. 885.

This volume contains *A Beleaguered City*, by Mrs. Oliphant; *The Return*, by Walter de la Mare; *The White People*, by Frances Hodgson Burnett; *The Terror*, by Arthur Machen; *Sweet Rocket*, by Mary Johnston; and *Portrait of Jennie*, by Robert Nathan.

E.W. contributed a general introduction (pp. 1–8) and fairly detailed individual introductions to each of the six novels.

13. *Stories of Christ and Christmas.* New York, David McKay Company, Inc., 1963. Pp. 336. Decorations by Peter Burchard.

E.W. contributed an introduction (pp. xi–xii) and one story: "The Soldier Who Saved the Child," by Julian Forrest.

14. *The Story of Jesus in the World's Literature.* New York, Creative Age Press, 1946. Pp. 479. Illustrations and decorations by Fritz Kredel.

    E.W. contributed an introduction (three pages, unnumbered) and one story: "The Child Who Saw Jesus" (pp. 199–203).

15. *When I Was a Child: An Anthology.* With an Introduction by Walter de la Mare. New York, E. P. Dutton & Company, Inc., 1946. Pp. 477.

    E.W. contributed a "Foreword" (pp. xxvii–xxix) and an introductory note to each of the forty-one selections.

D. Books Containing Introductions by E.W.

1. *The Art, Humor, and Humanity of Mark Twain,* edited by Minnie M. Brashear and Robert M. Rodney. Norman, University of Oklahoma Press, 1959.

2. *The Chimes,* by Charles Dickens. New York, The Limited Editions Club, 1931. Illustrated by Arthur Rackham.

    The introduction was reprinted substantially in Section A, #5.

3. *Dickens the Novelist,* by Sylvère Monod. Norman, University of Oklahoma Press, 1968.

4. *Great Expectations,* by Charles Dickens. New York, Pocket Books, 1956.

    Now published by Washington Square Press.

    Reprinted in substance in Section A, #5.

    Great Expectations, by Charles Dickens. "Guideline Book." New York, Harcourt, Brace & World, Inc., 1963.

    This "introduction" is technically an "Afterword."

    There is still another introduction to *Great Expectations* by E.W. in Section C, #9, where the text is also annotated.

5. *The House of the Seven Gables,* by Nathaniel Hawthorne. "A Perennial Classic." New York, Harper & Row, 1965.

6. *The Innocents Abroad,* by Mark Twain. New York, The

Limited Editions Club, 1962. Illustrated by Fritz Kredel. Also published by The Heritage Press.

7. *Life on the Mississippi,* by Mark Twain. New York, The Limited Editions Club, 1944. Illustrated by Thomas Hart Benton.
   Also published by The Heritage Press.

8. *Moll Flanders,* by Daniel Defoe. "A Perennial Classic." New York, Harper & Row, 1965.

9. *Pride and Prejudice,* by Jane Austen. "A Perennial Classic." New York, Harper & Row, 1965.

10. *The Prince and the Pauper,* by Mark Twain. New York, The Limited Editions Club, 1964. Illustrated by Clark Hutton.
    Also published by The Heritage Press.

11. *Robinson Crusoe,* by Daniel Defoe. "A Perennial Classic." New York, Harper & Row, 1965.

12. *The Scarlet Letter,* by Nathaniel Hawthorne. "A Perennial Classic." New York, Harper & Row, 1965.

13. *A Tale of Two Cities,* by Charles Dickens. New York, The Modern Library, 1950; revised, 1967.
    Reprinted in substance in Section A, #5.

14. *A Tramp Abroad,* by Mark Twain. New York, The Limited Editions Club, 1966.
    Also published by The Heritage Press.

15. *Two Years Before the Mast,* by Richard Henry Dana. "A Perennial Classic." New York, Harper & Row, 1965.

16. *The Wizard of Oz,* by L. Frank Baum. Chicago, The Reilly & Lee Co., 1956+.
    This "introduction," printed as an "Afterword," was written for the first Reilly & Lee edition of *The Wizard of Oz,* illustrated by Dale Ulrey, and published in 1956. Later Miss Ulrey's illustrations were replaced by modified versions of the original illustrations by W. W. Denslow. My "Afterword" was retained in the Denslow editions, but the only date appearing on them was still 1956.

217

INDEX

Index

221

Index